INSIGHT GUIDES

Created and Directed by Hans Höfer

GLASGOW

Edited by Marcus Brooke and Brian Bell
Photography by Douglas Corrance

Editorial Director: Brian Bell

Houghton Mifflin

APA PUBLICATIONS

When Apa Publications brought out its first guide-book (to Bali) in 1970, no-one reading it in Scotland would have imagined that Apa's blend of frank reporting and bold photojournalism could be applied to Glasgow. A lot has changed since then. Apa, with more than 100 titles under its belt, has become one of the world's top guide-book publishers. And Glasgow, skil-fully blowing its own trumpet while keeping its tongue firmly in its cheek, has transcended an image of street violence and industrial decay to take its turn as a European City of Culture.

Brian Bell, Apa's London-based editorial director, knew there was a story to tell. His Northern Irish roots gave him a clear insight into Glas-gow's cultural heritage and definitive sense of humour; and, as a national newspaper journalist in London, he

Bell

had first visited Glasgow not to report on inner-city problems but to see a Scottish Opera performance of *Die Meistersinger*.

Regrettably, though, he hadn't been born in the world's most vibrant city; so, to compensate for this oversight, he recruited as co-editor another old Apa hand, Glasgow-born **Marcus Brooke**. Having lived in various parts of the world and travelled in many while earning a living as a writer and photographer, Brooke pops back regu-larly to his native city to ascertain that it still stands and to survey its latest reincarnation.

Brooke

"The Gorbals," he notes, "has gone but these 'cosy' slums have been replaced by dreadful, unlovely hous-ing estates, and the gaps between haves and have-nots – there are many more of the former than before –

grows and grows. Theatre, which in my younger days thrived, is enjoying a renaissance, yet both it and art are often frowned upon unless they have political content – and a strong Glas-gow flavour."

One thing he misses is "the splen-did fleet of paddle steamers which would thrash their way down the River Clyde to the coast in no time at all, and the wonderful and colourful tram system which has been replaced by a frequently chaotic bus service". But he rejoices in the facelift given to much of the city centre: "The cleaning of the exterior of buildings has re-vealed to all what many knew: the magnificent architecture." In this book, Brooke has had ample scope to celebrate that new look: he has writ-ten the entire "Places" section, as well as several other chapters.

To capture the transformation visually, Bell turned to one of Scotland's most renowned photographers, **Douglas Corrance**, whose recent books include not only *The Eye in the Sky*, a photographic record of Glasgow from the air, but also Apa's *CityGuide: Edinburgh*.

Corrance

Corrance started his career on a local Inverness newspaper when he was given a Rollei one Friday night and told to learn how to use it – fast. Although he has lived in Edinburgh – "such a restful place" – since the mid-1970s, he spends half his working life in Glasgow, responding to its unrestful sense of fun and creativity.

Like Corrance, **Julie Davidson**, who wrote the History section, currently lives in Edinburgh but has close links with Glasgow, not least through her writing for the *Glasgow Herald*. An-other established Apa contributor, she also writes for Britain's national pa-pers and magazines and frequently analyses the nation's media for the

Davidson

television programme *What the Papers Say*. She has mixed feelings about the impact of tourism on Scotland generally and the way in which it sometimes falsifies the country's history into easily digestible myths. Glasgow, she feels, hardly needs myths: its reality is much more exciting.

For the crucial chapter on Glasgow's art tradition, Bell turned to **Naomi May**, a novelist and artist who, although born in Glasgow, grew up in southwest Scotland and now lives in London. Glaswegian taxi drivers, for her, sum up the city's attitude. "Instead of closing the partition between you, they open it up and start asking whether you're a visitor and what you're doing. Suddenly you can find yourself plunged into a deep philosophical and Biblical discussion."

It's a myth, of course, that visiting journalists wanting to know what's going on in a town turn to taxi drivers. In fact, they turn to other journalists. And so Bell set about recruiting the rest of this book's contributors from the pages of the *Glasgow Herald*.

Jack McLean, an award-winning writer and broadcaster, contributes a regular column to the *Herald*. He has lived away from Glasgow only three times: "in London, Dublin and – even weirder – Edinburgh. And each time I've come back, Glasgow's been better." The city, he thinks, "is an unlikely combination of political wiliness and Celtic imagination. One long-overdue development has been that the bright sparks who used to emigrate abroad and down south to London seeking their fortune have decided to remain here – or indeed to emigrate back. That's one of the reasons for the vitality of the city. Unlike Edinburgh, which is a quiet, Calvinistic place, Glasgow is a city for gypsies." Among McLean's contributions to this book is a chapter on pubs, a subject

McLean

he has researched with awe-inspiring thoroughness.

If pubs are a Glaswegian passion, so is football, a subject covered expertly by the *Glasgow Herald*'s **Ian Paul**. He admits that the Glaswegians' genuine love of football has tended to be sunk in the sea of publicity surrounding the frequently violent rivalry between supporters of the city's two great teams, Rangers and Celtic. But, like so many of Glasgow's images, this one too is changing, he thinks. "The broadening of the game's frontiers, especially the ever-expanding European commitments, has helped reduce the insularity of clubs and supporters."

Paul

Dublin-born **Anne Simpson**, chief assistant editor of the *Herald* and Scotland's leading writer on fashion and style, contributed an analysis of "Glasgow Chic". Not that "chic" is really the right word, she thinks – the city "is too full of jagged energy for that". It's more a kind of "physical swank, derived from its large Italian and Irish communities which have rarely been burdened by any puritan guilt about dressing up."

Dressing up depends, naturally, on having fashion-conscious retailers, and Simpson has also contributed a thorough shopping guide to the information-packed "Travel Tips" section of this book. The remainder of the section's information was packed by Marcus Brooke and by **Hilary MacPherson**, a writer whose experiences, while a student, included driving a milk-float in Glasgow.

This edition was fully updated by **James Sumner**, himself a native of Glasgow.

Simpson

MacPherson

CONTENTS

Preceding pages: office window in Sauchiehall Street; George Square at dusk.

"There's a lightness about the town, without heavy industry," said the Glasgow-born comedian Billy Connolly. "It's as if they've discovered how to work the sun-roof, or something."

His attitude conjures up the true spirit of Glaswegian resilience. Yesterday, soap-box orators raged against the hardships brought about by the closure of so many factories; today, they celebrate new opportunities, spicing their pronouncements with a characteristic dash of the surreal. The title of an academic study of Glasgow's regeneration hit the right melodramatic note: *The City That Refused To Die*.

Glasgow, in its industrial heyday, was known as the second city of the British Empire. Yet, paradoxically, it has also been called the least British of British cities. It has great vitality, but not a refined vitality. It is warm and vibrant, but not subtle. It likes to show itself off. It is in every sense Scottish and in no sense English. Because of its brashness, its nose for new trends and its willingness to experiment, it reminds many of an American city.

It is, for some, an acquired taste. One rather reserved visitor from the south of England, taken aback by the nosiness and apparent aggression of Glaswegians, suggested that, if the city were searching for a soul-mate overseas with which it might conclude a twinning arrangement, it need look no further than Tel Aviv.

Family feud: Self-assertion, of course, is often the flip-side of insecurity, a feeling fostered by many years of toffee-nosed sniping from its equally self-regarding sibling, Edinburgh – the "Athens of the North", just 40 miles (64 km) away to the east. The European Community unwittingly enflamed this interminable family feud by naming

Preceding pages: the Horseshoe pub; some of the city's "dear green places"; Glasgow's new skyline; city centre; young Glasgow at play. **Left**: buskers in Buchanan Street. **Right**: on parade at Glasgow Highland Games.

Glasgow as European City of Culture for 1990. The only people more surprised than the citizens of Edinburgh were the citizens of Glasgow.

However, they lost no time in celebrating their Cinderella dream come true – so much so that the poet and biographer Alan Bold likened their reaction to a wave of religious hysteria sweeping all before it. Obliterating its image as "razor city", Glasgow suddenly became God, rather as Liverpool in the 1960s

had been declared by Allen Ginsberg to be "the centre of the universe". It was a concept, said Bold, no more meaningful than the notion that Elvis Lives.

In fact, Glaswegians were simply demonstrating once more that their creed is not that of English understatement, much less that of Edinburgh hauteur, but an echo of the self-made American's maxim: "If you've got it, flaunt it."

For centuries, the ebullience of Glaswegians has either delighted or appalled visitors. In 1767, David Boswell described the city as "a place which I shall ever hold in contempt as being filled with a set of unmannerly, low-bred, narrow-minded wretches; the place itself, however, is really pretty, and were the present inhabitants taken out and drowned in the ocean, and others with generous souls put in their stead, it would be an honour to Scotland."

In 1934 George Blake painted a fairer picture in *The Heart of Scotland*. "This fantastic mixture of racial strains, this collection of survivors from one of the most exacting of social processes, is a dynamo of confident, ruthless, literal energy," he wrote. "The Glasgow man is downright, unpolished, direct, and immediate... He hates pretence, ceremo-

American echoes: But it is to America that most commentators have turned in search of apt comparisons. "Glasgow plays the part of Chicago to Edinburgh's Boston," wrote the inveterate traveller H.V. Morton. "Glasgow is a city of the glad hand and the smack on the back; Edinburgh is a city of silence until birth or brains open the social circle. In Glasgow a man is innocent until he is found guilty; in Edinburgh a man is guilty until he is found innocent. Glasgow is willing to believe the best of an unknown quantity; Edinburgh, the worst."

The grid-like layout of so many city streets also recalls America, and with good reason.

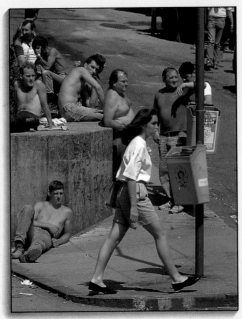

nial, form – and is at the same time capable of the most abysmal sentimentality. He is grave – and one of the world's most devastating humorists."

He also seems, to the outsider, to be exceedingly disputatious. In reality, this simply means that he enjoys a good argument. "Glaswegians are naturally scathing about each other and do not take their quarrelling seriously," says columnist Jack McLean, a contributor to this book. "They can have lifelong friendships in which the only time a civil word is spoken is at funerals – which, incidentally, they enjoy hugely too."

For Glasgow, like so many US cities, expanded rapidly, driven in its case by the engine of the Industrial Revolution. "The Clyde made Glasgow and Glasgow made the Clyde" is the saying that best sums up the role played by the river in the city's impulsive development as a port and one of the world's great shipbuilding centres.

And the speed at which it acquired wealth helped determine its character, too. "In its combination of riches and tastelessness upper-class Glasgow is very like the United States," wrote Edwin Muir in *Scottish Journey* in 1935.

But one man's tastelessness is another's zest. For that reason, Glasgow attracts film makers – and not just local boys like Bill Forsyth (*Gregory's Girl*, *Local Hero*). They view the place, as do its natives, as a character in its own right – a star, even.

And yet the iconoclasm in the Glaswegian character can't be suppressed. Although Glaswegians won't hear a word against their city from a foreigner (especially a foreigner from England or Edinburgh), they can be extremely critical of well-meaning attempts to "improve" it. This tendency to denigrate sends tourism officials into an apoplectic rage.

But then perhaps the tourism officials have

word "culture" because of its middle-class associations. "But it is a paradox that a people who had at one time an exaggerated reputation for violent drunkenness on Saturday night can really be so warm, generous and genuinely concerned for strangers as well as for each other. At the same time, they have a pronounced inferiority complex, particularly towards the English, and a humour that is self-deprecating, so that their best jokes are usually against themselves. Glaswegians are very quick and funny, when you can understand what they are saying."

But who cares about image, anyway? Glasgow's attitude towards the judgements of the

been set on making the place seem too respectable, too dull. The latest headline proclaiming an influx of foreign visitors will never seem as interesting as the story that begins: "Vandals set fire to drums of anti-vandal chemicals in a storage shed at Bilsland Drive, Glasgow, yesterday."

Inferiority complex: The Earl of Glasgow, by profession a television producer and director, thinks that Glaswegians distrust the

Left, sacred thoughts in Kelvingrove; secular thoughts in the city centre. **Above**, stall holder in the well-patronised Paddy's Market.

outside world is summed up in a tale told by Edinburgh journalist George Rosie. Having taken a train to Glasgow at a time when the European City of Culture hype was reaching a crescendo, Rosie was leaving Queen Street Station by taxi when he noticed the archetypal Glaswegian drunk, bottle in hand, throwing up violently into a waste bin.

"What's all that about?" Rosie asked the taxi driver. "I thought you fellows were supposed to be all cultured now."

"Oh we are, we are," replied the cabbie, quick as a flash. "See that coming up there? That's Beaujolais Nouveau."

DECISIVE DATES

AD 80: The Roman general Agricola arrives in Scotland and builds a line of forts between the Firths of Forth and Clyde. The Clyde valley is occupied by a Celtic tribe, the Damnonii, who establish trading links with the Romans.

AD 142: The Romans strengthen their northern frontier by building the Antonine Wall along the Forth-Clyde line.

AD 211: As the Romans retreat behind Hadrian's Wall, the Damnonii are absorbed into the larger unit of the Britons of Strathclyde.

AD 525: According to popular legend, the infant St Mungo is set adrift with his mother on a boat in the Forth. Raised in a Christian community in Fife, he then goes on to "found" Glasgow by building its first church by the side of the Molendinar Burn.

1015: The old kingdom of Strathclyde becomes part of Scotland under King Malcolm II.

1114–18: Bishop John Achaius is appointed and consecrated to the see of Glasgow, and begins building Glasgow Cathedral.

1136: The cathedral is consecrated in the presence of King David I.

1190: Glasgow Fair becomes an annual July holiday.

1297: Bishop Wishart of Glasgow organises a brief rebellion against the English King Edward I during Scotland's Wars of Independence.

1451: King James II accords the town a "grant of regality" and solicits a Papal Bull to found the University of Glasgow – the fourth oldest university in Great Britain.

1560: The Reformation is rubber-stamped by the Scots Parliament and Scotland is now officially Protestant.

1568: Mary Queen of Scots and her husband, the Earl of Bothwell, lose their final conflict with the Regent Moray and other Scots nobles at the Battle of Langside, just outside Glasgow.

1605: Glasgow begins to develop two unique institutions: the Merchants' House, which looked after indigent merchants' families, and the Trades House, which did the same for craftsmen.

1636: Glasgow becomes a Royal Burgh.

1644: Scotland is involved in England's bitter Civil War and Glasgow men fight with Oliver Cromwell in his decisive victory over the Royalists at Marston Moor.

1645: The Marquis of Montrose, harrying Scots Covenanters, enters Glasgow and "borrows" £50,000 Scots from the city. He attempts to restrain his Highland army from looting by hanging some of the ringleaders.

1650: Oliver Cromwell invades Scotland and enters Glasgow, where he behaves well, even tolerating a hostile sermon from the minister of the Barony.

1652: A devastating fire destroys one-third of the city's housing stock and leaves more than 1,000 families homeless.

1662: The years of the "Killing Time" of the Covenanting Wars begin, and numbers of Covenanters are executed in Glasgow.

1674: The first recorded cargo of tobacco is imported into the city from Virginia.

1707: The Union of the Parliaments gives Scotland access to the English colonies, and Glasgow's trade with America and the West Indies begins to make the city's fortune.

1715: Progress towards prosperity is briefly interrupted by the Jacobite uprising. Glasgow is scarcely involved, but contributes 500 men to the Duke of Argyll's government forces.

1740: Gentlemen's clubs begin to play a big part in the social lives of the "tobacco lords".

1745: Glasgow remains resolutely anti-Jacobite during the rising under Charles Edward Stuart. The Prince enters the city on his retreat from Derby and, it's said, is only persuaded to leave it intact by Cameron of Lochiel.

1775: First attempts to improve the navigability of the Clyde are made when the river is deepened up to the Broomielaw quay, in the heart of the city.

1783: Glasgow establishes a "Chamber of Commerce and Manufacturers".

1786: Cotton manufacturer and city benefactor David Dale opens the New Lanark mills and, with the coming of mechanised weaving, the Industrial Revolution gets under way.

1787: Handloom weavers in Calton maintain a four-month strike after manufacturers cut wage rates. Six weavers are killed and many wounded when the military fire on a demonstration.

1812: Henry Bell, a Glasgow engineer, becomes the first man to fit a steam engine to a boat and the Comet is launched on the Clyde – the first steamboat to go "doon the watter".

1831: The Glasgow and Garnkirk Railway opens – the first passenger-carrying line in Scotland.

1840: The dredging and enlargement of the Clyde to its present dimensions is completed. Glasgow's role as a major port is assured.

1840s: Glasgow's population is swelled by thousands of Irish immigrants escaping the effects of the potato famine in Ireland.

1848: The Bread Riots, violent and in some cases fatal confrontations between hungry demonstrators and the military, are one expression of a growing radicalism in the Glasgow working class, who are also active in the Chartist movement.

1832 and 1848: Outbreaks of cholera in the city expose the despair and deficiency of Glasgow's slums to outraged social reformers.

1860: The opening of the Loch Katrine reservoir brings a clean water supply to the city for the first time.

1868: Organised football begins with the forming of Queen's Park in 1867, and their first arranged match is played the following year.

1870: The university moves to its present site on Gilmorehill.

1872: Horse-drawn trams are licensed to serve the city.

1872: The first home international football match between Scotland and England.

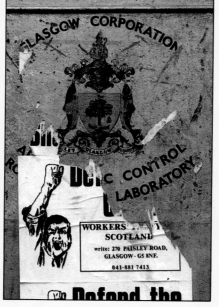

1887: Harry Lauder makes his first appearance in Glasgow, at the Scotia theatre.

1888: Glasgow's status as "Second City of the Empire" is consolidated by the International Exhibition, visited by Queen Victoria, who also opens the new City Chambers.

1896: The opening of Glasgow District Subway, later to be dubbed "the Clockwork Orange".

1898: The opening of the People's Palace, a museum and cultural centre for the working class population of the East End.

1899: The opening of Glasgow School of Art building designed by Charles Rennie Mackintosh, a pioneer of the "Modern Movement".

1901: A second International Exhibition, even more successful than the first.

1914: Suffragettes arm themselves with Indian clubs to resist the arrest of Mrs Pankhurst, who is speaking at St Andrew's Halls. Many are injured and imprisoned after police charge.

1915: Independent Labour Party leaders make Glasgow the focus of pacifist agitation. Jimmy Maxton and John Wheatley organise a strike of Clyde shipbuilders.

1916: Jimmy Maxton imprisoned after making an anti-war speech on Glasgow Green.

1919: Police and striking shipyard workers clash violently in George Square.

1922: In the General Election, Glasgow returns 10 ILP MPs out of 15 seats. The "Red Clydesiders" leave for Westminster.

1931: Work on the Queen Mary is suspended, confirming that Glasgow and the Clyde valley are gripped by the Depression.

1935: Two Glasgow novels are published: The Shipbuilders and No Mean City.

1938: The Empire Exhibition at Bellahouston Park is overshadowed by the prospect of war.

1939: The Athenia, sailing from Glasgow to Canada, is torpedoed by a German submarine and becomes the first shipping casualty of the war.

1941: Greenock and Clydebank become the targets of German saturation bombing.

1942: The founding of the Citizens' Theatre.

1946: The Clyde Valley plan prescribes massive slum clearance.

1971: The opening of the Kingston Bridge marks Glasgow's transformation into the "motorway city".

1972: Jimmy Reid leads the "sit-in" at Upper Clyde Shipbuilders' Govan yard.

1975: Glasgow becomes part of Strathclyde Region under local government reorganisation.

1976: The announcement of Glasgow Eastern Area Renewal (GEAR) is an early milestone on the route to renaissance.

1983: The founding of the annual Mayfest arts festival points to a new cultural confidence within the city.

1988: Glasgow is the site of the International Garden Festival.

1990: Glasgow, somewhat to its citizens' surprise, becomes European City of Culture.

1995: Glasgow strengthens its architectural pride by winning the coveted "1999 City of Architecture and Design" award.

Glaswegians take much pride in telling you that their city's name means "dear green place", from the Celtic *glas* (green) and *cu* (dear). This incongruous rebuttal of the old, grim industrial image tickles their sense of mischief. But, in fact, there's as much dispute about the genesis of the name as there is about the origins of Glasgow's patron saint, Kentigern or Mungo. This bastard princeling of the Celts was expelled with his dishonoured mother from the Lothians and drifted in an open boat across the Forth to Fife, where he found refuge with an early Christian called St Serf.

Wild bulls: The holy man became so fond of the boy that he changed his name from Kentigern to Mungo, "dear one", and sent him forth to convert the barbarians of Strathclyde. (Glaswegians are less inclined to recall that their cheery patron was an East Coast man.) His journey to a rudimentary settlement to the north of the River Clyde was magically effected by two wild bulls yoked to a cart. This, at any rate, is the most straightforward version of the St Mungo legend and places his death at the beginning of the 7th century, conveniently ignoring the fact that St Serf (or Servanus) post-dates this period by 200 years.

Further lore concerning Mungo's spiritual talent explains the robin, the tree, the salmon and the ring on Glasgow's coat of arms, each of which is associated with a somewhat homely miracle. He is credited, for example, with raising St Serf's pet robin from the dead after it had been killed by some young thugs; and in a tale of dubious morality St Mungo instructs a salmon to rescue the ring from the Clyde to spare the embarrassment of an adulterous Strathclyde queen.

But few dare challenge the central event of his story: Mungo it was who first established

a monastery on the banks of the Molendinar Burn, the modest tributary of the Clyde which the Victorians turned into an underground sewer. And Mungo it was who delivered the sermon which gave Glasgow its early motto: "Let Glasgow flourish by the preaching of the word." These sentiments take an abbreviated form today: "Let Glasgow flourish". This brisk piece of editing, transforming Glasgow's aspirations from the spiritual to the secular, was performed in 1866 by the

lawyer who designed the coat of arms, clearly taking his brief from the entrepreneurial spirit of the city's thrusting Victorians.

Although St Mungo gets the credit, Christianity had come to Strathclyde before the Lothian missionary arrived in his bull-cart. It's likely that St Columba's influence on the Scots and northern Picts had extended into Strathclyde by the end of the 6th century, and that the influence of St Ninian, Scotland's first saint, had spread northwards from his Wigtonshire heartland at an even earlier date. It has been argued, in fact, that the story of St Mungo has been confused with the better-documented story of St Ninian, who is said to have founded a cemetery on the site where Glasgow Cathedral later rose – the same site where Mungo built a wooden church.

These vague histories, whether fact or myth, are unlikely to have supplied the only impetus to the construction of the cathedral around 1124 and the consecration of Bishop John Achaius to the see of Glasgow. By then, the community must have had some substance, perhaps even the status of a market town. Although its original centre was established over half a mile to the north of a salmon-fishing village on the Clyde, the presence of that great waterway and the configu-

ration of its valley gave Glasgow all the natural advantages which seem obvious today. Another interpretation of the origins of its name suggests *glas cau*, meaning green hollows (according to one scholar, "the correct pronunciation, *Glesca*, is heard daily on the lips of Glaswegians") and the vast bowl of hills which contains the modern city was attractive territory to its earliest settlers: first Stone-Age hunters and fishers, whose relics have been found on the Clyde, then the agriculturalists who began clearing the forests of the valley, and then the first identifiable tribe, the Celtic Damnonii.

By this time the Romans had reached the Clyde, seeking a northern frontier for their province of Britannia. In AD 80 the provincial governor, the general Agricola, built a line of forts between the estuaries of Forth and Clyde as a temporary defence against the wild northern tribes whom the Romans called Caledonians. But before he could pursue his ambition to bring them to heel and occupy the rest of Scotland he was recalled to Rome leaving his fort at Castledykes, near what is now the town of Lanark, to develop trading links with the Druidical Damnonii of the Clyde valley.

Agricola's efforts were followed by the Emperor Hadrian, who had a more modest plan. He decided to write off the northern half of Britannia by building a restraining barrier between the estuaries of the Tyne and Solway, and Hadrian's Wall was raised between AD 122 and 128. Despite its massive stone fortifications, it wasn't strong enough to limit the activities of the tribes to the north and some 20 years later, when Antoninus Pius was emperor, the old Forth-Clyde line of forts was reinforced by a rampart of turf on stone foundations. Today, there are chunks of the Antonine Wall to be found at the bottom of the gardens of bungalows in Bearsden, the Glasgow suburb which is a byword for propriety.

After the Romans: The history of the Clyde valley then disappears into the Dark Ages, although it's known that the Damnonii were absorbed by the tribe of Britons who established the kingdom of Strathclyde, with Dumbarton, on the north bank of the Firth, as their capital. Shafts of light appear with the coming of Christianity and the St Mungo legend, and when that tangle of peoples called Britons, Scots and Picts finally coalesced under King Malcolm II in 1015. About this time something approximating the kingdom of Scotland came into being, with a southeast boundary marked by the River Tweed; and about this time Cleschu, Glasgu' or Glasgow became part of it.

It was not to be conspicuous by its presence for several centuries. Between building its cathedral in the 12th century and opening up trade with the Americas in the 17th, Glasgow's imprint on the military, political, social and commercial history of Scotland was sketchy. Except for a few incidents occuring now and then, it was pretty well by-passed by the bitter internecine conflicts of pre-Reformation Scotland and the running battles with the English. Most of Scotland's early trade, too, was conducted with the Low Countries from the East Coast ports, so its position near the Clyde estuary held no great advantage until British commerce began to look to the west.

It was even protected from the excesses of the sea empire of the Vikings, which was commanded from their base in Orkney. These Norsemen were not just the maurauders of

lish rule on Scotland, it was a Glasgow cleric, Bishop Wishart, who organised an early if brief resistance.

William Wallace, the first and arguably the greatest patriot of the Wars of Independence, was born near Glasgow, in Renfrewshire, and in 1305 betrayed to the English near Glasgow, at Robroyston. Two centuries later an enigmatic balladeer called Blind Harry chronicled his adventures in verse, describing various heroic acts performed in and around Glasgow. But Blind Harry's idea of history is reckoned to owe as much to folklore and his own imagination as it does to authentic record.

legend. Between the 10th and 13th centuries they attacked and colonised the western and northern seaboards of Scotland, but don't seem to have sailed their longboats up the Clyde as far as Glasgow presumably because the river was too shallow. But the city did have a minor role in Scotland's Wars of Independence. In 1297, when King Edward I of England, the "Hammer of the Scots", began his persistent attempts to impose Eng-

Left, Hadrian, builder of the Wall, remembered at the Hunterian Museum. Above, David I (left) and Malcolm IV, depicted on an 1159 charter.

Despite these interruptions Glasgow prospered steadily during the Middle Ages. The timber cathedral built by Bishop Achaius was consecrated in 1136, and when it was burnt down and destroyed some 50 years later a new cathedral was constructed and re-consecrated by Bishop Jocelin, the influential cleric who also secured a burgh charter from King William the Lion, rubber-stamping Glasgow's status as market town. By 1172 it was significant enough to be called *civitas*, city, in a papal bull and in 1190 the Glasgow Fair became an annual July holiday, making the expanded "Fair Fortnight" holiday of today one of the oldest fixtures in any local calendar.

Medieval Glasgow, like all cathedral towns, developed in the precincts of its church. Only a fragment remains (Provand's Lordship, the 15th-century manse of the Laird of Provan) but the pattern of streets round the cathedral follows much the same ground plan, and eventually it put out feelers towards the Clyde and brought the salmon-fishing village on its banks into the burgh. Scotland, like England, was very much an agricultural country until the late Middle Ages and the interface between town and country was less well defined than it is today.

All the Scottish burghs were given grants of land along with their charters, and a series of strips of arable land can still be traced in the city's foundations.

It was the function of the burghs to export the produce of coast and country – wool, hides, herring and salmon – and import manufactured goods and other commodities. The salmon-fishing village thus became important to Glasgow, along with the sea lochs of the Firth of Clyde and a considerable acreage of arable lands, commons and crofts. By the 15th century – and whatever the origins of its name – Glasgow was indeed the "dear green

place", with commercial rivalry brewing between it and the neighbouring burghs of Rutherglen, Renfrew and Dumbarton, "fort of the Britons", the ancient capital of Strathclyde. The 15th century, however, also ushered in an event which was to guarantee the eclipse of these neighbours. Few could compete with a town which had both cathedral and university.

Not so rotten: Another Glasgow cleric ambitious for his city was Bishop William Turnbull, who persuaded King James II to solicit a papal Bull authorising the founding of the University of Glasgow. In 1451, consequently, a new building rose among the thatched cottages and timbered houses round the cathedral (unlike Edinburgh, Glasgow didn't start building tenements for another four centuries), occupying a site on Rottenrow. Today, this wonderfully named street is sentimentally associated with its eponymous maternity hospital – "going into Rottenrow" has been a key experience for generations of Glasgow mothers – but the origins of the name are more majestic. It derives from the Gaelic *Rat-an-righ*, which means: "road of the king".

The university later moved to the High Street, and was rehoused again in 1870 on Gilmorehill, where the silhouette of the Victorian building now dominates the western skyline. It's the second oldest university in Scotland, pre-dated only by St Andrews, situated on the east coast of Fife, and the two towns rapidly became ecclesiastical as well as academic rivals.

When St Andrews was raised to an archbishopric in 1472, Glasgow set off in pursuit, and with the support of James IV and the Scots parliament won the necessary promotion from the Pope in 1492. This elevation "furthered the good repute and attraction of the western city", even if it "exaggerated the already top-heavy form of the ecclesiastical establishment of Scotland". And Glasgow's future importance – still two centuries away in commercial terms – was assured.

Left, St Vincent, a Dominican friar, at work. **Right,** James IV at prayer, from the *Vienna Book of Hours.*

MARIA D·G· SCOTIÆ REGINA, GALLIÆ DOTARIA, MAII 17·1568· AVXILII AB ELISABETHA
PROMISSI SPE ET OPINIONE DESCENDIT IN ANGLIAM· VBI CONTRA IVS GENTIVM, ET
FOEDERIS IVRATI FIDEM, ANNOS VNDEVIGINTI RETENTA, TANDEM HOSPITIS
ELISABETHÆ PARRICIDIO CHRIS.TI   MARTYRIBVS ADDITA, SANGVINIS LI-
BERALITER EFFVSI TESTI-   MONIO DEI LEGITIMVM CVLTV,
ET ECCLESIÆ ROMANÆ   FIDEM PROFESSA, CORONAM
MERVIT IN CŒLIS, ILLIS   TRIBVS ILLVSTRIOREM,
QVARV VSVM VIOLENTE   AMISIT IN TERRIS= 18·
·FEBRVAR·   1587·

Glasgow's quiet consolidation of its status as cathedral city, university town and thriving burgh was not seriously disrupted by the turbulent events of the 16th century, when the Reformation reached Scotland from Europe and a power struggle followed the return of Mary Stuart from France. As a leading ecclesiastical centre, it managed to escape the worst of the violence associated with the religious upheaval, most of which took place in the east. But in 1538, two young preachers of the reformed religion were brought to trial before the Archbishop of Glasgow, Gavin Dunbar.

Dunbar had no appetite for persecution. All over Scotland the accepted sentence for "heretics" was death at the stake. "I think it is better to spare these men, than to put them to death," he said. There is irony here. Today, the heartland of sectarian bigotry in Scotland is Glasgow – a misfortune which didn't befall the city until its social and religious fabric became entangled with that of Ireland in later centuries. But in the 16th century, it seems, Glasgow was a more tolerant place. Dunbar's clemency, however, was overturned by agents of the powerful and sanguinary Archbishop Beaton of St Andrews, who insisted that the preachers be burned.

Criminal offence: Eight years later Beaton himself was murdered and by 1560 Scotland's conversion to the Protestant religion was complete, ratified by Acts of Parliament which abolished the authority of the Pope and made the celebration of Mass a criminal offence. In England, the powers wrested from the Roman Catholic Church passed to the Crown, but in Scotland (more democratically) they became the province of the General Assembly, which was composed of lay and religious members. This meant that the Reformation was never popular with Scottish monarchs, and – with a young Roman

Catholic queen poised to reclaim her throne from her regents – the stage was set for a drama which still haunts the Scottish imagination to this day.

It's a drama which has also provided novelists and film-makers with one of their favourite characters: the tragic Queen of Scots, who lost her heart, her throne and her head. And the penultimate act of that drama took place in what is now the respectable inner suburb of Langside, on the south side of

Glasgow. Mary's story never fails to recall her beauty, courage and romantic spirit, but often neglects her performance as monarch, which was plain incompetent. She couldn't control her unruly nobles, she failed to reach a rapprochement with the leaders of the new religion (including the implacable John Knox) and her choice of consort was unreliable. When she and her third husband, the disreputable Earl of Bothwell, were accused of the mysterious murder of Bothwell's predecessor, Lord Darnley, the Scottish throne began to slip away from her.

Although Glasgow's citizens had been

Left, Mary Queen of Scots. **Right**, Samuel Sidley's 19th-century portrait of John Knox confronting Mary.

little involved in the power struggle which saw Mary imprisoned by her half-brother, the Earl of Moray, they were present in their thousands at her last-ditch attempt to recover her crown. When Mary escaped from Loch Leven Castle, rallied her forces and headed for Dumbarton Castle, which was one of her strongholds, she was intercepted by Regent Moray and his army on the hill of Langside. Many of the Regent's forces were Glaswegians, and they held the high ground. The Queen's army was routed and Mary and Bothwell fled – him to madness and death in a Danish jail, her to the "mercy" of her cousin Elizabeth, Queen of England, which meant

king of the united nations, although increasingly, thereafter, alliances were made and challenged along sectarian, rather than national, lines.

Religion as well as politics underpinned the wars of the 17th century: the Civil War in England and the bitter conflicts between hardline Presbyterian "Covenanters" and Episcopalian Royalists in Scotland. Despite some interventions by their bishops and city fathers, Glaswegians were largely spared any heavy involvement in these troubles, and continued to improve the standing of their city as a centre of entrepreneurial excellence. By the early 17th century the guilds of

long years of imprisonment and eventual execution at Fotheringay.

There is a certain inevitability about Mary's story. No Roman Catholic monarch could ever sit comfortably on a throne whose authority was so powerfully challenged by the Protestant Church. The repercussions of the Reformation were to harass both Scotland and England for another two centuries – until, in fact, the final routing of the Stuart dynasty at Culloden in 1746. Nor did the hostilities between Scotland and England end with the Union of the Crowns in 1606, when Mary's son James became the first

their merchants and craftsmen were celebrated for their skill and enterprise, and the town's population nudged 8,000.

In 1643 England's civil war spilled over into Scotland. The English Parliamentarians, led by Oliver Cromwell, sought help from Scots Presbyterians in ousting the inadequate Charles I, another hapless Stuart king, and the minutes of Glasgow Town Council record the recruitment of men who took part in Cromwell's victory at Marston Moor. Within a year or two, however, Glasgow was making nervous overtures to the Royalist Marquis of Montrose, who had just trounced

Covenanting forces in a battle near the city. Montrose occupied Glasgow peacefully enough, although he couldn't prevent his Highlanders doing a spot of looting in the prosperous Saltmarket and Gallowgate. What's more, he is still in debt to the town council – to the tune of 50,000 Scottish pounds, borrowed and never repaid.

Glasgow was also required to entertain Oliver Cromwell after his invasion of Scotland. The Protector, as the general called himself, was treated to a hostile sermon in the Barony Church, but got his revenge by inviting the minister to supper and holding a prayer meeting which lasted until three

Burgeoning trade: One of the best assessments of Glasgow's economic potential at this time came from an agent of Cromwell, Thomas Tucker, who predicted a golden future "were she not checqued and kept under by the shallowness of her river." The sandbanks which had protected Glasgow from the Vikings were now hampering her growth, but despite them she ranked with Montrose and Kirkcaldy as sea ports second only to the flourishing Leith. The 12 vessels owned by the city and numerous smaller boats ferried coal to Ireland and returned with "hoopes, ringes, barrell-staves, meale, oates, and butter", took cloth, coal and her-

o'clock in the morning. The city also had some serious domestic worries around this time. In 1647 there was an outbreak of plague which was so severe it drove the university population from its lodgings to the coastal town of Irvine, and five years later more than 1,000 families were made homeless in a fire which destroyed one-third of Glasgow's housing stock.

Left, David Rizzio, murdered in front of Mary in 1566 (painting by John Opie). **Above**, a group of Covenanters pledging to protect their threatened Presbyterian heritage.

ring to France in exchange for salt, pepper, raisins and prunes, fetched timber from Norway and plied the harbours of Scotland's own west coast and islands.

Tucker noticed something even more significant. "Here hath likewise been some who have adventured as far as Barbadoes." It was the first intimation that Glasgow was beginning to look across the Atlantic. But as the city took steps to improve the prospects for its sea-going trade by building the first quay at the Broomielaw and then opening a harbour at what is now Port Glasgow, nearly 20 miles (32 km) down river, there were more bloody interruptions: the restoration of the monarchy was followed by the brutal Covenanting wars, when another Stuart king, Charles II, tried to impose an episcopalian structure on the increasingly zealous ministry of the Presbyterian church.

For all the tension in its dealings with Cromwell, Glasgow was essentially a Puritan city. When, in 1662, the restored monarch appointed an Archbishop of Glasgow with hefty civil powers, his authority was ignored by ministers, and these dissenters were banished from their churches and manses. The spectre of the "killing time" stalked central and southern Scotland, with

the Covenanters hunted like vermin. Many were executed in Glasgow in 1666, and again in 1684, with their heads publicly displayed, and the Tolbooth was packed with prisoners.

This savagery was not the monopoly of the king's side. When the Covenanters gained a temporary advantage over their most successful enemy, Graham of Claverhouse, and chased his troops out of Glasgow, they performed some frightful atrocities at the home of the Bishop of Argyll. They disinterred the Bishop's two recently dead children from their graves in the chapel and ran their swords through their corpses.

With the so-called "bloodless revolution" of 1688 (it wasn't bloodless in Ireland) and the displacement of the Stuart dynasty by the Protestant William and Mary of Orange, Glasgow was able to pursue its austere religious impulses in peace. The town council mounted a campaign against debauchery, forbidding citizens or visitors from drinking in taverns after 10 o'clock at night on weekdays "or in tyme of sermon, or thereafter, on the Sabbath dayes." (The "10 o'clock bell" persisted in Scotland until the reform of the licensing laws in the 1970s).

And godliness was accompanied by cleanliness. An ordinance of 1696 prohibited the casting "out att the windows be day or night, wither on fore or back streets, or in lanes, or closses, any excrement, dirt, or urine, or other filth, or water foul or clean." The high-living people of Edinburgh, meanwhile, continued to hurl the contents of their chamberpots out of their tenement windows for another few decades.

Last barrier: As the 18th century got under way, there came the moment which set the seal on Glasgow's economic future. Although the English Navigation Acts prevented other countries, including Scotland, from trading with English colonies, Glasgow ships had sometimes managed to circumnavigate the rule book. In 1674, the city's records note the first cargo of tobacco from Virginia. These 40 hogsheads of weed were the harbingers of a trade which was to make Glasgow's fortune, and in 1707 the last impediment to this trade was removed by the Act of Union, which gave Scotland access to England's colonies.

In Glasgow, as elsewhere, the people rioted against the forfeit of Scotland's sovereignty to Westminster, and the city's Member of Parliament voted against the union of the two parliaments. But it guaranteed the prosperity which was to carry Glasgow through the 18th century to an economic base able to exploit the Industrial Revolution and turn the town on the Clyde into the Second City of the Empire.

Left, intimations of Glasgow's future as a major port. **Right**, memorial to the persecution of the Covenanters.

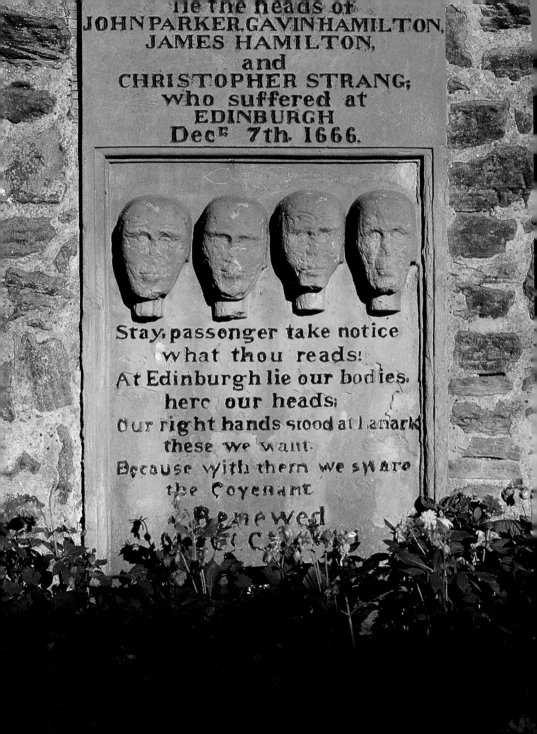

lie the heads of
JOHN PARKER, GAVIN HAMILTON,
JAMES HAMILTON,
and
CHRISTOPHER STRANG;
who suffered at
EDINBURGH
Decᵣ 7th 1666.

Stay, passenger take notice
what thou reads!
At Edinburgh lie our bodies.
here our heads:
Our right hands stood at Lanark
these we want.
Because with them we sware
the Covenant
Renewed
MDCCXXVII

THE INDUSTRIAL REVOLUTION

The most quoted writer on Glasgow in the 18th century is Daniel Defoe. His celebrated judgement – "'tis the cleanest and beautifulness, and best built city in Britain, London excepted" – was to be recalled wistfully by mid-20th century writers observing its industrial grime and material decline. The author of *Robinson Crusoe* (who found the prototype for his castaway, Alexander Selkirk, in the Fife fishing village of Lower Largo) was sent to Scotland by the English Government to consolidate support for the Union of the Parliaments. This generally sympathetic spy made another four trips between 1724 and 1726 before publishing the third volume of his *Tour Thro' the Whole Island of Great Britain*; and during this period he updated his notes on Glasgow.

He was already an enthusiast for the city, and now found it charged with economic vigour. The trading boom with the Colonies was well under way. "I am ass'red that they send nearly fifty sail to Virginia, New England, and other English colonies in America, and are every year increasing…" Glasgow was importing not only tobacco but sugar, which Defoe called the "home trade of the city", and its two handsome sugar-baking houses were kept fully employed. From the molasses a large distillery produced spirits "which they call'd Glasgow brandy". Other important industries were curing herring and manufacturing cloth, including fine muslins and linen.

But tobacco was pre-eminent in the city's fortunes. Geography gave Glasgow's ships an advantage. They could make the Atlantic crossing more quickly than vessels from ports in the south, and importers were able to undercut all their English competitors when they re-exported the weed to France and other parts of Europe. They also developed the custom of sailing up rivers to plantation landings and trading goods for tobacco on the spot, which encouraged the resentful merchants of Whitehaven, Lancaster, Liverpool and Bristol to accuse them of evading custom duties. In 1721, however, an official inquiry cleared Glasgow's traders of this charge, and remarked that it had been brought in a "spirit of envy".

The "tobacco lords" became a class of their own. Their warehouses and mansions have mostly gone, swept away by the Victo-

rians who raised the massive fabric of a new "Merchant City" in that eastern enclave of the city centre which has been resuscitated by restoration and property development to become the aspirants' symbol of the New Glasgow. But their influence still remains. By re-deploying their capital, they laid the foundation for the growth of banking in the west of Scotland, founding several banks. They also used their profits to buy country estates and send their sons on the Grand Tour of Europe.

Edinburgh, what's more, was not the only Scottish city to suffer from deference to the

Preceding pages: David Morier's portrayal of Culloden, painted in 1746. Left, *First Steamboat on the Clyde,* **by John Knox. Right, the much quoted Daniel Defoe.**

English ruling class. Some of the more pretentious merchants deserted the Presbyterian Church for the Scottish Episcopal Church and despatched their sons to England to be tutored by Anglican clerics.

Their fief was centred on the Trongate. These upwardly mobile merchants, in the process of transforming themselves from middle-class to landed gentry, claimed exclusive rights to patrol the Trongate's pavements. Their daily perambulations, in all the finery of satin suits, powdered wigs and gold-topped canes, took them to the Tontine Coffee House at noon to drink their "meridian" – claret or whisky – and read the news-

and earlier in 1745, when the city had a brush with Bonnie Prince Charlie and his army of Jacobites. Glasgow, like much of the Lowlands, was hostile to the adventure of the Pretender to the throne, which had passed securely to the Hanover family. But the Roman Catholic Highlands were still sympathetic to the ambitions of the old Stuart dynasty and by September 1745, after their victory over the Hanoverian troops of Sir John Cope at Prestonpans, the Jacobites had control of Edinburgh.

Glasgow's allegiance hadn't changed since the earlier Jacobite Rebellion of 1715, when it contributed 500 men to the Hanoverian

papers, freshly arrived from Edinburgh and London by stage-coach. Lesser Glaswegians were unimpressed by their display. It's said that the coffee room waiter distributed the newspapers by throwing a bundle in the air and letting the wealthy worthies scramble for them.

The even tenor of Glasgow's prosperous progress was interrupted only twice by external events in the 18th century: once by the outbreak of the American War of Independence, when tobacco imports slumped between 1775 and 1777, only to recover in 1778, although not to their pre-war volume;

forces of the Duke of Argyll. But, with the popular prince in the capital, the city was required to donate £5,000 and £500 in goods to his cause.

Two months later, fatally retreating from England, Charles and his army occupied Glasgow itself and the prince proclaimed himself Regent at the Cross. He took up residence at Shawfield Mansion and extracted "6,000 short cloth coats, 12,000 linen shirts, 6,000 pairs of shoes, and the like number of pairs of tartan hose" from the city by way of penalty for its Hanoverian sympathies. Despite some ceremonial wooing and all the prince's charm, support for the cause was dismal, and Charles could find only 60 Glaswegians willing to join his army.

He left the city early in the New Year, taking two magistrates as hostages for the goods still missing from his inventory, but by April he was on his "flight through the heather" after defeat at Culloden – the last pitched battle fought on mainland Britain. He was bitter about Glasgow. "Nowhere," he said, "have I found so few friends as in Glasgow."

The Glasgow of the the prince's time was still very much the dear green place, and it remained so until the end of the century. An

and was acquired by the burgh in 1662. Prosperous Glaswegians sent their servants to do the laundry at the wash-house there, and to this day Glasgow women have the right to dry their washing on the Green.

Unlike Edinburgh, which had piped water by the end of the 18th century, the city still drew its supplies from the Clyde and public wells. Sewage was collected from back courts by horse and cart, although the first sewer (for the benefit of gentlefolk) was laid in 1790 between the new squares of St George and St Enoch, where sheep still grazed. As the century advanced, the diet of Glaswegians became more elaborate (and possibly

18th-century local historian, John M'Ure, described the city streets as "surrounded with corn-fields, kitchen and flower gardens and beautiful orchards, abounding with fruits of all sorts", and many of the tobacco merchants' new mansions had their own large gardens and orchards.

Then there was Glasgow Green. This great pasture beside the Clyde had been the common grazing ground of the medieval town,

Left, an 18th-century tobacco lord, John Glassford, at home. **Above**, a Glasgow shopkeeper in the 1790s, by an unknown artist.

less wholesome) as their simple breakfasts of porridge and herring and suppers of broth, salt beef, boiled fowl or Clyde salmon were supplanted by fancier fare.

Demon drink: With the new prosperity came Glasgow's (and Scotland's) reputation for heavy drinking. While the humble took to the proliferating taverns the affluent drank in their homes – claret or punch, rather than whisky – and in some households a servant was dedicated to the task of loosening cravats after dinner, so that guests who had drunk themselves insensible wouldn't choke.

Towards the end of the 1700s, social life

for gentlemen centred more and more on clubs and coffee houses, while the ladies, as ever, stayed in the drawing room. The lowly had to be content with their taverns or drinking shops – little grocery-shops, often run by women, where it was customary to tipple wine and spirits in a back room. Otherwise, they turned for entertainment to such free pastimes as stone-throwing competitions, or inexpensive ones like the New Year's Day tradition in Govan of cock-shooting, which cost a penny a shot for the sport of shooting a cock tied to a stake.

But there was change in the air. The city of merchants and professional men was soon to

mary in 1792. This likeable, far-sighted manufacturer brought mechanised weaving to the Clyde valley and in 1786 founded the New Lanark cotton mills, which not only prospered but – although they employed men, women and children – became a model for industrial and social organisation. Dale's daughter married the innovative social engineer Robert Owen, who used New Lanark as the laboratory for his ideas.

But the infant cotton industry had its troubles. In 1787 the handloom weavers of the Glasgow suburb of Calton went on strike for four months when their employers cut their rates of pay by 25 percent. This organised

be transformed. In the last quarter of the century its population almost doubled as immigrants arrived from the Highlands to find work in a new industry. Cotton was replacing tobacco as Glasgow's heftiest economic plank, and by 1792 one commentator was able to observe: "The traveller approaching this city, beholds before him, nothing but spires, buildings and smoke." The Industrial Revolution was under way.

The greatest name associated with Glasgow's cotton industry is David Dale, who was also one of the city's major benefactors, supporting the building of the Royal Infir-

withdrawal of labour was an early example of the radicalism which was to become a tradition on the Clyde, but the strike was brutally put down when magistrates called in the military. A confrontation near the Drygate bridge ended when three weavers died in a hail of bullets and many more were wounded. The soldiers were rewarded with free shoes and stockings.

At the turn of the century the city's population was 47,000, and from then on it exploded in a manner which has caused Glasgow to be called an "instant city". By 1830 it had quadrupled to 200,000 and by 1870 it was half a million. In that time, the Industrial Revolution took Glasgow from cotton-weaving town to "Workhorse of the World" as all the ingredients for its future in heavy engineering and shipbuilding came together with the arrival of the steam engine, invented by a Scot, James Watt.

The Clyde had been made navigable to the heart of the city at the Broomielaw (a process begun in the 1780s) and the building of Port Dundas, at the west end of the Forth-Clyde canal, linked Glasgow to the shipping lanes of Europe. The coalfields of Lanarkshire fuelled the ironworks of the Clyde valley; and there was a ready supply of cheap labour

"doon the watter", is described by a chronicler who credits a local man with the birth of steam navigation: "At that period (1812) Mr Henry Bell, an ingenious, untutored engineer, and Citizen of Glasgow, fitted up, or it may be said, without the hazard of impropriety, that he invented the steam-propelling system and applied it to his boat, the Comet... After various experiments, the Comet was at length propelled on the Clyde by an engine of three horse power."

The early 1800s also saw the planning of the new merchant city to the east of George Square. Surviving buildings such as the Trades House in Glassford Street and

in crofters cleared from the land by the "improving" estate owners of the Highlands and hungry Irish immigrants driven across the sea by the potato famine of the 1840s.

The new century saw, too, the beginnings of a "leisure industry" whose remnants remain today in excursions on the Clyde, although its repercussions were far more fundamental to the city's economy. The launch of the *Comet*, the first of generations of steamboats which were to ferry Glaswegians

Left, the Gorbals before they became a notorious slum. **Above**, John Knox's *Trongate of Glasgow*.

Hutcheson's Hospital followed the classical forms which influenced Georgian architecture, although much of it was to be overwhelmed by later Victorian building. But the century also produced an architecture destined to become notoriously synonymous with Glasgow: the lofty tenement, which soon came under pressure from the swell of population.

The social consequences were terrible, and bred a reputation which was to dog Glasgow, justly and unjustly, into the second half of the 20th century. In 1839 a Parliamentary report on housing in Great Britain made this contribution: "I have seen human degradation in some of the worst places, both in England and abroad, but I did not believe until I had visited the wynds of Glasgow that so large an amount of filth, crime, misery and disease existed in one spot in any civilised country." In 1842 Edwin Chadwick, documenting the *Sanitary Condition of the Labouring Population of Great Britain*, called the city "possibly the filthiest and unhealthiest of all the British towns of this period… in the courts of Argyle Street there were no privies or drains, and the dung heaps received all the filth which the swarms of wretched inhabitants could give."

in Glasgow died before their fifth birthday, and a report on the city's mortality bills for 1851 moved its author to make this heart-wringing plea: "The want of care on the part of the mother, called to toil beyond her home, which is left filthy and neglected, the want thereby of nature's nutriment to her child, who, when crying to others for food, is too often only soothed by opiates, or when assailed by disease, is permitted to die without the aid of medical skill or nutritious appliances, are all elements in this frightful waste of life. Can nothing be suggested to meet this cruel calamity?"

Mothers were called to toil beyond the

Despite the new building, despite the vigour of its entrepreneurial class, the dear green place, "the beautifulness city" was becoming an urban Hades. (Housing problems were to haunt Glasgow for another century: in 1924 a Member of Parliament for the city called his home town "earth's nearest suburb to hell".) Until a clean water supply was provided with the opening of the Loch Katrine reservoir in 1859, typhus and cholera were endemic.

Smallpox was also commonplace and the infant mortality rate one of the worst in Europe. In 1850 one half of all children born

home by necessity. But if poverty and squalor bred disease and drunkenness (the easy availability of whisky was a solace which only compounded these problems) they also provided fertile ground for radical politics. Glasgow's contribution to the Chartist movement which, throughout the middle of the 19th century, agitated for universal male suffrage, was energetic. Trade unions became more and more assertive.

In 1848, provoked by hunger and unemployment and encouraged by the political climate (in February of that year the Communist Manifesto was issued), a mass of demonstrators assembled on Glasgow Green in a series of protests which became known as the Bread Riots. They marched through the streets looting shops, and the crisis came to a head when the military fired on the crowd, killing six and wounding others, including blameless by-standers.

As the century advanced, however, and piecemeal progress towards male suffrage was made, the Glasgow Chartists entered municipal politics as civic reformers. The Victorian conscience was at last being roused and improvements in the city's services got under way. In 1863 the first medical officer of health was appointed, and in 1875 the

Lauriston (Gorbals fleetingly enjoyed a life as an affluent suburb before its decline) but prosperous Victorians were now moving west to Charing Cross, and beyond to Hillhead and the environs of the Botanic Gardens, which were laid out in 1842.

Rich rewards: Despite the Stygian picture painted by social reformers of the period, the city was moving handsomely towards the apotheosis of its economic and civic achievements. By the second half of the century, it was well on course for its destiny as Second City of the Empire.

The Victorians embarked on that proud and prolonged exercise in aspirational build-

Public Health Act brought pollution from industrial chimneys under some kind of control. The slums and their entrenched problems remained, and many of their ills spread from the city centre to the east and its suburbs, where more and more of Glasgow's escalating population were finding labour in the ironworks and coalfields of Lanarkshire.

The city was expanding fast. Development to the south of the Clyde had taken place between 1800 and 1830 in Gorbals and

Left, Andrew Shanks's *The Saltmarket in 1849.*
Above, David Small's *Broomielaw.*

ing which dominates the city's character today. Churches, hospitals, theatres, banks, public buildings, shipping offices, shops and veritable temples of commerce were raised by architects who also turned the humble tenement into Glasgow's most distinctive domestic building. In the suburbs to the west and north, in the flourishing shipbuilding communities of Govan and Partick and Clydebank, streets of confident dignity were planned for both bourgeois and working-class families, their tenement flats differing only in capacity and decorative detail. New city parks were a central part of the Victorian vision, and today there are more than 70 – "more green space per head of population than any other city in Europe," according to pub statisticians.

With engineering and shipbuilding now its main industries, Glasgow logically took an aggressive interest in transport systems. Railway companies were founded and promptly did battle for status as well as custom, vying with each other to build the most magnificent stations and hotels. Railway bridges were raised over the Clyde and, in the 1880s, suburban railway networks and a tramway system were developed.

In 1896 one of the earliest underground

railways in the country was opened. Glasgow District Subway, now running in the livery which has given it the sobriquet "the Clockwork Orange", is the only British system which, American-style, calls itself "the Subway".

Rapid expansion, too, was taking place in Glasgow's earliest transport system. By 1872 the docks and wharves and maritime life of the Clyde had become a tourist attraction. *Tweed's Guide* of the year urges the visitor to Glasgow not to ignore them, or "he'll miss one of its greatest marvels if he neglects to spend a few hours strolling along the quays

of the harbour. He may have seen much of shipping in his travels… but he has probably never witnessed a greater triumph of human industry, enterprise, and sagacity than Glasgow Harbour."

From these quays the products of the city's engineering works – the massive locomotives which pulled the British Empire's trains and the boilers and machinery which powered its ships – were dispatched all over the world; and from the Clyde's shipyards the ships themselves set forth. Glasgow's industrial status was internationally confirmed, while the city's cultural life had both local energy and universal appeal.

In the last two decades of the century the "Glasgow Boys", a school of painters despised by the Scottish artistic establishment, were invited to exhibit in major galleries in Europe and America; and in 1899 the new School of Art was opened – designed by Charles Rennie Mackintosh, who was to become a hero of the Modern Movement. Popular culture, as elsewhere, centred on the music hall. In 1887 Harry Lauder made his first appearance in the city at the Scotia theatre, to be told by its manageress: "Gang hame and practice, Harry, I'll gie ye a week's engagement when the winter comes round."

Two exhibitions marked the zenith of Glasgow's confidence. The International Exhibition of 1888 was held in Kelvingrove Park and splendidly visited by Queen Victoria, who was also in town "to perform the ceremony of opening the new Municipal Buildings lately erected in George-square for the City Corporation"; and in 1901 an even more successful International Exhibition was attended by Tsar Nicholas II.

As the century turned on that high note, the development of the steam-turbine engine on the Clyde seemed to guarantee limitless labour for its engineers and workforce, and an even more golden future for the Second City. The most pessimistic Glaswegian could not have predicted that within three decades it would be afflicted with decline and gripped by despair.

Left, Lavery's portrait of Queen Victoria at the Glasgow Exhibition of 1888. **Right**, the other side of the story – High Street slums in 1868.

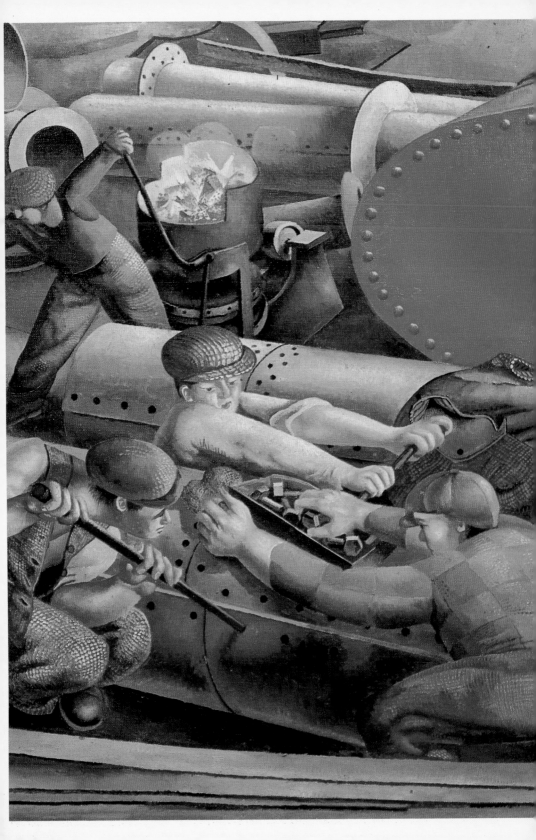

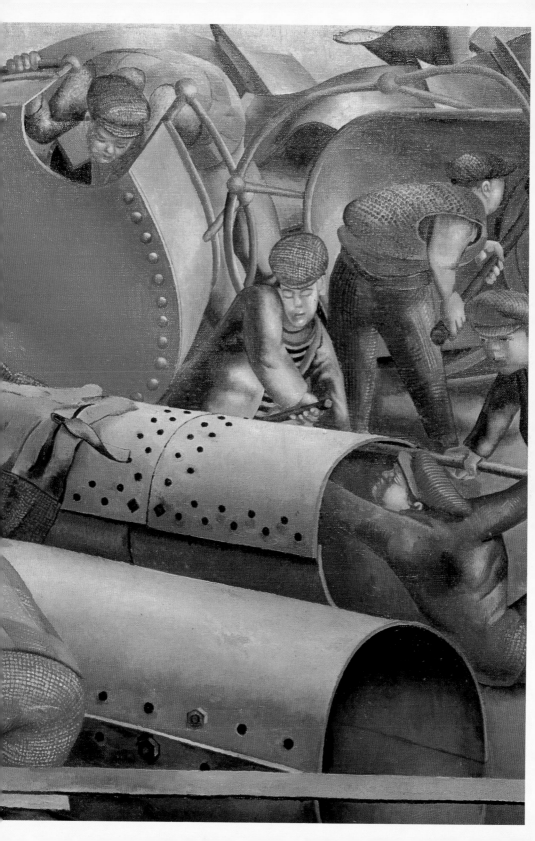

"It was in a sense a procession that he witnessed, the high, tragic pageant of the Clyde. Yard after yard passed by, the berths empty, the grass growing about the sinking keel-blocks. He remembered how, in the brave days, there would be scores of ships ready for the launching along this reach, their sterns hanging over the tide, and how the men at work on them on high stagings would turn from the job and tug off their caps and cheer the new ship setting out to sea. And now only the gaunt, dumb poles and groups of men, workless, watching in silence…"

George Blake's novel *The Shipbuilders*, published in 1935, is a work of fiction which has helped cement in folk memory the image of the "high, tragic pageant of the Clyde" which still persists to this day. Writing in an eloquent essay which challenged the more destructive aspects of its "debilitating nostalgia", Alf Young, Scotland's leading economic and industrial journalist, confessed: "I, too, can walk round that room in the Museum of Transport and feel my heart ache, measuring case after case of hand-crafted Clyde-built ship models against the silent dereliction that grips much of the river today."

The Shipbuilders wasn't the only novel to come out of Glasgow in 1935. Even more potent, in its impact on public perceptions of Glasgow, was *No Mean City*, by Alexander McArthur and H. Kingsley Long, which was notoriously successful and still sells well. This "terrible story of drink, poverty, moral corruption and brutality" introduced the razor gangs of Calton, Bridgeton and the Gorbals to a wider public and confirmed the city's reputation for violence. Although today Glasgow is no more violent than any other comparable city – and less so than some – the slur has stuck.

The ghostly Clyde and the spectre of violence: the two images which have haunted Glasgow were not invented by works of fiction. There is reality in them both, and indeed many (male) Glaswegians have come to relish their city's primacy as a town of "wee hard men". When the visions of the Second City began to dissipate after World War I the huge unemployed workforce contained the ingredients of a potentially explosive social mix: the historical combativeness of the Scot and the constitutional reckless-

ness of the Irish. Nor was Glasgow's industrial diversity to save it from the worst effects of the Great Depression in the 1930s.

Secret of success: How did the confident economic infrastructure of the Victorian city crumble so swiftly? The first decade of the 20th century was entered on a high tide of contracts for the Clyde, where the volume of shipbuilding had grown from about 100,000 tons in the early 1860s to 750,000 tons by 1913. In 1915, when more than 60,000 men were employed in Clyde shipyards and marine engineering works, the Town Clerk was able to point with pride to a variety of other industries: the continuing prominence of textiles, as well as pottery and glass-making, distilleries, breweries, tan-works, dye-works and paper manufacture. "Accordingly," he added, with premature complacency, "Glasgow does not feel any of those universal depressions which so frequently occur in places limited to one or two branches of manufacture or commerce."

Glasgow's economy was also able to provide all the basic services for its citizens out of the municipal purse – a fact which astonished an American professor of civic administration who visited the city in 1905. "Enthusiasm and interest, devotion and pride

just below the surface of Glasgow's political consciousness since the start of the Industrial Revolution. This was the period when the Independent Labour Party, inspired by the magnetic Jimmy Maxton and his colleague John Wheatley, made Glasgow a focus of pacifist agitation. In 1915 they organised an all-out strike on the Clyde and in 1916 Maxton was imprisoned for the speech he made at an anti-war demonstration on Glasgow Green on May Day.

Woman power: Suffragettes, too, were active in the city (supported by many members of the ILP) and armed themselves with Indian clubs to help resist the arrest of the

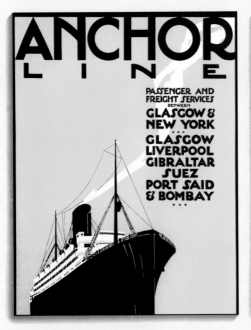

– these are the characteristics of Glasgow citizenship," he wrote. "I have talked with the heads of the city departments, with a score of town councillors, with police and fire officials, with clerks, bath-house custodians and conductors on the tram-cars – with all sorts of men, Tories and Liberals, Radicals and Socialists, from the Lord Provost down to the cab-driver. And this is the only citizenship I have been able to find."

This solid spirit of unity was to be challenged by World War I, which not only falsely inflated the shipbuilding boom but inflamed the radical instinct which had been

movement's leader, Mrs Pankhurst, when she visited Glasgow in 1914. Witnesses reported that they were brutally treated by the police force, who charged the platform at St Andrew's Halls where the Suffragette leader was speaking. (Similar charges were made against the Glasgow police when they broke up a demonstration of strikers in George Square five years later.)

The fires kindled by the ILP were further fuelled when the war ended and the first intimations of decline produced a wave of unemployment. There was a reduction in the demand for new ships – partly because confiscated German ships were being re-sold – and the yards began a programme of "rationalisation". Glasgow's locomotive engineering works, almost as important as shipbuilding to the city, were also affected when the control of Scotland's railways moved south after a series of company mergers.

By 1922 the unemployment figures had reached 80,000, and the city's famed diversity was being undermined, too. The great conurbation of the Clyde Valley was almost entirely dependent on heavy industry, and when the decline of the 1920s was followed by the Depression of the 1930s Glasgow's service and consumer industries were se-

ness of the people of these islands", was soon to come under pressure from the inevitable compromises of practising politics. John Wheatley became a minister in the Labour Government of 1924, and was the architect of the far-reaching Housing Act which allowed the building of 74,000 local authority houses in Scotland; but conflict was growing between the Labour Party and the ILP, who were soon to lose two of their Glasgow MPs, Emmanuel Shinwell and Tom Johnston (a future and most distinguished Secretary of State for Scotland) to the larger party.

The significance of the ILP dwindled in the 1930s, but the totems bequeathed by the

verely affected by the miseries of the Clyde Valley population, as well as its own.

In the General Election of 1922, 10 out of Glasgow's 15 seats were won by the ILP. The "Red Clydesiders" were off to Westminster, cheered onto the night train by thousands of supporters gathered at St Enoch Station. But their noble manifesto, dedicated "to the reconciliation and unity of the nations of the world and the development and happi-

Left, early 20th-century poster; and a male view of local sufragettes. **Above**, traffic jam on Jamaica Bridge as early as 1924.

Red Clydesiders have never quite disappeared from the political landscape of Glasgow and its river valley; while Jimmy Maxton, the purist of their idealists, remains the greatest folk-hero of the Scottish Left. Their spirit was reinvoked most memorably in 1972, when four of the five remaining yards on the Upper Clyde were threatened with closure and shop steward Jimmy Reid organised the Govan "sit-in". Such was the success of this orderly and prolonged occupation of the Upper Clyde Shipbuilders' yard that the government put up the money for the formation of an amalgamated Govan

Shipbuilders and only a few hundred jobs were lost. Today, Govan Shipbuilders survive – under Norwegian ownership.

Sense of humour: Throughout the first half of the century, despite the chronic poverty of many of its citizens and the periodic hardships of its workforce, Glasgow never lost the capacity to enjoy itself. Apart from its flourishing street, pub and football cultures, it became the centre of Scotland's music hall industry (even today, as writer Jack House has said, "most Scotch comics either belong to Glasgow or pretend that they do") and it was an early enthusiast for the cinema. By 1917 there were 100 picture houses in the

The years of World War II – despite the devastating saturation bombing of the shipbuilding towns of Greenock and Clydebank – were vigorous ones for the Clyde, which had an early taste of disaster when a Glasgow ship, the passenger liner *Athenia*, became the first shipping casualty of the war: it was sunk en route to Canada by a German submarine on 3 September 1939. The yards were busy again and Glasgow, like Liverpool, became a major port for merchant shipping into wartime Britain, as the southern ports were exposed to greater bombing risks. The city centre was left relatively unscathed by the Luftwaffe, but after the spring raids of 1941

city, more than any per head of population in the country, and in 1929 the "talkies" came to Glasgow with *The Singing Fool*.

At a higher level, the "second Scottish Enlightenment", which the city enjoyed in the early part of the century, found a permanent monument in the Citizens' Theatre, which was founded in 1942 by the playwright James Bridie and Dr Tom Honeyman, director of Glasgow Art Gallery. Wartime servicemen stationed in Glasgow also discovered a city devoted to ballroom dancing, with its palatial dance halls not at all discouraged by blackout restrictions.

only seven houses were still standing in Clydebank and nearly 1,500 people had been killed.

Although the shipyards were kept active into the 1950s with replacement orders, the writing was again on the wall for the Clyde's greatest industry. The war had already seen off the last of Glasgow's regular transatlantic passenger and cargo services, and sea traffic was declining everywhere as air travel developed. In the 1930s the great Cunard liners *Queen Mary* and *Queen Elizabeth* had been built and launched on the Clyde, and an echo of those days was recalled when Cunard commissioned the *QE2*. But her launch in 1967 was to mark the passing of the majestic line ship (now given over to cruising) on the Clyde.

The river's vitality got a boost in the 1970s when the opening up of the North Sea oil fields brought new work on supply vessels and oil platforms. By this time, however, Glasgow was no longer looking to the Clyde for its salvation. Glasgow had other problems, many of them self-inflicted.

In the post-war years the city's priority was housing. The malaise of the slums persisted, and they had to be cleared. The Clyde Valley plan of 1946 prescribed systematic

In all, 85,000 tenement houses were demolished and a network of urban motorways changed the face of the city centre and swept away whole communities. A new multi-storey Gorbals rose from the rubble of the old.

In 20 years the city had transformed itself into something modern, rational and unlikeable. There was a price to pay. The population had declined from more than a million in 1951 to less than 900,000 in 1971, but many of those who moved to the New Towns were young and vigorous wage-earners. The urban motorways also encouraged the middle class to flee the city in increasing numbers to new private estates in the suburbs, and the

depopulation, "overspill" New Towns and massive peripheral estates. With hindsight there was much that was wrong with this vision, but the planners believed they had the best interests of the city and its people at heart. Throughout the 1950s and 1960s thousands of Glaswegians were rehoused in the New Towns of East Kilbride, Cumbernauld and Irvine and thousands more were given brave new council homes in Green Belt estates such as Easterhouse and Castlemilk.

Left, shipbuilding, a dying industry. <u>Above</u>, Glasgow's attempt to solve its housing problem.

old working class districts which – however rotten their fabric or legion their problems – had given Glasgow a coherent social character, were now being dismantled.

The new high-rises of the Gorbals and the isolated sprawl of Easterhouse were creating as many problems as they solved. The city had already lost much of its heart, and it was now in danger of losing its soul. "The problem is," said the late Geoffrey Shaw, who was housing convenor when Glasgow became part of Strathclyde Region under local government reorganisation in 1975, "that while people could live with violence and poverty, we've never quite learned to live with concrete."

Then, in 1976, came the imaginative stroke which was to redefine planning policy and become one of the milestones on the route to renaissance. GEAR was launched. The regeneration of 4,000 acres (1,600 hectares) of the East End – Glasgow Eastern Area Renewal – has been the most ambitious scheme of its kind in Western Europe, and it started a momentum which produced a whole series of initiatives. Glasgow finally realised that many of its tenement buildings were not only sound but handsome. Rehabilitation and stone-cleaning replaced demolition. Whole

buildings; the opening of an adventurous new museum in Pollok Country Park to house the eclectic and long-neglected Burrell Collection; and, in 1988, the prodigious International Garden Festival which, along with the Scottish Exhibition Centre opened in 1985, successfully converted some of the wasteland of empty docks and weedy wharves on the banks of the Clyde from an area of barren stillness to one of fertile activity.

Glasgow is still a city in transition. While its morale is high and its looks have improved the residue of decades of unemployment, bad housing and social debilitation remains. But over the past 20 years it has

communities, including the people of the East End, were more closely involved in planning decisions and the design of local authority housing. And, recognising that it had what the advertising industry call an "image problem", the city began to look to its public relations.

There followed the dynamic "Glasgow's Miles Better" campaign; new co-operation between local authority and private enterprise to revitalise the old "Merchant City" of derelict warehouses and gap sites and bring people back to live there; the cleaning and display of the Victorian city with its splendid

revived its own spirit in a manner which is startling, if not downright miraculous. If its elevation to European City of Culture in 1990 marked the apogee of its renaissance, there are many who still believe its economic base is unsound. However, in its progress from dear green place to post-industrial metropolis, the city has shown a capacity to reinvent itself over and over again. The will to do so remains. Whatever its future, Glasgow will always have one.

Above, concert on Glasgow Green by internationally successful local pop group Wet Wet Wet.

THE CITY THAT REINVENTED ITSELF

At the start of the 1980s Glasgow was down, if not out. In the 1970s it had made national headlines when workers took over the Upper Clyde Shipyard. Much of the world then decided that the waters of the Clyde flowed red and investors returned their money, if not to their sporrans, at least to their banks. Then, during the 1980s, Glasgow, for some of its inhabitants at any rate, proved that there is life after death – or, at least, after moribundity. How was it done?

The city had suffered previous declines and yet, like the phoenix, had arisen. In 1776, when the Americans decided they had had their fill of colonialism, the tobacco industry on which Glasgow was founded virtually disappeared overnight and the city had to re-invent itself. And so it went: ups and downs. First, there was tobacco; then linen and textiles; then heavy engineering and shipbuilding. Each time the city was in the van of its chosen speciality, and each time was boom time until, inevitably, the bubble burst.

The city's regeneration commenced with a detailed analysis of the decline of its heavy engineering, shipbuilding and manufacturing and how it might pursue a programme of economic regeneration. McKinsey and Company, the consultants, suggested a fourfold attack: put life back into the inner city; expand the retail sector within the city; attract large companies to relocate in Glasgow; and develop tourism. Such proposals were standard enough medicine for industrial cities on the skids, but for Glasgow the prescription worked.

One feature which, for centuries, has set Glasgow apart from other comparable cities is that it has always enjoyed a strong partnership between its industrialists and the City Fathers – who, frequently, have been one and the same. Private and public sectors often work hand in hand with massive institutional involvement. In this respect Glasgow is more like a village than a metropolis. Then again, no city has a middle class which is so conscious of its contribution to high culture.

In 1983, the then Lord Provost, Michael Kelly,

GLASGOW'S MILES BETTER

approached John Struthers of the advertising company of that name and so was born the city's remarkably successful "Glasgow's Miles Better" campaign. At first it was directed solely at Glaswegians and its aim was to make them "walk tall", but nine months after Mr Happy, the smirking sunburst emblem of the campaign, had lit up the city it was proposed that he should travel further afield and attempt to attract businessmen and even tourists to Glasgow. The public sector had no funds and it was the private sector which carried the can for the next four years. The total cost was well under £1 million which, for such a campaign, is mere bawbees.

It was fortuitous that, coincidentally with the birth of Mr Happy, the Burrell Collection, which had been sitting for aeons in basements until the terms of Sir William Burrell's legacy could be fulfilled, finally found its home, and the art world – which also includes much of the money world – was abuzz with anticipation.

It was because of the successful "Miles Better" campaign that Glasgow was chosen as the Garden Festival city for 1988 and its handling of that six-month extravaganza brought much kudos. And so, to the amazement of one and all – Glasgow was chosen to be the European City of Culture in 1990. Suddenly – or was it all very gradual and just had not been noticed by those outside of the city? – Glasgow was the "in-place" not only in the UK but in Europe and the US. Glasgow was back on the map: surely it could not be that bad a place after all? Investors and multinationals, eternally flexible, abandoned their image of the "Red Clyde".

Many feel that since 1990, Glasgow has drifted, into lethargy and inertia, the impressive achievements of recent years either brushed aside or even forgotten in what has continued to be a difficult economic climate. However, the definitive spirit of Glasgow lives on, as it always will, and its fighting edge has, against all the obstacles and barriers which have been put in its way, helped maintain the pride and strength that the city has always had. Such values, it seems, have paid off once again – in 1996 Glasgow hosted its very own Festival of Visual Arts, and in 1999 it will be the prestigious title-holder of the "UK City of Architecture and Design" award. ∎

Highlanders and Irish, Italians and Jews, Chinese and Ghanaians, Poles and Greeks and many different peoples from the Indian sub-continent all make their home in Glasgow. Some have been assimilated, others have not. Some claim racial intolerance, others are more satisfied with their lot.

For many, Glasgow has proved a sucessful melting-pot. As early as 1905, Michael Simons, a Jew, was Deputy Lieutenant of the County of the City of Glasgow. In recent years the city has had a Jewish Lord Provost, or Mayor (who, incidentally, became the Deputy Speaker of the House of Commons), a Roman Catholic Chief of Police (until a few years ago, the number on the force who "kicked with the left foot" was negligible), and the present Director of Education is a second-generation Italian.

But the path to racial peace has not been smooth. "Dirty, lazy, untrustworthy, thieving" are just some of the adjectives which were uttered and recorded in a Glasgow council meeting in the 18th century. These words did not describe immigrants from foreign lands but referred to the Highlanders who had come south to live in Glasgow. A century later, the same adjectives were used to describe Irish immigrants.

Integrated at last: Glasgow, therefore, has had a long experience, a long history, of racial intolerance. Yet those Highlanders and the Irish who originally formed a subgroup based on religion and language were ultimately integrated, as were in the 20th century the Jews and the Italians and other European minorities.

Even those from the Indian sub-continent who are not yet integrated (and some of whom are racially harassed) consider Glasgow as their home rather than looking backwards and eastwards to India as do their brethren in, for example, the city of Bradford. Second-generation Chinese refer to themselves as "Chinks" in broad Glasgow

accents and have taken on board that colourful Glasgow speech which the visitor might assume to be derogatory but which is in reality affectionate and which Glaswegians even apply to their own kith and kin. "Aye, he's a wee keelie" (Yes, he is a small rascal). Or "Away doon to the Tally and buy yerself an ice-cream" (Go down to the Italians and buy an ice-cream.)

Racial prejudice does exist in Glasgow. However, Glasgow would be, if not at the

bottom, then very close to the bottom of any harassment league table which included cities in the United States, France and Germany, or in the rest of Britain. While the Glasgow Hindi claims racial harassment by the natives, he is turning his face and moving southwards because of bedevilment by fellow countrymen from the Indian sub-continent: the Pakistanis.

On the other hand, those antagonisms which are common in the homeland tend to disappear among immigrants: divided they fall, united they stand. And so, whereas in Kashmir the Indian and Pakistani may be at

Preceding pages: winning the race for racial equality. Left and right, Glasgow's melting pot.

loggerheads, in Glasgow they are all Kashmiris and business partnerships are formed between Indians and Pakistanis. (Incidentally, when they use the word "black" to refer to themselves it naturally has a political and not a pejorative meaning and does not denote skin colour.)

Enquire of a Chinese whether he is Hakka or Cantonese and he looks uncomprehendingly; in Glasgow all Chinese are... Chinese. Many of the city's Iranians and Iraquis, most of whom are students, are firm friends and would like to make Glasgow their home.

The first major influx of Chinese and Indians in the early 1950s was the result of direct

invitations by the City Fathers, who needed people to work both on the buses and in the hospitals. Labourers were not required nor invited. Although the Indians had been born in villages, they were well-educated and the jobs they took were way below their educational achievements. Gradually, they abandoned their original jobs; nowadays they are no longer on the buses but rather have established their own businesses.

The acceptance of these immigrants and those who preceded them might be due, at least in part, to the fact that they, like most Glaswegians, place a great value on educa-

tion. The Chinese, the Indians and the Jews would top any poll to determine which peoples are most enthralled by education.

It is difficult to assess the number of people from the Indian sub-continent who live in Greater Glasgow but the figure is in the region of 50,000. Pakistanis outnumber Indians by about two to one; there is also a substantial Bangladeshi community and some who, irrespective of their religion, classify themselves as Kashmiris.

Most Indians are from the Punjab and they dominate the Race Councils while the Pakistanis dominate the political scene and vote Labour. Hindus are found in business and law while all groups from the Indian sub-continent appear to be involved in the restaurant business or the running of small general stores. The small general store of Mr Bashirman, a Pakistani Glaswegian who is now a millionaire Justice of the Peace, grew and grew by concentrating on the sale of that which is dear to so many of his fellow citizens: whisky. In many fields, it is noticeable how closely the Pakistanis have followed in the paths the Jews trod a century ago.

Desirable residences: Ghetto life as such is unknown but there are large enclaves of blacks in the Pollokshields and Govan districts in the south of the city and Woodlands in the west. Those who have made it move to Bishopbriggs and Bearsden, the latter outside even Greater Glasgow – although only 6 miles (10 km) from the city centre.

The community does not believe in parochial schools but language is not lost. Some city secondary schools offer Hindi as a language, for both blacks and whites, and primary schools have black teachers assigned to work alongside the white teachers. The Glasgow Mosque and Islamic Centre is a city landmark. The Sikhs have three temples. There is a Hindu Temple and an Asia-Christian Fellowship.

In Dilip Deb, the community boasts Scotland's only black lawyer and in Gurneet Mattu they have the country's only black playwright. One black bookshop exists – the Crosshill Asian Bookshop – but, surprisingly for a land which produced Tagore, it is run by a Scot, Martin Watson. Black clubs and societies abound, including the Alien

Arts Theatre Group and the Asian Artistes Association.

The vast majority of Greater Glasgow's Chinese community, which numbers between 8,000 and 10,000 – nobody is certain of the precise number – are Cantonese or Hakkas from the Hong Kong New Territories or are first-generation descendants of immigrants, most of whom arrived in Glasgow in the 1950s. They left their country for the same reason that the Highlanders had abandoned their native heath 200 years before and that the Irish had said goodbye to Erin 100 years later: because of the collapse of agriculture and fishing in their own land. A few mem-

days. Instruction for the 400 students is in Cantonese, although older students are sometimes taught in Mandarin.

Nearly all the Chinese work in the catering industry and greater Glasgow has dozens of Chinese restaurants. Only a few of the younger generation are professional persons, though when this is translated into percentage terms the figure might even be above the Glasgow average. Many are Catholics but Confucianism still reigns in the home and these are the principles – and, in some few instances, those of the triads – to which the Glasgow Chinese kowtow.

In the 1980s Glasgow escaped the race

bers of the community are from Malaysia, Singapore and the Republic of China.

Glasgow does not have a Chinatown and the Chinese live throughout the city. Most have homes near the Art School which, coincidentally, is situated close to the casinos. Those who have "made it" reside out of town in Bearsden. Two Chinese schools, one of which accepts students until the age of 12 and the other until the age of 18, hold Chinese language and culture classes on Satur-

Left, the city has a strong Jewish tradition. Above, Asian shopkeepers stay open until late.

riots which plagued English cities of a comparable size. It is usually claimed that this is because the city, apart from a small number of Ghanaians, does not have an Afro-Caribbean population and because of the political passiveness of its blacks. However, most authorities suggest that the reason was that the breeding grounds which fomented these riots in Birmingham and Liverpool did not exist in Glasgow, whose inner city slums had largely been replaced by peripheral housing estates where few blacks lived.

That Catholic-Protestant intolerance which was formerly such an integral part of the

Glasgow scene has, if not disappeared, then greatly diminished. Nowadays, the large annual Orange Day (Protestant) parade is peaceful and the great battles at Ibrox and Parkhead between the Blue and the Green (Rangers and Celtic) supporters are noisy and the air filled with taunting words rather than with weapons: much bark but little bite. The end of religious intolerance on the football field was signalled in the summer of 1989 when Protestant Rangers signed Mo Johnson, a renowned Catholic player. All forecast riots when the two rivals met: nothing actually happened.

Many Chinese and the blacks are con-

vinced that cessation of hostilities between the Catholics and the Protestants has resulted in both these groups seeking alternative outlets for their intolerance – namely, in *their* harassment. When tolerance against one group is removed, must it be replaced with intolerance against another group? Does centuries of intolerance result in an immutable genotype?

Italians form an especially cohesive group. They first arrived in Glasgow at the start of the 20th century and today they number about 20,000. Most came from the region between Rome and Naples or from Lucca, a province of Tuscany. (Practically every member of the not inconsiderable Italian populace of Greenock and Gourock, which were formerly ports, is from La Spezia in Liguria, which had a maritime civilization before the Roman era.) On arrival, they sought work which nobody else did and at which they, with lack of language and absence of capital, could succeed and so they opened fish-and-chip shops and then ice-cream shops and finally restaurants.

Today they are found in all the professions and in retail and wholesale business, but not in politics. The community is integrated yet maintains its identity with Italian Associations where both culture and language are taught. It has an Italian chaplain.

The Jewish experience: Jews have had a more chequered history. Tom Honeyman, who was director of the Glasgow Art Galleries and co-founder of the Citizens' Theatre, once said: "The trouble with Glasgow Jews is that there are not enough of them." And today, more than half a century after Honeyman made this remark, the outstanding role which Glasgow Jewry plays in the city's art scene, mainly through patronage, belies their numbers. The city has a community of about 9,000 Jews, although with intermarriage this figure is constantly being eroded.

One factor which might have made Glasgow tolerant of its Jewish minority is that some of those Highlanders who arrived in the big city in the 18th century bore Christian names such as Isaac and Abraham and came to regard the Jews as aboriginal Presbyterians. Indeed, some Glaswegians who came from the Highlands firmly believe that they belong to one of the 10 Lost Tribes. To balance this, there are Glasgow Jews with the name Campbell. And has any other city in the world a Jewish bagpipe band?

Yet, even today, bigotry exists: not a few of Glasgow's private golf clubs refuse to accept Jewish members. The Jewish community resolved this slight by the simple expedient of forming their own club, which is open to all Glaswegians, irrespective of race, colour or religion.

Left, musical integration. Right, street trader.

KEEPING PACE WITH "THE PATTER"

If, when in Glasgow, you hear a *wee bachle* (a small, often somewhat misshapen person) calling "Hey Jimmie", do not ignore him: chances are that, whether your name is Gilbert, Rufus or Lord McClan, he is addressing *you*. Lady McClan, Genevieve or Elspeth are likely to be simply addressed as *Mrs Wummin*.

The visitor does not need to know the patter in order to survive, but a knowledge of it will add considerably to the pleasure of a stay. The patter is especially strong in abuse which is more often affectionate than it is aggressive and, ever conscious to changes, especially in the social conditions of the city, it is constantly evolving.

Glaswegians are hospitable and the visitor might well be invited for "a refreshment" – a popular euphemism for an alcoholic drink. En route to the pub your host might say: "*Ah'll hiv tae go tae the hole in the wa' afore we hit the boozer.*" ("I must stop at the bank's cash dispenser before we reach the public house.")

Once in the pub Jimmie may meet some of his pals and invite them for a drink. *S'ma bell: whit'r ye fur?* means, to use another vernacular, "My Shout". Responses might include *C'n ah git a wee nippy sweetie?* ("May I have a small glass of whisky?"); *Jist geeza voddy* ("I shall merely have a vodka"), or the classical *Ah'll hiv a hauf and hauf.* The last named is a half a pint of beer and a half-measure of whisky. One Jimmie more coy – in Glasgow? – than his pals might say: "*Wouldny say eeichie or ochie*" ("I wouldn't say yes or no").

Naturally, the talk will get around to previous blow-outs. *That wis a rare wee sesh last Setterday: Jimmie wis fu' as a wulk.* (That was a splendid drinking evening last Saturday: Jimmie was drunk as a whelk). Other Jimmies would have been *steamin', stotious, oot of their brains* or *wellied.* (The neophyte must take care not to confuse *wellies* and *wallies*; the former are gumboots while the latter are dentures.)

As he *stoated oot* the pub, Jimmie said to his pals: *See yeez the morra then.* ("See you tomor-row".) *Yeez* is the plural of *ye* (you) while *yeez yins* means "those others" or "those persons". Thus, standing at a bus stop one is almost certain to hear the *wummen* talking: *Yeez yins wid fair scunner ye* ("Those people really irritate you") or *Awa ye go ya mug ye*, which translates as "Get lost", with the use of the double *ye* increasing the vehemence of the remark.

Eavesdropping at a bus stop is a great way to increase one's knowledge of the patter – or to leave one utterly flummoxed. I bumped into *thingmyjig* yesterday; *she's got a mooth oan her like the Clyde Tunnel.* Her companion refers to *thingmyjig* as *hingmy* or *hingwy* (even broader Glasgow versions of whatsisname) and further tears her apart by adding *A've no come across sumdy as donnert as her.* ("I've never met anyone so stupid.")

Donnert is but one of a host of words is used to describe the sanity of one's neighbours. They include *gommy, bampot, nutter, tumshie* and *eejit* or, somewhat more politely, *awa' wi the fairies.* Not quite questioning sanity but suggesting a dreamy person or someone not quite at grips with matters is the phrase *fair glaikit.*

Young love, of course, has its own patter. *Wis that Mary I seed ye with last nicht? I canna stand the sicht o' hir: she's so peely-wally and her hair is like straw hingin oot a midden. Yon lassie's a richt wee brammer; ye'll never get aff w' her.* ("That girl is quite stunning: you will never make it with her.") Or, *have ye seen that burd Jimmie's guan wi noo? She's a wee stoater.* ("Have you seen the girl that Jimmy is presently going out with? She is stunning.")

The girls also have their say. *You mibby think he's somethin, but ah think he's hacket* ("You might think he is attractive but I think he is ugly") or *Ah mind him: whit a nyaff: he's a wee keelie*: ("I remember him: an irritating person: a small nothing.") *Keelie* is a common term for Glaswegians which can be either insulting or affectionate. However, the visitor best not attempt to use it until he is expert with the patter; basically, it means a hooligan.

Dearie mearie – whit time dae ye ca' this? Ah mist be aff. Ta ta for noo. ("Dear me – is that the time? I must be leaving. Goodbye for now.") ∎

The toughest Glasgow pubs, the sports writer Hugh McIlvanney once declared, could be taken by the Red Army in three days – or a day and a half if tactical nuclear weapons were used. This, like all aphorisms about Glasgow, is part-myth and part-fact – and a bit less fact now than it used to be. For Glasgow's pubs, like Glasgow's everything, are changing.

Take the legendary *The Saracen Head*, for instance – still known everywhere as "The Sarry Heid". Situated in the Gallowgate area of Glasgow's east end, this establishment was at one stage perhaps the most notorious public house in the city. Originally dating back to the 18th century, it was once a haven for tramps, thieves, hawkers, writers, poets and artists who would come here regularly to spend their hours fervently discussing the hopes and dilemmas of the outside world, playing fisticuffs with one another, or peacefully resting their merry heads, snoozing away the drowsy effects of just one to many whiskies. Today, this image has been cast aside and now, after recently being subjected to some extensive refurbishment, the pub is geared to a more younger, "fashionable" clientele.

Serious pursuit: In Glasgow, drinking is a passion. The west of Scotland has more pubs per head of population than anywhere else in Europe, and more drinkers too. The Irish/Highland mix has meant that drinking is a serious pursuit in the city and teetotallism is regarded with contempt. As Scots comedian Will Fyffe once put it: "When you're teetotal, ach, when you're teetotal, you have a nasty feeling that everybody's your boss".

The ubiquitous "wee hauf" – Glaswegian dialect for *half* – is a small whisky. When you add a chaser of a half-pint of beer, you get the famed request from the Glaswegian toper for a "hauf and a hauf".

Left, a powerful relic of the past – the infamous *Saracen Head* before undergoing its recent refurbishment to become a "healthier" pub. Right, the wee "haul and hauf".

At one time the normal measure of whisky was a half-gill. Today the measure is a quarter-gill, though probably most Scottish pubs sell a fifth-of-a-gill measure. A sixth-gill – the normal volume in England – is regarded with derision, and all whisky drinkers try to take their ease in pubs which sell quarter-gills – "quarter-gill shops".

Visitors can easily be confused by much of this terminology. The normal request for a whisky in Glasgow is "a half". You might

hear a drinker ask for "a dram". If you happen to hear someone ask for "a nip", you can rest assure that the fellow is from Edinburgh, or somewhere in the east of Scotland. And if you're offered "a glass" of whisky, expect a double – sometimes known as a "gentleman's measure".

Other euphemisms for the amber fluid are: "a wee toddy", "a nippy sweetie", or sometimes in Glaswegians of Irish origin "a ball of malt". It doesn't really matter what you call it, however, Glasgow is a great whisky-drinking city.

After some years when the white spirits

such as gin, vodka, or Bacardi were clearly gaining ground among Glaswegian drinkers, whisky has made a comeback, even among the young. This is not due to the fashion for single malts which has become prevalent in England, for Scottish bars have always carried a considerable number of fine single malts. Indeed, one pub – *The Pot Still* in Hope Street – devotes itself to the purveying nearly every whisky you can think of.

Most whisky drinkers, however, still order a blended whisky to which they also add a little water or sometimes lemonade. Few Scots take soda water. It is a myth that Scotsmen drink their liquor neat: whisky

improves in aroma and taste with a little water in it. The English dilute whisky with soda because their tap water is so vile; Glasgow's tap water is clear and pure, straight from the lovely Loch Katrine. But, water or not, you will be astonished at the sheer range of whiskies, and indeed other spirits, which even a modest pub carries.

Beer is drunk in plenty too, and not only as a half-pint chaser. A number of pubs have imported English beers, in the form of real ale, but the normal beer sold is called "heavy" instead of "bitter". Scottish beers are stronger and usually sweeter than English ales and the

visitor should treat them with respect. Lager is widely drunk, especially by the young, and every bar stocks a large variety of expensive German and continental lagers and pils, both on draught and in bottle. There are several wine bars in the city but they too mainly trade in beers and spirits.

The wine bar began making an appearance in Glasgow a few years ago, and at that time there was a certain resistance because of an old and contemptuous nomenclature in which certain very low dives were known as "wine shops". Such places sold, not table wines, but dessert wines, and very cheap ones at that. The wines were often mixed with whisky to provide a potent brew. They were mixed, too, with methylated spirits by the less well-off denizens, a mixture known, poetically, as "electric soup".

"It's a well-run shop," you will hear natives declaring, or of a publican that "he keeps a clean wee shop". But then pubs are, after all, exactly that: shops. Another term, sometimes used to denote a rough establishment, is *howff*, meaning a somewhat squalid house – in this case, a public one.

Rules of the game: But all this is academic. What matters is that you enjoy drinking in Glasgow's pubs; to ensure that you do, you need to know some basic rules of etiquette. First, a warning: do not be alarmed by the high level of energy used by Glaswegians in pub arguments. Glaswegians are not temperate in drink or discussion and they go to pubs to argue. They are naturally disputatious and enjoy arguments hugely.

Arguments almost never lead to violence: you will find that Glasgow pubs, no matter how vibrant, enjoy a high level of personal conduct, mainly because such offences would lead to being "barred", a truly dreadful fate to anyone living in a culture so dependant on the pub as a social focus. Any dispute likely to lead to fisticuffs would be conducted outside and round the corner, and it would be bad form to involve anybody else other than the protagonists.

Visitors and strangers, especially from foreign parts, are welcomed in Glasgow bars and you will find a natural curiosity on the part of bar staff and customers. It is best to wait for them to inaugurate a conversation, though an idle observation on your part to a lone drinker may be permitted. Do not try to enter a strange company, as you will be rebuffed. Glaswegians will think you to be the constabulary, in plain clothes, looking for information. Now we come to a vital point. If you should be invited into company, you will have joined the "round". Each member in the round takes it in turn to buy drinks for all the others, and a failure to meet this obligation will be met with quite ferocious contumely. Even if the last bell goes, signalling the approach of closing time, you must try and squeeze in your round of drinks before the final shutters of the bar come

ephone booths, with many a citizen using his local as an office, as extensions to universities and colleges – it is not unusual to find professors conducting informal tutorials in a West End pub – and even as public lavatories, for publicans recognise the city's lack of public conveniences. As the old spit-and-sawdust establishments have gone (much to the regret of many citizens), all the bars in the city possess ladies' toilets now.

Naturally, there are couple of exceptions. One is the famous *Heraghty's Bar* on Glasgow's southside. Once a gloriously ramshackle place, it is now revamped into one of the most lovely pubs in the UK but, true to

down for the night.

Do not be surprised either at the local habit of ordering another set of refreshments long before the first drink is finished. It is not uncommon to find a Glaswegian with four whiskies set in front of him. And the English practice of using the same glass all night is not followed in Scotland: it is illegal, in fact.

Glasgow pubs are not unlike those of Dublin in that they are used as more than drinking places. Some fulfill the role of public tel-

tradition, still does not have a ladies' toilet and the womenfolk simply use the lavatory in the pub next door. Nobody seems to find anything odd about this arrangement.

You will find that Glasgow pubs are invariably rather noisy, but not, blessedly, because of muzak – although there are disco-type pubs for the young, most pubs eschew background music – but because Glaswegians are noisy people generally, drunk or sober. You will find them friendly in the pubs – perhaps too friendly on occasion – and all they will ask of you is that you are friendly back.

Left, stained glass in the Griffin. **Above**, peace is a pint in a familiar public house.

There is a very old Glasgow joke about the Rangers supporter whose wife, in the middle of a family agrument, accuses him of loving Rangers more than her. "Rangers?" he booms, "I love *Celtic* more than you."

If the joke does nothing to alleviate the reputation the Glaswegian male has acquired for a particularly virile brand of chauvinism, it does offer a glimpse of the manic obsession the city possesses for the people's game. The notoriety of the contests between Rangers and Celtic has gone around the world and back again, yet there is much more to the Glaswegians' love of football than the abhorrent bigotries which masquerade under religious banners.

It is also interesting to note that this enormous working-class obsession was started in 1867 by middle-class Highlanders. Football in the city was to become the symbol of the labouring class of the 20th century, but it owes its roots to a collection of young Highland tradesmen and embryo businessmen who formed that living bastion to amateurism, Queen's Park.

Founding fathers: The gentlemen who were to found Queen's, the oldest Scottish football club, had come down from the north where the Highland clearances had scattered the populace towards the Central Belt. The Glasgow in which they chose to settle had also been invaded by Irishmen fleeing famine and destitution, but the mature young men who watched some YMCA lads playing football on Queen's Park Recreation Ground had come to town with the intention of improving their trading prospects.

Perhaps some of them could be termed the Yuppies of their day, but at any rate they liked what they saw, decided to form their club and, by a margin of one vote, chose to call it Queen's Park, which was to become the world's most famous amateur club.

Two Hampden Parks were utilised before they settled on the current site which has also

become the home of the Scottish national team. So successful was the amateur team that it was eight years before it lost a game. Its success can be measured less dramatically nowadays but the fact that it survives at all in a business that is the epitome of professionalism is remarkable enough.

If the old stadium, outdated and uncomfortable, is the subject of much criticism today, any visitor with a sporting soul who ventures out to Mount Florida on a match

day will surely see and hear and sense the great world stars, the huge crowds, the swell of excitement.

Cheap at the price: Why the working (and non-working) men chose this game as their escape from drudgery, poverty and the bleakness of the overcrowded slums in the "ghetto" sections of the city is not difficult to guess. Football, unlike other activities, costs nothing – apart from a ball of sorts, often one made of cloth. Position a couple of jackets as goal-posts, station a sentry at each end of the street to look out for the "polis" (the police), and the game was on.

Left, guess which team he supports? **Right**, the old rivals Rangers and Celtic in action.

Maybe more accurately than any other picture, the image of the raggedy child kicking a ball along a street lit by bleak gas lamps captures the meaning of what sport meant to the Glaswegian. It was the vision of senior football as an escape route to relative wealth, not to mention a rather comfortable and untaxing lifestyle, which fired the teenagers from the slums of the Gorbals before World War II and the great sprawling housing schemes of the 1940s and 1950s.

Yet the two teams towards which they mostly gravitated, spiritually and materially, were spawned in humble enough circumstances. Rangers was founded because some

It is fascinating to recall that the mighty club which was to become a candidate as the most powerful in Britain, as well as one of the richest, was treated with some disdain by Queen's Park in those formative years. Queen's, as the élite of the game, was not disposed to play a team without a proper ground. Today the amateurs from the south side battle away gallantly in the lower reaches of Scottish football while Rangers, in its magnificent custom-built stadium at Ibrox, enjoys the trappings that go with a multi-million pound business.

Although it was a long distance short of that eminence by the time Celtic came into

lads who enjoyed rowing down the Clyde fancied the idea of playing this new ball game on Glasgow Green. The oarsmen got together in 1873 and "borrowed" the name of an English rugby club, to become Rangers Football Club. Brothers by the name of McNeill were instrumental in founding the club, although one of them, William, was allowed to make his contribution only after he threatened to take the ball, his personal property, away.

From those tender beginnings in 1873 Rangers hustled around a few different grounds until it reached Ibrox 14 years later.

being, Rangers had been around long enough to have established a sound base. It was in 1888 that Celtic was given birth, fathered by Irish immigrants for predominantly charitable reasons. The Catholics who had settled mainly in the east end of Glasgow had endured severe poverty for decades and many a parish priest had attempted to start a football team in the hope of raising badly-needed funds for the poor.

None succeeded until a group of prominent men among the Irish community, moti-

Above, fans at a Rangers-Celtic match.

vated particularly by a businessman, John Glass, realised the dream of the West Scotland immigrants by launching Celtic. They played their first game on 28 May 1888, beating Rangers 5 to 2, and thus began the series of derbies which has grown to such notoriety. Yet in those early years there was none of the deep hostility that has proved such an embarrassment to the city. In fact, nearly all the matches they played were friendlies in the true sense of the word.

Religious divide: Gradually, however, the polarisation of the two sets of supporters produced an intense, unhealthy rivalry. Its foundations lay in a number of sociological causes, among them the Presbyterian resentment not only of the Irish Catholic expansion in their city but also of the immigrants' willingness to accept lower rates of pay, and the importation of the Belfast religious divides whose manifestations unhappily continue across the Irish Sea.

The rift between the clubs grew wider as the crowds grew bigger and no less bitter. Rangers' adherence to an unwritten but firmly applied "No Catholics" rule did nothing to reduce the feelings of persecution among the minority, imagined or otherwise.

However distasteful these Old Firm matches became, the fact is that the sharpness of the clubs' rivalry probably hoisted the standard of football in the country to a level it might otherwise never have reached. The demands at either end of the city to succeed inevitably meant keeping up with the other lot and, showing a neat appreciation of the *mores* of capitalist competition, the finest exponents of the workers' game responded to market forces.

There have been riots, on and off the field, and considering the genetic combinations that spawned the supporters of both clubs that can hardly come as a surprise. There is no prevalence of passive resistance in the Irish or Scottish antecedents but a corollary of the rivalry has been a remarkable domination of football in their country. At the time of writing, for instance, Rangers has won the league championship 45 times, Celtic 35; but, in the Scottish Cup, Celtic has been successful 30 times, against 26 by Rangers.

There is hope, too, that the bad, or at least the worst, days are past. Rangers' highly publicised signing of a prominent Catholic player in 1989 demonstrated clearly enough the changing times. And the broadening of the game's frontiers, especially the ever expanding European commitments, has helped to reduce the insularity of clubs and supporters. For a long time, in any case, the great majority of the Glasgow populace has rejected and fumed at the match-day restoration of the ancient hatreds and bigotries.

The Glaswegians' genuine love of football has tended to be sunk in the sea of publicity that has carried news of the Old Firm supporters' antics to every corner of the world. But it is there in an extraordinary devotion that is greater than any commitment to a single team. Less passionate, of course, but heart-felt, the city's love affair with the sport in general is best illustrated by the fact that for most of the century it has supported six senior teams.

Even today five remain: Celtic, Rangers, Queen's Park, Partick Thistle and Clyde. One other, Third Lanark, was mismanaged into liquidation in 1967, but Thistle and Clyde soldier on gallantly in the shadow of the big two.

Army of sympathisers: Thistle, from Partick, close to the heart of the city, were established in 1876 and ever since has been the alternative team for many with leanings to either Celtic or Rangers. Likewise Clyde, from the southern side, which, having been forced to leave its own ground for economical reasons, has been sharing Thistle's ground, Firhill, for some time. Each of them has a loyal, if tiny, band of genuine fans, augmented by an army of sympathisers throughout the city. They are alive and have survived testing times only because of this deep attachment to football.

But nothing, even devotion, can be guaranteed forever and the challenge of the 21st century awaits the people's game within the Glasgow boundaries. As yet, football is still attracting booming crowds and still discovering new talents. But perhaps there are signs that things could be different after the millennium. For the moment, however, it is still the game. Or, to use the Glasgow vernacular, *ra gemme.*

That such a commercial, philistine city as "dear, dirty Glasgow" should have had the nerve to turn itself into a cultural mecca seems, at first glance, like typical civic cheek. Yet it's the same aggressive dynamism that once built great ships which is now promoting the lavish public galleries and bustling sale rooms and propelling its young native painters towards the glittering prizes of New York recognition. Civic pride, as ever, is unbounded. Where else would taxi drivers

who frittered away his substance on sensory delights disapproved of by the kirk (church). Besides, the arts were the concern of genteel Edinburgh, which Glasgow, second city of the British Empire, had long surpassed. Practical achievements, linked to sound finance, were what mattered. "Edinburgh may *be* the capital," the saying went, "but we *have* the capital."

Given the austerity of the kirk, which frowned on "outer show", it's strange that

regale the visitor with the glories of *our* Burrell Collection or *our* Charles Rennie Mackintosh?

A hundred years ago, in the 1890s, Francis Newbery, principal of Glasgow School of Art, prophesied that his city would one day emulate the cultural prestige of Venice, Paris and Amsterdam. At the time this seemed an absurd boast – typically Glaswegian. For the place was then run by dour, hard-headed businessmen, while its intellectuals directed their energy to useful pursuits such as medicine, engineering and the law.

The artist was of little account, a mere idler

Scotland should be the only British region with a distinctive school of painting. This originated in 18th-century Edinburgh, where there was a sudden flowering of intellectual activity. In addition to scientists, philosophers and men of letters, the "Athens of the North" also produced Alan Ramsay, court painter to George III, Henry Raeburn, knighted by George IV, the genre painter David Wilkie, and in architecture the brothers Adam whose aerial neo-classicism became the craze of Europe.

Glasgow was still a minor town. Not until the 19th century did it become a great industrial centre, much richer than Edinburgh and jealous of its cultural edge. Ever since, as in Italy during the Renaissance, inter-city rivalry has helped foster the arts. Glasgow opened Scotland's first museum, the Hunterian, in 1807; its now famous School of Art in 1840; then a permanent civic collection, the McLellan Galleries; and an exhibition centre, the Glasgow Institute of Fine Arts. As early as 1867, the Glasgow Art Club was formed, conferring "respectability" on that

had made good: Dr William Hunter (of the Hunterian), who rose to fame as a pioneer of obstetrics; Archibald McLellan, who grew rich more prosaically as a coach builder; and later, the most munificent of all, shipowner William Burrell.

The Glasgow Boys: Initially, the pictorial style of Scottish art was controlled by the Edinburgh establishment. But in the 1870s a rebellion was mounted by a group of young painters, dubbed derisively the Glasgow

doubtful creature, the practising artist.

Snobbery, too, played its part. In an era of new money, acquiring fine paintings gave tone to the self-made man. But unworthy cravings for status were balanced by Presbyterian virtue, which insisted that social debts be repaid. Before 1900, Glasgow's public collections were built up almost entirely through private donations from men who

Boys. Their leader was James Guthrie; others included Arthur Melville, George Henry, John Lavery, Edward Hornel and Joseph Crawhall.

Rejecting the polished technique and grandiose, often moralising subjects of the academic "Gluepots", they broke with convention by abandoning their studios to paint in the open air, choosing scenes from peasant life: a goose girl, a cabbage patch, munching cattle. Inspired by Whistler and the Dutch and French Realists, their sketchy brushwork, luscious colours and, above all, their proletarian themes offended both the prim

Preceding pages: painting a backdrop in a Glasgow theatre. <u>Left</u>, the Hunterian Gallery. <u>Above</u>, Lavery's *Mrs Stewart-Clark* and Fergusson's *Voiles Indiennes*.

and the newly genteel. So they fled, disgusted, to Paris.

Years later, when they were acclaimed in Europe's capitals and in distant New York, Glasgow pride was tickled – after all, who from Edinburgh could compete? – and their pictures became highly prized (as well as priced). In contrast to the rarefied dabblings emanating from Edinburgh, their honest, earthy vigour were seen as being essentially Glaswegian.

But suspicion and prejudice were still directed at their great contemporary, Charles Rennie Mackintosh, creator of the Glasgow Style. Mocked as a drunken "tea-room de-

produced a second generation of rebels, the Scottish Colourists: J.D. Fergusson, Leslie Hunter, S.J. Peploe and F.C.B. Cadell. Oppressed by Scotland's mean-spirited philistinism, they too fled to Paris to join the *avant garde*.

Flouting tradition in the manner of Matisse and the Fauves (wild beasts), the Colourists painted vibrant, joyful pictures in which tonal shading was replaced by pure colour and perspective flattened into a dancing, linear rhythm. In 1914, when the outbreak of World War I forced them to return, they startled the wary Scots by portraying them and their grey landscape bathed in Gallic sunshine.

signer" and abandoning his architectural dreams in favour of small but exquisite watercolours, "Toshie" died prematurely and in exile. *(See panel, page 152).*

Having gained wealth and respectability, many of the Glasgow Boys lost their freshness. Hornel retreated into orientalism, Lavery painted modish society portraits in Edwardian London, and Guthrie became a conservative president of the Royal Scottish Academy he had once scorned.

Their success, however, gave younger artists the courage to experiment, and the next generation (this time mainly from Edinburgh)

Once again, a pattern was repeated. The war over, they continued to exhibit in Paris, and success abroad made them (belatedly) so popular at home that Fergusson, who spent his last 20 years in Glasgow, was given a major retrospective, at the city's expense, and an honorary degree from its university.

Surprisingly sensuous: From then on, the status of the artist, once marginal, was assured. Despite a gloomy climate and religious puritanism, Scottish art has at all times been surprisingly buoyant, sensuous and, on the whole, considerably lacking in angst. Influenced by Post-Impressionism and their own Colourists, painters in the 1930s found a ready market for the bright landscapes, fruit, flowers and fishing boats, which they rendered with uninhibited gusto. (Glasgow-trained James Cowie was unusual in his formal restraint.)

But such cheerful preoccupation with the local scene led to parochialism, and the loss of contact with the European mainstream frustrated younger artists. After World War II, many of Glasgow's most talented painters – such as the romantic neo-cubists Robert Colquhoun and Robert MacBryde, icono-clast Bruce MacLean and abstract expressionist Alan Gouk – all bolted to London.

namic leadership was the first hint of the improbable form in which Glasgow would be resurrected: from grim steelworks and shipyards to European City of Culture.

As the economic crisis deepened, Glaswegians were slow to realise their cultural assets. Years passed before Pollok House, with its fine Spanish paintings, quietly opened its doors. The Hunterian then expanded to show (among other works redeemed from the shadows) a collection of Whistlers rivalled only by the Freer in Washington DC; these had been bequeathed in gratitude because, in 1891, Glasgow Boy E.A. Walton had persuaded the City Fathers to buy a

Among the gifted few who worked on in isolation was Cowie's pupil Joan Eardley, whose ragged street kids are a poignant record of the Glasgow slums.

After 1945, heavy industry, the basis of Glasgow's wealth, plunged into decline and the city seemed moribund. In the circumstances, it seemed to many a scandal that Tom Honeyman, director of the Kelvingrove Art Gallery and Museum, should squander £8,200 on a Dali *Crucifixion*. Yet his dy-

Left, the Glasgow art market is buoyant. **Above**, music meets painting at the City Arts Centre.

portrait of the Scots philosopher Thomas Carlyle – Whistler's first public sale.

But these treasures slumbered. It was not until 1983 that the world's aesthetes began to buy air tickets for Glasgow and costly art tours added the city to their brochures, alongside Florence, Athens and Leningrad. The reason was the opening of the Burrell Collection, after 40 shameful years in storage. The four million people who visited the Burrell in its first three years became aware that the city held further delights; now Kelvingrove is an even greater tourist attraction.

Another factor contributing to Glasgow's

cultural prestige was a new curiosity about the art produced by the Scots themselves. From the late 1960s, the London Fine Art Society had been promoting the long-forgotten Glasgow Boys, slowly at first but with increasing success, and in time they included the Colourists. Scottish art is now valued so highly that, when Peploe's *Girl in White* was sold in 1988, it was the most expensive picture to come under the auctioneer's hammer that year, fetching more than £500,000. What's more, it was sold not in London but in Glasgow.

Media fever has spurred the great art auctioneers Sotheby's, Christie's and Phillips to

tion, the building McLennan gifted to the city with his collection (now in Kelvingrove) has been refurbished for major exhibitions of contemporary art. Big business sponsors, too, have been attracted..

Another factor in the "Glasgow phenomenon" is the vitality of its young painters, whose vast canvases take up space in major galleries throughout the UK and in the US. It all started with the critical stir caused by the 1982 degree show of three graduating students: Steven Campbell, Adrian Wiszniewski and Ken Currie. As Wiszniewski put it: "You get one Glasgow artist and he's a freak, two and they're a movement."

cash in with all the attendant hype and razzmatazz and to despatch their agents to scour Scotland for neglected talent. As a result, even minor artists, who painted bright lochs and glens between the wars, have captured a public which prefers their "parochialism" to the ugliness, gloom or sheer gimmickry of the latest international fashion. In Glasgow's salerooms, foreign dealers – including Japanese on the look-out for orientalist Hornels – jostle alongside Glaswegians proudly investing in "their own".

In 1970, there was only one commercial gallery; now there are more than 30. In addi-

Bored with the abstraction and tricksy effects admired by the modern art elite, the students aimed to create an imagery for the troubled world they saw around them and, through political or literary allusion, to express "the confused spirit of the age". Scottish hedonism and the *belle peinture* practised in Edinburgh were also rejected in favour of figurative painting, muscular and hard-edged, on a monumental scale.

Instead of flighty Paris, they looked to German Expressionism and the doom-laden visions of an uncharacteristically tormented Scot, John Bellany. Currie, obsessed with the old industrial Glasgow and the militant trade unions on the Clyde, describes his work as "epic socialist humanism". The more lyrical Wiszniewski, son of Polish immigrants, has adapted Slavic folk art to convey nostalgia for the past, disillusion with the present.

But, although their themes are sober, the execution is flamboyant, rather jolly. The most effervescent of the three, Steven Campbell, draws inspiration from the writers P.G. Wodehouse and Bram Stoker (author of *Dracula*) to cock a snook at the art boffins with titles like *Nasal and Facial Hair, Reactions to Various Disasters*.

Overnight, Campbell's exuberant fantasies became the rage of New York, whose dealers raced to Glasgow to compete for other new "finds". The city's students were quick to spot a bandwagon, and the School of Art's midsummer degree show became such a lively event that, in 1985, the police had to close surrounding roads to traffic on the opening night.

In the same year, the Third Eye Centre, now the Glasgow Centre for Contemporary

The new wave: a Steven Campbell (left) and Ken Currie's *The Self-Taught Man* **(above).**

Arts, mounted its first exhibition, *New Image Glasgow*, which featured, with the now famous trio, rugged "realists" Stephen Barclay and Peter Howson and the more romantic Italian-Scot Mario Rossi. Although their styles varied, what the "Glasgow Pups" had in common was an extrovert and macho brutalism, often lightened (however glum the subject) by a jokey irreverence reminiscent of Glasgow pantomime.

Behind the scenes: Crucial to this youthful boom is the role of the Glasgow School of Art, where academic discipline was never "liberalised", as in England. The tradition of sound technique was reinforced when Jack Knox took over the Fine Art Department in 1981. "Clyde-taught," he said, "should mean Clyde-built." Drilled with Presbyterian thoroughness, his students would emerge as accomplished draughtsmen and, when taking a trip south to the London galleries, these young Glaswegians – never short on confidence – would decide that their work was not only as good as that of the resented English but *better*.

Exploiting the glamour of a building designed by Mackintosh, the School also organises its own enterprises such as guided tours and a shop. All exhibits are on sale at the annual degree show; in 1986 all of Stephen Conroy's paintings were sold before they were even hung.

Conroys now grace New York's Museum of Metropolitan Art, which has a student and teacher exchange scheme with Glasgow. Among transatlantic visitors was a former School of Art student, Steven Campbell, who had settled in the US but returned to Glasgow to lecture on "How to paint a picture the New York critics will like".

A visual feast: Finally, Glasgow again claimed its much-deserved stake in the arts world in 1996 by hosting its very own Festival of Visual Arts, a feast of exhibitions, art and design events. It was the largest cultural event the city had enjoyed since all the activities of 1990, when Glasgow was the proud wearer of the coveted European Capital of Culture crown. A major feature of the Festival was the opening of the Gallery of Modern Art, Glasgow's first-ever monument to the aesthetics of the avant-garde.

A major part of Glasgow's renaissance is a flourishing of the performing arts. This covers the entire gamut from Grand Opera to Rock and from classical ballet to Indian dance. In the 1980s the city inaugurated a Mayfest, a Folk Festival, a Jazz Festival and Street Biz, all of which are now well-established annual events.

The nearly month-long Mayfest, held since 1985, brings together all the performing arts – and much, much more. Originally meant for the hoi polloi in the outlying districts who were starved of entertainment, the Mayfest has grown and grown to become one of Britain's largest art festivals. More than 100 different groups perform at a score of venues and offer classical and folk music, theatre and ballet and a host of other activities from all over the world.

Jazz musicians come into their own during the Annual Jazz Festival in June when such luminaries as Stéphane Grappelli and Oscar Peterson light up the scene. The one-week International Folk Festival in July attracts traditional music and dance groups from all over the world while in August Street Biz keeps the pot boiling by bringing mimes, magicians and musicians to the city. And, as if that isn't enough, August is the month of the big blow when the city hosts the World Pipe Band Championships.

Peculiar entertainment: Glasgow has a long tradition of theatre and, as early as the 18th century, the city abounded with such places of entertainment. The vast majority of these were not venues for serious thespians but music halls which spawned a long line of comedians, including Harry Lauder, Will Fyffe and Tommy Lorne, whose fame spread far beyond Glasgow. And then, the city was for long the premier place in all Britain for that peculiar Christmas theatrical entertainment known as pantomime: indeed, the pantomime season at the Princess Theatre, which is now occupied by the internationally renowned Citizens' Theatre, lasted for more than eight months.

Today, commercial theatre, if not quite dead, is almost moribund. The Royal (home of Scottish Opera), the King's and the Pavilion are the only venues which mount purely commercial shows. In addition, a number of venues are available which professional and amateur companies can rent. These include the tiny 90-seat Glasgow Centre for Contemporary Arts auditorium which opened in

1993, the cavernous The Tramway where such unusual productions have been performed as Peter Brook's *Carmen* and *Mahabaharata*, and the Mitchell and Royal Scottish Academy of Music Drama theatres.

Four well-established Glasgow-based groups mount occasional productions. Best known is the Citizens', which has its own theatre which is available to other companies in its somewhat long off-season (approximately May to September). Then there is the Tron and the 7:84 each of whose theatres are also available to other companies. Finally there is the Wildcat, which is just that – a

Left, the Theatre Royal. **Right**, a Scottish Opera production of *Das Rheingold*.

splinter group formed by, among others, breakaway 7:84 founders. Both 7:84 and Wildcat, although loathe to admit it, have their roots in the theatre of James Bridie, who had attempted to establish a wholly Scottish theatre in the mid-1940s.

The Tron was founded in 1978 to fill the gap caused by the burning down of the Close in 1973 and by 1981 was a theatre club occupying its present premises. Although the bar is still popular, it is no longer a club. Plays presented here tend to have political overtones and a Scottish flavour, although the artistic director, Michael Body, would not admit to the latter. Foreign works, some

performed by companies from overseas, are not neglected, possibly because Body worked in theatre in Russia.

Both the 7:84 and the Wildcat are madly Glaswegian and very socialist. Theatre to them is meaningless without social content which is a cry one also hears from many young Glasgwegians in the other arts. The popular entertainer Billy Connolly said of them: "Political theatre is fine, but so is theatre without politics. In fact, it's better. I'm bored with middle-class boys telling me about socialism." Incidentally, Connolly is not too popular with the Glasgow theatrical fraternity: although a Scottish comic in the line of Harry Lauder, Will Fyffe and Tommy Lorne, he stands accused of having sold out to the establishment, hobnobbing with royalty and society and having forgotten his roots in Partick.

When John McGrath, the founder of the 7:84, was its artistic director, the plays the company presented were out-and-out Marxist. Now, since David Hayman took over, the group's productions are populist rather than agitprop and have included those two Glasgow classics, *No Mean City* and the *Gorbals Story*.

Cocking a snook: The Wildcat, which beats the socialist drum with musical accompaniments, was formed by John McGrath's brother-in-law, writer-director David McLellan, and his sister. Two of their great successes, which it is doubtful if the non-Glaswegian will understand, are *The Steamie* and *The Celtic Story*. The desire to be ethnic and Scottish and cock a snook at the establishment was seen when Michael Tremblay produced a play, *The Guid Sisters,* in broad Glasgow patois which had been translated from Quebecois, the patois of the French Canadians of Quebec.

The Cits Theatre, on the other hand, wants its actors to be understood by all and to speak, if not Oxford, at least the Queen's English. Its productions are flamboyant, deviant, biting and anti-establishment, yet not with a specific left-wing content.

Glasgow has a prolific group of playwrights, several of whom are involved in other arts, and nearly all of whom are ethnic and fail to see the point in writing a play unless it has social content. They, like many other Glaswegians, do not look kindly on the establishment, whether it be in Edinburgh or in London, and are constantly worried about whether they should cast their votes for the Scottish Nationalists or for the Labour Party. Recent election results clearly show their decision to favour Labour.

It was in the 1970s that John Byrne, who still paints and designs sets, stirred the public with his *Slab Boys,* the first part of a trilogy. Hector McMillan and Liz Lochhead, the latter a poet and left-wing feminist as well as a dramatist, are both noted for their Scottish ethnicity, while the plays of John McGrath are both Marxist and populist. Tom McGrath (no relation of John) is a poet, musician and dramatist with a strong interest in the Scottish scene. Ian Heggie's fame has spread far beyond the bounds of Scotland with such ethnic plays as *A Wholly Healthy Glasgow* and *American Bagpipes*.

Glasgow, which once had more cinemas *per capita* than any other country in Europe, has a small, inchoate, respected film industry. It was at its strongest in the 1950s when John Grierson impressed all with his *The Drifters, Coal Face, Night Mail* and then *This Wonderful World.*

much time in the US, is probably still the best-known Glasgow film name.

Maybe it's the influence of the waters of the River Clyde, but Glasgow is awash with music. The city is home to half a dozen major classical groups, an active pop scene, several first-class choral groups, a vibrant jazz scene and Scottish Opera. True, the shame of Glasgow for quarter of a century was that, after the burning down of St Andrew's Halls, the city lacked a decent concert hall and classical music was performed in the acoustically excellent but somewhat parochial City Halls. That, however, was rectified with the opening in 1990 of a purpose-built 2,500-seat

Most studios today consist of two men and a dog – and one of the men is probably moonlighting for other companies. Lack of capital means that small-screen productions and commercials are produced rather than large-screen feature films. The best-known feature films are Bill Forsyth's *Gregory's Girl,* which he followed with *Local Hero* and *Comfort and Joy.* All have backgrounds which are familiar to any who come from Glasgow. Forsyth, although now spending

Left, training for the Scottish Ballet. Above, tomorrow's musicians, at the City Arts Centre.

International Concert Hall.

Another relatively new venue is the Royal Scottish Academy of Music and Drama which has two small, jewel-box concert halls. Kelvingrove Art Gallery and Museum is a superb venue for large choral works which involve an organ, while Kelvin Hall and the Scottish Conference and Exhibition Centre readily await the masses who wish to applaud at Promenade or pop concerts respectively. Chamber music and choral ensembles enjoy performing in the Sir Henry Wood Concert Hall.

The city is home to the Royal Scottish

National Orchestra (RSNO) the Scottish BBC Symphony Orchestra, the Scottish Youth Orchestra and Scottish Opera. Both the Scottish BBC Symphony and the RSNO put on regular concerts which can be enjoyed during the evening. An all-too-brief Promenade season by the RSNO enlivens summer nights.

Glasgow has, in the past, given birth to a number of rock bands that have managed to make it big, not just throughout the country, but also throughout Europe and the United States. Probably the best example of this is Simple Minds, a rock group hailing from Bearsden, a suburb of North Glasgow, who have enjoyed many hit singles and albums,

club goers. Dance music in particular has, over the past few years, consistently played a prominent part in the redefining of popular youth culture and can commonly be heard pumping its powerful rhythms in many of Glasgow's dynamic nightspots. Similarly, rock and indie music are also a strong musical feature of the city. There are a great many unknown bands in Glasgow, the members of which trying desperately hard to establish a keen following of fans, as their predecessors did before them, and perpetually longing for that special day when they catch the gleaming eye of an individual with influence – a local talent scout, perhaps, or a record com-

and to this day still succeed in effortlessly filling up concert halls and football parks with thousands of enthusiastic followers. Other Glasgow-based groups that have enjoyed similar success over recent years include Wet Wet Wet, Hue and Cry, The Blue Nile, Deacon Blue, The Silencers, The River Detectives and Texas.

Nowadays, Glasgow is still fashionable for music which is aimed at the younger generation – popular music, both dance and rock/independent (universally known as "indie") music, continues to thrive and appeal to the tastes of a whole mass of pub and

pany representative on the lookout for fresh, upcoming bands.

But why, all things considered, have there been relatively more successful bands from Glasgow than from other UK cities of comparable size? Is it because tenements bring youths together and lead to them forming musical groups when in former years they might have formed street gangs? Will this enthusiasm last, or will it have fizzled out by the end of the decade? Fashion looms less large for jazz enthusiasts; they are catered for at half a dozen venues throughout the city.

Scottish Opera, which is based in Glasgow, began its life in 1962 with one week of performances and since then has become, apart from one rather bad hiccup due to financial problems in the late 1970s, a force to be reckoned with internationally. If Scottish Opera can be said to have an ethos which differentiates it from other international companies, it is a desire to employ theatrical-style directors; in this, they take the lead in Britain, together with the English National Opera with whom they occasionally mount co-productions. Yet, as one director said: "We don't do everything wacky." Strange, then, that they have not become more involved with the Citizens', whose directors

now has been the 1982 production of *Das Rheingold*, with its minimal startling blue-and-gold set, as the first part of Wagner's *Ring Cycle*. A huge success, this production attracted audiences from all over Europe and the US. Notable among more recent productions is *Die Fledermaus,* directed by Simon Callow and set in contemporary Glasgow.

John Mauceri, Scottish Opera's American-born music director and artistic chief, justifies his mounting of serious musicals – if such justification is necessary – by stating that "popular is not the opposite of serious." Bernstein and Weill are among his favourites and the former's *Candide* won for Scot-

have been invited to mount operas for several international companies. Recently, supertitles have been introduced.

Local fieldmouse: Even before the present company was formed under the leadership of dynamic Sir Alexander Gibson and Peter Hemmings opera was not unknown to Glasgow. In the 1930s, the then second city in the empire premiered *The Trojans.* Undoubtedly, the highlight of Scottish opera until

Left, the Scottish National Orchestra at the Exhibition Centre. **Above**, saucy opera goes down well at the Theatre Royal.

tish Opera the SWET (Society of West End Theatre) award for best musical.

The average Glaswegian's attitude to opera was revealed when, in the very early days of the company, an unemployed working man was interviewed in a "Man on the Street" television programme. Not a viewer was surprised when his response to the question of whether or not the city council should subsidise opera was No. However, he went on to add: "Educate the bairns in the school and they'll flock to see opera and to pay for it and there'll be nae need for subsidies". His knowledge of the economics of opera may have been somewhat shaky, but his attitude was admirable.

In 1971, Scottish Opera for Youth was formed as the educational branch of Scottish Opera and offers an unusual programme of music-drama for schoolchildren who are not a passive audience but who are involved in the productions many of which are rock operas. A third group, Opera-Go-Round, tours the hamlets and islands of the country and performs operas with a small cast and a pianist. The programme is not only *La Bohème* and *Tosca* but includes Janacek.

Vocal exercise: Glasgow, much to the outsider's surprise, is home to a substantial

When the current Scottish Ballet was formed in 1969 and located in Glasgow, it soon attracted a committed audience. Peter Darrell, its founder, believed in earthy and believable productions. Nobody dies of a broken heart in his ballets: rather they commit suicide. In his *Swan Lake* the hero does not conventionally wander off into the woods and encounter swans in a pond: he has an opium-induced dream.

Darrell also believed in productions which provoked their viewers. Before coming to Glasgow, his *Out of Darkness* both shocked and galvanised London audiences. Since Darrell's death in 1982, the company has had

amount of choirs. One of the most famous is the Phoenix which arose from the ashes of the Orpheus, a Glasgow choir renowned throughout Britain but which died with its founder and conductor Sir Hugh Robertson in the 1960s.

The John Currie Singers is a chamber choir which performs baroque, classical and modern works and also commissions new works on a regular basis. The Cappella Nova specialises in unaccompanied choral music, while the Scottish National Chorus and the New Glasgow Singers continue to be leaders in their field.

an international commitment, in terms of both dancers and choreographers, and delights in employing younger choreographers and directors. Hands are stretched both eastwards and westwards and a long-term commitment with the Kirov and its director Oleg Vinogradov began with Vinogradov creating for Scottish Ballet his first-ever, and highly successful, non-traditional *Petrushka*. For the younger generation, the company has a strong school commitment.

Above, a popular local band perform on stage at the People's Palace.

BILLY CONNOLLY AND GLASWEGIAN HUMOUR

If English comics invariably died a Friday-night death in the Glasgow Empire, Scottish clowns could never make the transfer south of the border – except for Sir Harry Lauder, who was more of an icon than a comedian. Until, that is, Billy Connolly. The "Big Yin" (literally the Big One) was taken to the English breast early on, and has now an impressive international following.

Scottish comics had always been parochial and more: they had been stand-up laughter-makers with silly catchphrases, juvenile gestures, inane jokes, and evidently not a thought in their heads. Perhaps the only exception to this, the sublime Chic Murray, despite his flights of surrealistic fancy, never expressed himself in Connolly's analytical sociological exegesis. Connolly was the first British comic to go beyond a laugh: there was a point to his patter.

Into his 50s now, Billy Connolly (pictured here in his hairy heyday) has been a star for nearly 25 years. Hailing from Partick, an insignificant district of Glasgow, and then being brought up in the Drumchapel housing estate – which he once described as "a desert wi' windows" – Connolly went on to serve his apprenticeship in the Govan shipyards. It was an ideal university for a professional funnyman.

In fact, he launched his career not as a clown but as a musician. Glasgow in the early 1960s was abuzz with folk clubs and folk musicians. It was where the action was. Connolly found himself sitting in with musicians, students, teachers, lawyers, and the Glasgow intelligentsia in pubs like the Marland Bar in the city's George Street. It was then that he discovered literature and ideas, and above all, music and style – his own style.

His wizard's beard dates from that time, as does the Jesus hairstyle and the banjo. Connolly chose this difficult instrument because there were too many superb guitarists around at the time, and because Bluegrass folk music was especially popular in the Glasgow folk scene of the early 1960s. He also became known as what Glaswegians call "a patter merchant". Glasgow, rich in such individuals, came to recognise Billy as a master. And it was his patter, rather than his banjo-playing, that the folkies came to admire.

He started with odd unpaid appearances in the clubs which abounded at the time, and then a few semi-professional gigs in London and elsewhere. Then he founded The Humblebums with his pal, Tam Harvey. Tam, an engaging fellow, tired of the pressure of constant gigging, and after a first LP, left to be replaced by the talented singer-songwriter Gerry Rafferty. Humblebums Two became increasingly a vehicle for Rafferty's haunting songs and Billy came to speak more. His incidental soliloquies got longer and longer and, when Rafferty got the offer to move into the pop world's big time, Connolly transformed himself into a comedian first and foremost.

He was, in this role, an almost instant success. Glaswegians had heard patter like his before, but never so sustained – Connolly can do two to three hours virtually non-stop – and never with such imagination. His jokes developed into long, rambling, monologues which were scatological, even eschatological, and very robust indeed. He once described his appearance as back-up to Elton John on a US tour: "I went down like a fart in a space suit." And what an eye and an ear for observation. Talking of a favourite subject, the wee Glasgow housewife, he noted that she had "corn-beef legs through sitting too close to the electric fire." The packed audiences loved it. They cheered like football crowds at every fresh insight that interpreted their own loves and experiences.

Soon Connolly proved he could repeat his success with audiences outside Scotland. He began to spend more time in London, then divorced his wife to marry the fashionable comedienne Pamela Stephenson. But many Scots resented this success; they felt somehow betrayed. They felt further aggrieved when Connolly started hob-nobbing with chat-show hosts and royalty, tried to break into American television, and espoused vegetarianism. Even more astonishingly, he gave up drinking.

Gradually, most Glaswegians have come to terms with the Big Yin, and in truth Connolly is now back as a favoured son. His fans are at long last proud that Billy has the same effect on audiences everywhere: their own representative. ∎

Glasgow is a city of superlatives – the first, the best, the highest, the most – and these claims are not the rantings of chauvinists but are based on fact. During its heyday in the second half of the 19th century, Glasgow built and built and that is the heritage which it offers the visitor: magnificent buildings which have recently been freed of grime and, in many instances, recycled. Its name, *Glasgu,* may mean the "Green Place" and it can boast more than 70 parks, but its city squares are not leafy green oases; rather, they consist of a handsome building surrounded by other buildings. And so, in the following pages, attention has been paid to architecture.

The realignment of boundaries in 1973 meant that the city's population shrank, but it remains the focal point for Greater Glasgow, a conurbation of more than two million people which can rival most European cities with its array of galleries, theatres and restaurants. The new boundaries are closely followed in the ensuing pages. All the chapters, other than the last two, deal with places within the city. The penultimate chapter covers Greater Glasgow and the final one suggests half- and full-day trips.

Because the city sits in a basin surrounded by hills and because it is built on 36 drumlins (hills) it has many splendid view points. For those whose appetite for exercise is not satisfied by climbing the drumlins, the city has many public tennis courts, bowling greens, indoor swimming pools and several ice-rinks. There are also 50 golf courses within the city limits and 90 courses within 20 miles (32 km) of the city centre. Spread the net a wee bit wider and within 30 miles (48 km) there are about 150 courses.

Glasgow is easy to get out off and within 30 minutes the visitor can be at Loch Lomond or, in twice that time, in the Trossachs or the Burns Country. And it's only 50 minutes by rail or road to Edinburgh, Scotland's other great city, which is giving Glasgow a run for its money in both the industrial and cultural arenas. Not that anyone in Glasgow, of course, could imagine why you would possibly want to visit Edinburgh.

Those who, failing to follow the directions on the ensuing pages, find themselves lost should take care. No, they will not be mugged; but on seeking information from locals they might believe they are being answered in a foreign tongue. What's more, their thick-accented informant is liable to delay their progress by inviting them for a "refreshment" before taking them by the arm and leading them to their destination.

Preceding pages: a night out at the Scottish Exhibition and Conference Centre; an Orange parade; antique shop in the city's West End. **Left**, thrills 'n' spills on a fun-packed merry-go-round.

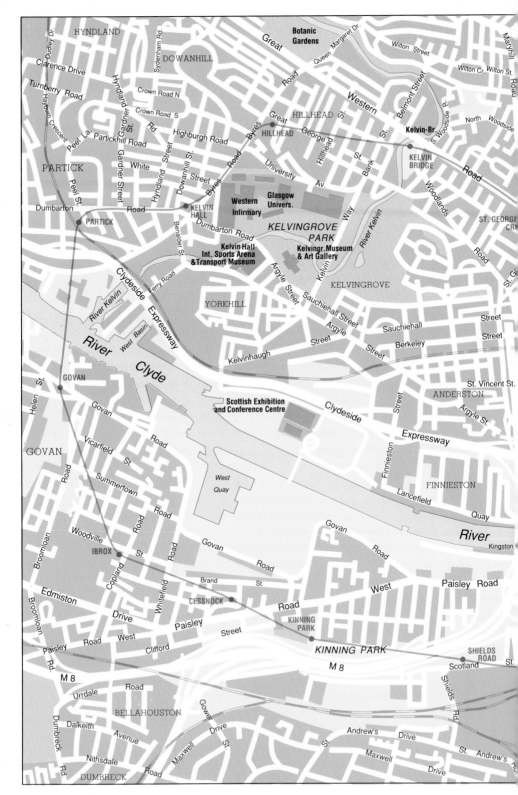

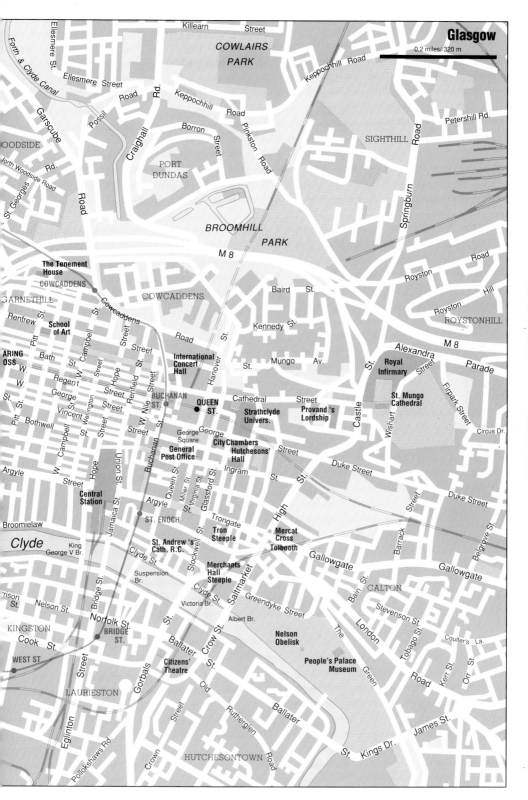

Glasgow

0,2 miles/ 320 m

Killearn Street

COWLAIRS PARK

Keppochhill Road

Forth & Clyde Canal

Ellesmere St.

Ellesmere Street

Keppochhill Road

Borron Street

Possil

Craignall Rd.

OODSIDE

North Woodside Road

Garscube

St. Georges

Road

PORT DUNDAS

Pinkston Road

Petershill Rd.

SIGHTHILL

Springburn Road

Royston Road

Royston Hill

Royston

ROYSTONHILL

BROOMHILL PARK

M 8

M 8

The Tenement House

COWCADDENS

GARNETHILL

Renfrew

Pitt

School of Art

Cowcaddens

St.

COWCADDENS

Road

Baird St.

Kennedy St.

Alexandra Parade

Firpark Street

ARING OSS

Bath

St.

Campbell

St.

Renfield Street

Hope

Street

Street

W.

Regent

Street

W.

St.

George

St.

Vincent

Street

Wellington

Street

Street

International Concert Hall

Hanover St.

Mungo Av.

St.

Royal Infirmary

St.

Wishart St.

Castle St.

Circus Dr.

BUCHANAN ST.

W. Nile Street

QUEEN ST.

Cathedral

Street

St. Mungo Cathedral

Bothwell

St.

Pitt St.

Campbell St.

Buchanan Street

George Square

Strathclyde Univers.

George Street

Provand's Lordship

Argyle

W.

Street

Hope St.

Union St.

City Chambers

General Post Office

Hutchesons' Hall

Ingram

St.

Duke Street

Duke Street

Central Station

Jamaica St.

Queen St.

Miller St.

Virginia St.

Glassford St.

Argyle

Trongate

High St.

Mercat Cross Tolbooth

Gallowgate

Barrack St.

Belgrove St.

Gallowgate

Clyde

Broomielaw

King George V Br.

ST. ENOCH

Clyde St.

Stockwell St.

Tron Steeple

St. Andrew's Cath. R.C.

Merchants Hall Steeple

Saltmarket

Greendyke Street

CALTON

Bain St.

London Road

Stevenson St.

Tobago St.

Coulter's La.

Suspension Br.

Victoria Br.

Albert Br.

Clyde St.

rison St.

Nelson St.

Bridge St.

KINGSTON

Cook St.

WEST ST.

BRIDGE ST.

Norfolk St.

Street

Gorbals

Street

Ballater St.

Crow St.

Old

Citizens' Theatre

Nelson Obelisk

People's Palace Museum

The Green

Kerr St.

Orr St.

Road

James St.

LAURIESTON

Eglinton

Pollokshaws Rd.

Crown

Street

Rutherglen

Ballater

St.

Kings Dr.

HUTCHESONTOWN

Adm: R: et Doctissimus
D: D: Leonardus Jansen
Pastor in Vet Weis Vigilan-
tissimus hanc donauit
fenestrā amp: D: Decani
Cap: Tolp: Anno 1681

OLD GLASGOW

It all began in 543 when St Mungo arrived in *Glasgu* ("the beloved green place") and built a timber-and-wattle house of worship on the banks of the **Molendinar Burn** in the northeastern part of present-day Glasgow. Historically, the next 600 years is a void. But then, on 7 July 1136, Bishop John Achaius consecrated a church in the presence of King David I. And so Glasgow, as it is today, began.

However, the splendid yet gloomy edifice with a verdigris roof, standing in **Cathedral Square** at the top of **High Street**, is not that church. It was destroyed, probably by fire. The present **Cathedral**, smaller than any of its great English equivalents, was possibly built, at least in part, by Bishop Jocelyn (1174–99) and the existing choir and crypt are from the time of Bishop William de Bondington (1233–58). The first Bishop of Glasgow, Robert Blacader (1483–1508) completed the building.

A perfect example of pre-Reformation Gothic architecture by an unknown architect, the Cathedral has an importance which spreads far beyond the Molendinar Burn, far beyond the River Clyde and far beyond Glasgow: it was the only cathedral on the Scottish mainland to survive the rapacious Reformation at the start of the 16th century. This was because Archbishop Beaton fled to France, taking with him most of Cathedral's relics, jewels and ornaments, where they still remain.

The craftsmen of the Trades House, supported by some of the inhabitants of the neighbouring royal burgh of Rutherglen, rallied round and persuaded the Reformers to spare the fabric. However, the lead-covering of the Cathedral roof was torn off and the altars, vestments and statues were destroyed, together with a valuable library.

The exterior of the building, awkwardly placed on a slope above the Molendinar Burn (now culverted) and with almost non-existent transepts, belies the beauty of the interior. Enter and be impressed by the magnificent nave which is separated from the aisles by two rows of massive clustered columns. The loftiness and the narrowness of the aisles, the stained-glass windows and the soaring columns all form a subdued medieval vista somewhat enlivened by regimental flags.

The choir, which is about the same length but somewhat higher than the nave, is almost shut off from it by a superbly carved rood screen, on the corbels of which are carved the Seven Deadly Sins. The choir is a beautiful example of early Gothic and is separated from the aisles by clustered columns with flowered capitals.

Beyond the choir is the exquisite Lady Chapel with rich, light columns topped by florid capitals supporting a groined roof and lancet windows. A desire to beautify the cathedral in the middle of the 19th century badly misfired when

Left, window at Provand's Lordship. **Right**, Glasgow Cathedral.

the church elders, in the belief that no local (or, for that matter, British) artisans could produce stained-glass windows to match the glories of their Cathedral, placed an order for l23 windows with Old Testament scenes with the Royal Bavarian Stained Glass Establishment in Munich. Less than l00 years elasped and these windows had to be removed and replaced by the work of local artisans which, it is hoped, will last rather longer.

Patron saint: From the nave, a flight of steps descends to the **Lower Church** which occupies most of the crypt. (Although the word crypt conjures up visions of a dark underground chamber it is, as seen here, not necessarily so.) This Lower Church is one of the glories of Scottish medieval architecture and is especially renowned for its fan vaulting which springs from a forest of columns. Four of these surround the tomb of St Mungo, patron saint of Glasgow, who was buried here in 603.

In medieval times, tens of thousands of pilgrims came to this spot and, in 451, the Pope decreed that it should be esteemed as meritorious to make a pilgrimage to Glasgow Cathedral as to Rome itself. Hanging on a wall behind the tomb is the handsome St Kentigern Tapestry. Kentigern ("Chief Lord") is a more formal name for St Mungo ("Dear One"). It was in this Lower Church, then the Barony Church, that Sir Walter Scott set one of the many Glasgow scenes in his novel *Rob Roy*.

The **Blacader Aisle** in the southest corner of the Lower Church is said to occupy the site of a cemetery consecrated at the start of the 5th century by St Ninian. Now it stands as it was built during the primacy of Archbishop Blacader. Especially interesting are the late medieval carved bosses.

On leaving the cathedral precincts turn left and then left again to enter the **Necropolis**, one of Britain's, even Europe's, great Victorian cemeteries. It is reached by crossing the **Bridge of Sighs** under which flows the now culverted

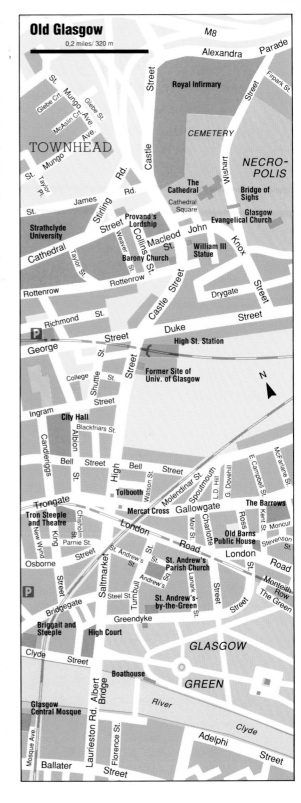

Old Glasgow

0,2 miles/ 320 m

Molendinar Burn. The necropolis is often compared to the celebrated Père Lachaise in Paris and many of the tombs in that part first reached are of spectacular proportions and distinguished design. Doric temples, Egyptian vaults, neo-Gothic towers, Moorish kiosks, tombs designed by "Greek" Thomson and Charles Rennie Mackintosh, Glasgow's two greatest architects, are all on display. At the extreme northwest corner of the Necropolis a column marks the entrance to the "Jews' Enclosure": outside this enclosure are the tombs of Jews who married Gentiles.

Towering above all, on the summit of the hill, John Knox stands atop a soaring Doric column apparently shaking his fist at the Cathedral whose congregants, in his day, followed Rome, and which he would have so loved to have seen destroyed. Superb views of the eastern part of the city can be enjoyed from the summit of the Necropolis and there are also excellent views of the eastern suburbs and the hills to the south.

A stony stare in the Necropolis.

The black foreboding building in the foreground which tends to overshadow the Cathedral is the **Royal Infirmary**. Here in 1865 – not in the exisiting building but in one demolished in the 1920s – Joseph Lister introduced the antiseptic system which revolutionised modern surgery and which caused a United States ambassador to Britain to say: "My Lord, it is not a profession, it is not a nation, it is humanity itself which, with uncovered head, salutes you."

Leave the Necropolis and cross High Street to an undistinguished, stone, three-storey, crow-stepped building. The **Provand's Lordship**, built in 1471 and the oldest house in Glasgow, was originally built for the priest in charge of St Nicholas Hospital. It later became the town house of the Canon of Barlanark whose rectory was designated the Lordship of Provan. Because King James II and James IV were Canons of Glasgow it is possible that either or both may have stayed here.

More certain, yet not positive, is a

visit in 1567 of Mary Queen of Scots, who spent several days here arranging for Darnley, her husband, who was suffering from "a great fever of the pox" to be transferred to Edinburgh. Others claim that the purpose of Mary's visit was to plan the murder of Darnley and present as evidence the infamous Casket Letters which were apparently written in Glasgow in January 1567.

During the 19th century and the early part of the 20th, the building had many occupants and at different times was an alehouse, a sweetshop and a cabinet-maker's establishment. Now, it is a museum with furniture and domestic articles. Especially interesting is the reconstruction of an early 16th-century pre-Reformation room occupied by Cuthbert Simon, the clerk to the Cathedral and a notary public.

Joy in worship: Religion is not abandoned on leaving the Cathedral. The two Barony churches, one on either side of the road, stand a couple of hundred yards down High Street. To the left, and back from the road, is the beautiful white Barony North Church (1878) in rich Italianate style with the four evangelists standing atop the balustrade. Here, one feels, is a church whose members take joy in worship. Once a United Presbyterian kirk, this is now the **Glasgow Evangelical Church**.

That on the right, the red sandstone **Barony Church** (1886–90) which, by its mere size, lays fair claim to being a cathedral rather than a church, has recently been recycled and will become the main ceremonial hall of the **University of Strathclyde** which is rapidly colonising this part of the city. It is remarkable how the wheel has turned full cycle, for it was here, on **Rottenrow**, that in 1451 Bishop William Turnbull founded the University of Glasgow. Today, Rottenrow is "The Village" of the University of Strathclyde with most of its halls of residence. Some of these are new, some are recycled tenements; the whole makes an attractive ensemble.

Provand's Lordship: the oldest house in the city.

A bronze equestrian statue on top of an 8-ft (nearly 3-metre) plinth which stands in a small park between the Evangelical church and the High Street has a world-wide following. And not all of these followers are fanatic Protestants who see Catholicism as a threat: William III (1650–1702), who is the horseman represented here, was a Catholic zealot. Rather, they know that this is probably the only bronze statue in the world with a movable part: in strong winds, the horse's tail sways slightly.

It is about here that the battle of the Bell o' the Brae was fought in 1300 between the English, led by Early Percy, and the Scots, led by William Wallace. The conflict was short and bloody and the good guys – the Scots – were victorious. And the reason for the battle's odd name? A bell was rung regularly here by an old woman when funeral processions passed on their way to the adjacent Necropolis.

Continue down High Street passing, at the intersection with **Duke Street**, handsome, red sandstone tenements with attractive baronial touches which were built in 1905. A plaque at the suburban railway station on the left which fronts a large open space marks the second site of the University of Glasgow. It moved to here from Rottenrow in 1470 and here it remained until moving to Gilmorehill in 1870.

Soon this area will again resound to the voices and footsteps of students. However, they will now be from the University of Strathclyde as that campus spreads further and further eastwards from its beginnings close to George Square in the city centre. Some outstanding recyling is visible in this part of the city. And so, 1,000 yards (1 km) after leaving the Cathedral arrive at **Glasgow Cross**, which is dominated by the steeple of the Tolbooth.

The **Tolbooth**, a stark, severe, seven-storey, stone traffic policeman wearing a crown, stands amidst swirling traffic at an intersection of five roads and is a constant thorn in the flesh of the god of

traffic flow (but then, do gods have flesh?). The tower, built in 1636 and 126 ft (38 metres) high has always been a policeman, for this is the spot where those entering the city would pay a toll. The tower is all that remains of the original Tolbooth Building which extended to the west and the north and which was used as offices by the town council until 1814.

The jail mentioned by Sir Walter Scott in his tale of *Rob Roy* was also in this building which came to be called the Tontine rather than the Tolbooth Building and which by the end of the 1700s, the town council having moved, became Glasgow's most renowned hotel and the terminus for stagecoaches coming from and going to Edinburgh and London. It also served as Glasgow's Exchange and here, on the Plainstanes, a stretch of paving fronting the hotel, the tobacco lords, dressed in scarlet coats, cocked hats and full-bottomed wigs would stroll, much to the contempt of well-established old-money, and flick

their gold headed canes at any riff-raff who dared to tread on their territory.

Glasgow Cross continued to thrive as the heart of the city until 1846 when the iron road came to George Square (the first rail connection with Edinburgh was made in 1842; with London in 1846) which then became the city centre. Here, too, stands the **Mercat Cross**, a 1929 replica of the original, which was removed in 1659 and which marked the site of the first Glasgow market dating back to the 12th century. It consists of an octagonal base with a balustraded roof on which stands a slender column supporting a heraldic unicorn. A gallows once stood at this spot.

The **Tron Steeple** dominates the first part of **Trongate** which is that road running west from Glasgow Cross. This squat, four-stage steeple was part of a church which was built between the end of the 16th and the beginning of the 17th century. (The arches in the steeple are 19th-century additions.) The church was destroyed in a spectacular fire in 1793 which was started by hooligan elements of the Hell-Fire Club who, while warming themselves by the watchman's fire, stoked it too high in order to prove their immunity to the heat in Hell. Only the steeple survived and, in 1793, a new church, designed by John Adam, was constructed.

The clock faces on the dial were first illuminated by gas reflectors in the winter of 1821, the first steeple in Britain to be so lit. Then, when the Trongate was widened in 1825, the open Tudor-style arched vault was carved into the steeple base. Since 1980 the church has been the home of the **Tron Theatre**.

The Trongate very soon gives rise to **Argyle Street**, the city's most popular shopping thoroughfare. Argyle Street has long had a special attraction for the ordinary folk of Glasgow and the words in a guidebook to the city written more than 100 years ago are still almost true: "...from day-break till night the human and vehicular tide never ceases to ebb and flow along this great artery. There is

The Tollbooth by night.

no other street in the city like it. There are finer streets, more fashionable streets, streets with grander buildings in them. But Argyle Street has something of all, and as a thoroughfare for the transport of everything to everywhere has no rival." The description is "almost true" because much of the street is now pedestrianised.

Thirsty work: Time for a "refreshment" – the word "drink" is taboo in genteel Glasgow society – at the **Tolbooth Bar** at the southeast corner of the Cross. It was here that one of Glasgow's greatest contributions to modern civilisation – the *hauf an' hauf* – was introduced. This is a half-measure of whisky washed down by a half-pint of draft beer. Having downed the whisky, upturn the glass over the beer and knock hard on the bottom of the glass to be sure that "ne'er a drap is lost".

Continue south from the Tolbooth Bar down the **Saltmarket** which, last century, was a sorry indictment of *homo sapiens*. Here, in an area of about 300 sq. yards (251 sq. metres) were some 150 *shebeens* (illicit stills) and 200 brothels. Indeed, the Laigh Kirk Close at 59 Trongate contained 20 brothels and three *shebeens*. Into this section crowded the Irish, who had left their native land for Glasgow during the time of the great potato famine, known as the Hungry Forties (1840s). It was said of the Irish of those days that if they had any money they emigrated to America; if they had only a little they went to Liverpool; and if they had none at all they came to Glasgow.

Turn left into St Andrew's Square, dominated by a church of that name; it was the official place of worship for the City Fathers as testified to by the Glasgow coat of arms being sculpted in the tympanum of the pediment. (Observe that both the fish and the bell are missing.) **St Andrew's Parish Church** (1739–56) is reminiscent of London's St-Martin-in-the-Fields, although the steeple is somewhat slimmer. The soaring hexastyle Corinthian portico cre-

Traffic clogs
the Trongate.

ated such a stir that, after the centring was removed, Naismith, the mason, slept beneath it to demonstrate his faith.

The rococo interior, adorned with stucco figures and huge Corinthian columns supporting the gallery is just as grand as the exterior. The wood is said to have been brought from the Caribbean and the United States in ships owned by the tobacco lords who worshipped here. The church now serves a dual purpose and the visitor is as likely to hear the sound of performers as he is the word of the Lord.

Exit from the south side of St Andrew's Square and reach, after 100 yards, on the edge of Glasgow Green, **St-Andrew's-by-the-Green**, a jewel-box of Georgian architecture (1750–51). This, the fourth oldest building in Glasgow, was the first Episcopalian church in Scotland. When built, just four years after the Battle of Culloden, no love was lost between the Glasgow Presbyterians with their Covenanter traditions and the Episcopalians, or

"Piskies", with their Jacobite sympathies. To make matters worse, the "English Chapel", as it was dubbed, was the garrison church of the scarcely popular Regiment of Foot which was stationed nearby and – can it be believed? – the cushions on the seats were "stuffed and covered with green cloth" and the organ was played. Not surprisingly, the church earned for itself the sobriquet the "Kirk o' Whistles".

In its early days the church had a rich congregation but, over the years, it fell in desuetude and was on the verge of being demolished when, in 1985, Mr Giles Davies, himself a "Piskie", turned up and quickly decided that the building could be recyled into offices for the Christian Action (Glasgow) Housing Association, which he heads. Visitors are welcome to view the handsome interior elegantly decorated with panelled wood and dark blue carpeting.

Observe the ancient stones in the little graveyard to the east of the building. One of these remembers the unfortunate Captain Wemyss Erskine Sutherland and his wife Sarah, who were drowned in the Clyde when the *Comet* steam-boat was run down by the *Ayr* in 1825. Another remembers the fate that befell Jane Eliza Madden in 1871 when she was "run over by an omnibus" and exhorts: "All little Children that survey The emblem'd Wheel that crush'd me down, Be cautious, as you carelessly play. For shafts of death fly thick around."

Drunkards and vagabonds: Six hundred yards further, on the right, stands the imposing Doric facade of the **High Court**, the scene on 28 July 1865 of the last public hanging in the city. On that day, no less than 30,000 persons made their way to the judiciary buildings to attend upon one Dr Pritchard, an English practioner who had settled in Glasgow. As a doctor he was not much more than a quack, but he shone as a ladies' man and a lecturer. The vast crowd, described as "drunkards, thieves, and vagabonds", had not come to hear Dr Pritchard, however; they wanted to see

Glad rags by St Andrew's Church.

him hanged for poisoning his wife and his mother-in-law.

Facing the High Court is the entrance to **Glasgow Green** which the city adopted as its first public park in 1662, thus making it Britain's oldest such park. Some make the extravagant claim that the Green is the most important historic site in all Scotland while others say that the history of the Green is the history of Glasgow. Come what may, when first mentioned in 1178 it was essentially nothing more than a village green without a duck pond – although it had and still has the River Clyde as its southern boundary – where cattle grazed and continued to graze until 1870: sheep for much longer. Even today, those receiving the Freedom of the City are entitled to graze a flock of sheep on the Green and to hang out their washing in front of the City Chambers.

The Green has been and still is the site of political rallies, sporting events and pop concerts. Here, too, buxom lassies hitched up their skirts and petticoats and clambered into the *boins* (tubs) to trample their laundry, an event which was a great attraction for sightseers.

Collins Fountain, which stands at this entrance to the Green, has a significance which far belies its modest size. This fountain remembers Sir William Collins (1789–1853), of the eponymous publishing house, which still has its headquarters in Glasgow and which owes much of its success to the printing of Bibles and religious literature. Sir William was a great temperance man and indeed, under his leadership, the European temperance movement began in Glasgow. Great were the meetings in favour of temperance which took place on Glasgow Green.

Several structures at the west end of the park are worthy of at least a passing glance. The **Nelson Monument**, a 146-ft (44-metre) soaring column was the first monument in Britain to celebrate the admiral's victory at Trafalgar and was paid for by public subscription. Nearby, Queen Victoria stands only 40

Handy advice at Glasgow Fair.

ft (12 metres) above the ground atop the **Doulton Fountain** and her widespread Empire. This terracotta extravaganza was Doulton's gift to the 1888 Empire Exhibition, held in Kelvingrove Park.

The solid isolated **McLennan's Arch**, which stands about 100 yards northwest of these two monuments, is proof that Glasgwegians have always had a respect for heritage. The arch, the work of Robert Adam, was part of the Atheneum in Ingram Street and was moved to its present position when that building was demolished.

Few will observe a large boulder with some rough hieroglyphics immediately to the south of the Monument. Yet this marks the spot where in 1765 the Industrial Revolution was conceived. To quote James Watt, its midwife: "I had gone to take a walk... I had entered the Green... I was thinking upon the engine at the time... when the idea came into my mind that, as steam was an elastic body, it would rush into a vacuum, and if a communication were made between the cylinder and an exhausted vessel, it would rush into it and might be condensed without cooling the cylinder."

That part of the Green between the Collins Fountain and the Nelson Monument was to Glasgow what Orators' Corner in Hyde Park is to London. Here, in traditional Scottish fashion, the Roman Catholics thundered against the Protestants while "Unitarians, Trinitarians, Good Templars, Good Tipplers, Quack Doctors all gave tongue". This is one of Scotland's great battlefields, where a thousand battles have been fought for political freedom – first for one man, one vote, and then for one woman, one vote; wars against social injustice; wars against the demon drink – the Green has seen them all.

Popular culture: Over at the northeast of the Green stand two large impressive, yet disparate, buildings, constructed towards the end of the 19th century. The solid, red sandstone, renaissance-style **People's Palace** is not Glasgow's answer to London's Buckingham Palace or Edinburgh's Holyrood Palace but rather it is a tribute to the working people of the city. This is emphasised by the decoration on the facade of allegorical figures representing shipbuilding, engineering, the textile industry, mathematical science, painting and sculpture. Within its walls, the collection is devoted exclusively to Glasgow: its history, its culture, its achievements and social conditions.

Many of the happenings on Glasgow Green can be conjured up by looking at some of the items on display. The lid of a large, burrwood snuffbox graphically depicts the women tramping their washing on the Green; a bust of Harry Alfred Long (1826–1905) recalls one of the Green's greatest religious orators who "defended the doctrines of grace on Glasgow Green for more than 20 years"; and here are the letters which Bonnie Prince Charlie sent in 1746 to the city magistrates with demands for clothing for his 10,000 troops.

One ground floor room is devoted to

Bird's-eye view of the People's Palace.

112

fascinating tableaux of medieval Glasgow while another depicts Glasgow in the 18th century at the time of the Tobacco Lords. The first floor is chock-a-block with Glaswegiana bric-a-brac relating to commerce and religion, entertainment and sports, arts and crafts and famous Glasgow personalities. Here are entertainer Billy Connolly's "banana wellies" and here is the Saracen Head Punch Bowl, a large tin-glazed earthenware bowl capable of holding five gallons (20 litres) and symbolic of those days when excessive drinking was both a virtue and an accomplishment. The inside is painted with the Glasgow coat of arms and the legend: "Success to the Town of Glasgow". The bowl was used at the Saracen's Head, once a main coaching inn.

The upper floor has splendid stained-glass windows recovered from churches which are now defunct; eight major canvasses, packed with social content, of Ken Currie, one of the Glasgow Boys II School and part of a tearoom decorated in Glasgow Style by George Walton for Miss Cranston.

An integral part of the building, at the rear, is the large glass conservatory. The **Winter Gardens**, the Kibble Palace of the East End, a "treasure house of the beautiful in shrub and flower", is a splendid bolt-hole on a grey winter's day and a delightful spot on any day.

The large pastiche of orange-and-yellow glazed bricks and blue mosaic across the road from the People's Palace was built in 1889 as Templeton's Carpet Factory. Nowadays, this building of battlements, arches and pointed and circular windows is the **Templeton Business Centre**. William Leiper, its architect, when asked to name his favourite building, replied: "The Doge's Palace in Venice". One would have loved to have seen the look on his face when he was told to go ahead and build a similar building on Glasgow Green.

Back on the Green, that part to the east is the **Fleshers' Haugh** which should not be approached by those in

Templeton's, from carpet factory to business centre.

fear of flying missiles – namely, footballs. Here is where those two great Glasgow protagonists, Rangers and Celtic, had their first touch of the ball.

Great gatherings have been held on this part of the Green. In 1746 Bonnie Prince Charlie, much to the annoyance of most of the populace, set up camp for his 10,000 troops here and, after receiving "6,000 short cloath coats, 12,000 linen shirts, 6,000 pairs of shoes, and the like number of pairs of tartan hose and blue bonnets" from the city, reviewed these troops. (Glasgow craftsmen, accustomed to supplying large quantities of shoes and clothing to America, met the order within three weeks.) More recently the Fleshers' Haugh has had much larger crowds for pop concerts by such local groups as Wet Wet Wet.

Sporting activities have always been a feature of the Green. Glasgow's first golf course, an eight-hole affair, was laid out in 1730 on this flat sward of grass and it is reported that after the game the players would retire to the Burns Barns Tavern, now the **Old Barns**, at the corner of Ross and London Road. In Victorian times, by far the most popular activity was swimming in the River Clyde. Even though the water must have been much purer than it is today, because salmon were then caught and the nets dried on the Green, it is difficult to conjure up images of demure, discrete, Victorian ladies emerging from the bathing boxes which lined the river bank.

More recently the Green has been the site for the finish of the **Glasgow Marathon** which, however, has failed to emulate the success of the London, New York, Chicago or a host of other marathons and has now become a somewhat parochial half-marathon. On the other hand, rowing, which in Victorian times was the most popular sporting activity of the Green, is enjoying a resurgence. The Green's two boathouses are to be joined by others and soon the former three-day regatta will be revived and races once again rowed from opposite the Monument to Rutherglen.

Below, best foot forward at the Glasgow Marathon. Right, tenements in St Vincent's Crescent.

TENEMENT LIFE

One in five Glasgwegians lives in a tenement and such flats are much sought after. Basically, a tenement is a three- or four-storey-building of red or grey sandstone with a number of apartments on each level. Tenements are not free-standing but are joined together: the largest stretch for 600 yards, although more usually they are about 100 yards long.

The only major difference between a superior tenement flat and a posh apartment is that the latter has an elegant entrance, carpeted lobbies and elevators. Some, even in the poorer parts of the city are from the drawing boards of distinguished architects such as "Greek" Thomson. Some have bow windows, others have cornices, and still others are embellished with falderals. The best flats can have five, six, even I0 large rooms with exquisitely moulded high ceilings.

To view some of these elegant tenements, board the train at Central Station for a 10-minute journey to Maxwell Park. Then one can see why middle-class Glaswegians still scoff at their English counterparts who live in "little boxes" with a small plot of land.

A tenement is entered through a close which, at its worst, is little more than a hole in the front wall which penetrates through the building to the back court. The street entrance to the close is the "close mouth" while the rear part, beyond the stairway, is the "back close". (Correctly, the close refers to the court at the rear of the building but has come to mean the building's entrance.)

A stairway rises from the middle of the close to the two or three levels of the building, each with two or three flats. At its best, the close stands at the top of a flight of stairs, is fronted by a portico and is entered through a door and the stairway is illuminated by painted glass windows with light also entering through a handsome skylight.

Aesthetically, many handsome Glasgow tenements are degraded by their closes. Glasgow is damp; Glasgow can be windy; and so, moisture condenses on the walls and rubbish gathers in the close. Further diminishing the salubriousness is

the fact that many tenements have shops on the ground floor with a side entrance in the close. When, after World War II, closes were improved by the simple expedient of placing a door at both the front and the back, some tenements were enormously improved.

The decor of the close walls often indicates the quality of the flats within the close. Poorer tenements have closes which are simply white-washed and plastered; in better-class tenements the lower part of the close-wall is painted, often with a stencilled pattern above. Still better tenements have closes with an easily-cleaned tiled dado to about shoulder height creating the so-called "wally close". In the best tenements, tiles continue up the stairway.

So why all the talk of Gorbals slums? These were tenements whose flats had only one or two rooms and which were devoid of any plumbing. Shared toilets, if not in the back green, would be on the landing at the top of each flight of stairs.

More than a dozen people lived in one room and those fortunate enough to have two rooms would take in lodgers. In the I880s, a quarter of Glaswegians lived in one apartment; lodgers were taken in by 14 percent of those dwelling in one-room flats and by 27 percent of those with two-room houses. Girls slept in a concealed bed in a recess in the sitting room while boys occupied a similar bed in the kitchen. The bottom drawer of a chest of drawers could – and did – serve both as a crib for an infant and, often soon after, as its coffin.

Manny Shinwell, a renowned Red Clydesider who became a veteran Member of Parliament, once recalled his early days: "Later my father took me to Glasgow. We lived in the Gorbals. It was terrible, one lavatory to three families and no such thing as a bath... Drunkenness? People were floating across the streets."

In the "good old days", being a tenement dweller meant enjoying free entertainment. Singers, accordion players or violinists and, on occasions, one-man bands would perform regularly around the back greens. And there was no need, after the performance, for the buskers to beg for money: the generous Glaswegians would throw open their windows and toss out a penny. ∎

ALONG THE RIVER

That oft-repeated and formerly well-earned cliché "The Clyde made Glasgow; Glasgow made the Clyde" is no longer pertinent and, today, might even be considered impertinent. Nowadays, Glasgow scarcely depends on the river for its economic survival, although the river is, under the direction of city planners, being used more and more for recreation purposes. To this end, the **Clyde Walkway**, a handsome paved way, rich with flowers for much of the year, stretches from the King Albert Bridge, at the western end of Glasgow Green, to Stobcross, 2 miles (3 km) downstream.

The Walkway has not attracted as many hand-in-hand strollers as expected but rather is a new haven for friendly and somnambulant drunks who now often find their solace in beaujolais wine rather than in meths and whisky. Yet plans are afoot to extend the Walkway upstream for a further 4 miles (6 km) to Rutherglen. This will certainly delight crews who use this stretch of water, and once again the river, as it was in Victorian days, may be busy with skiffs and rowing boats.

The Walkway to the west from **Albert Bridge**, the first of five vehicular bridges in the heart of the city (there is also the pedestrian suspension bridge), occupies the space between the river and **Clyde Place**. The latter is flanked on its northern side by some interesting and attractive buildings.

The **Briggait**, which stands between Albert and Victoria bridges, the next bridge to the west and possibly the most handsome of the five, is a cream-and-green baroque extravaganza from the 19th century which was formerly the fish market and which in 1986 was converted into a shopping and restaurant complex. In spite of its handsome exterior with banded columns, winged sea horses flanking a very young Queen Victoria and Glasgow coats of arms and a splendid airy cast-iron interior, the conversion was not an economic success: the Briggait closed within 18 months of opening. It may yet have its day – possibly as a nightclub.

Behind the Briggait peeks the 164-ft (50-metre) **Merchants' Steeple** (the **Briggait Steeple**) which was built in the middle of the 17th century and is topped by a sailing ship. The steeple is all that remains of the old Merchants' House. When Port Glasgow was, in fact as well as in name, the port for Glasgow, city merchants would climb to the balconies of the square towers of diminishing dimensions in order to watch their dream boats come home.

A most successful market is invariably in progress behind the Briggait in the arches; these support the rail tracks which went in and out of the now defunct St Enoch's station and in vacant ground around these arches. **Paddy's Market** is the city's best flea market and the opportunist might just be fortunate enough to pick up a treasure: don't depend on it, though.

Return to upmarket at **Kings Court**, a small new V-shaped shopping complex which is readily recognisable by its glass canopy, azure-and-violet wrought-iron supports and the cupola which tops the base of the V. It stands opposite Paddy's Market.

Before continuing along the Clyde Walkway, stroll northwards for a couple of hundred yards on **Stockwell Street** to no. 27, where a plaque marks the house in which James McGill, the founder of Canada's McGill University, was born on 6 October 1744.

The clipper moored on the other side of the Victoria bridge is the *S.V. Carrick* which was built in 1864 in Sunderland – shame on you, Glasgow – as the *City of Adelaide*; it set the record, which still stands, for the voyage between Adelaide and London. The time taken to cover the 12,000 miles (19,200 km) was 65 days. The *Carrick*, a contemporary of the *Cutty Sark,* has been a Glasgow land-

mark for a quarter of a century and is the club house of members of the Royal Naval Volunteer Reserve.

Across the road from the Carrick is the relatively small **St Andrew's Cathedral** which is shatteringly reflected in the adjacent Diocese building. The consecration of the cathedral in 1816 signalled the entry into public life of the city's rapidly expanding Roman Catholic community, which now numbers one in three of all Glaswegians. Architecturally, the cathedral is spiky linear Gothic with traceried octagonal towers flanking the great window which overlooks the river.

The **Customs House Building** (1840), recognisable by its engaged Doric columns and prominent coat of arms, is about 200 metres further along the road. At this point, make the shortest of detours into **Jamaica Street** to view the beautifully proportioned **Gardner's building (The Iron Building)** (1855–56) which is a landmark not only in the architecture of Glasgow but in that of

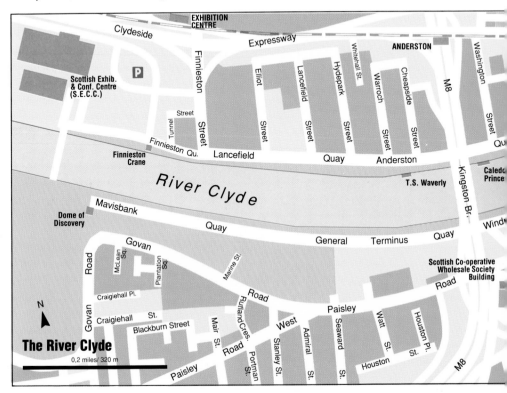

The River Clyde

0,2 miles/ 320 m

Europe. This furniture store, constructed of wrought and cast-iron and glass, exhibits unmatched refinement and restraint. The fenestration subtly changes from floor to floor with the arch shapes flattening as they get lower. Observe the delicate balustrades at the base of each window.

Return to the Clyde Walkway and pass under the railway bridge, over which trains pass in order to enter Central Station. This is the departure point for river excursion boats. Cross Jamaica Bridge and Clyde Street has become the **Broomielaw**, in its heyday the busiest spot on the river; from here, up to 50 passenger steamers would depart each day for Port Glasgow, Greenock, Gourock, Helensburgh and the islands in the Firth. These were the forerunners of today's suburban trains.

When moorings were not available, steamers would tie up across the river at Bridge Quay, now called **Clyde Place Quay**. The result was often "a regatta of demented chimney pots".

Now, where paddle steamers fought for moorings, all that can be seen – and this at Clyde Place Quay – is what appears to be a floating conservatory. This is the last **Renfrew ferry**, a breed of craft which was pulled to and fro by cables across the Clyde at Renfrew. They have been replaced by a bridge; the ferry is now a discothèque.

Occupying the city side of the Broomielaw, at the corner of **Oswald Street**, is the headquarters of the **Clyde Port Authority** (formerly the Clyde Navigation Trust). In some respects this outstanding building is a *trompe l'oeil* for, although the handsome frontage topped by a giant Neptune and the entrance flanked by stone carved boats, suggests a spectacular building, the gracious interior is very small.

Further along the Broomielaw, beyond James Watt Street where the great man lived in a pedimented villa, is the former **Glasgow Seamen's Institution**, now a "Nite Spot". The building is readily recognisable by an undistinguished

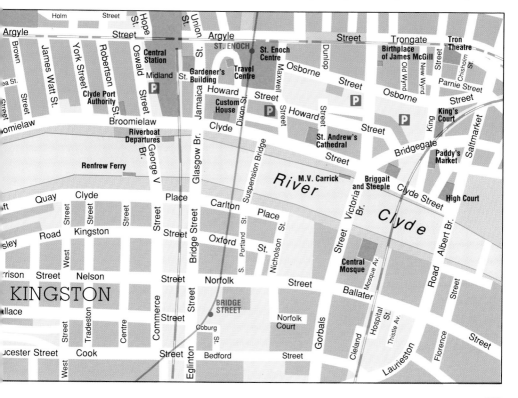

green dome and by bas reliefs of different types of craft, all Clyde-built, on its walls. Much more entertainment is offered by the white, 6,000-ton *Caledonian Princess (Tuxedo Princess)*, moored in the lee of the sky-high **Kingston Bridge**, which is a couple of hundred yards further downstream. This former car ferry, a hedonist's delight, has two discos, a piano bar, six other bars and a restaurant and is open until the wee sma' hours.

Across the river, on the other bank – and even dwarfing the Ring Road, which it stands alongside – is a French renaissance palace which was actually built as a Victorian warehouse: the headquarters of the **Scottish Co-operative Society**. It is reasonable to see in this masive pile echoes of the City Chambers for rumour circulated – and was vehemently denied by the architects – that the plan for this building was their unsuccessful submission for the City Chambers competition. During its existence the Society was not just the working classes' favourite retail store, especially for provisions; it was also a vehicle for political education, a social club with choirs and drama groups, a bank through the medium of the Co-op "share book" and quarterly dividends – in a word, an alternative society.

Tea tycoon: Back at the Broomielaw and a couple of hundred yards to the northwest is where Thomas Lipton, the son of Northern Irish parents who owned a grocery store in the Gorbals, set up his own "Irish Butter and Ham Market" soon after returning to Glasgow from the United States. In becoming a millionaire, Lipton cut out middlemen, brought produce direct from the Emerald Isle and blended "Lipton's Tea" to suit the different waters in towns where his chain had branches.

Above all, he was a marketing man *par excellence*. Every day two pigs were driven up from the quay wearing a banner which proclaimed "I'm on my way to Lipton's, the best place in town for bacon"; and at Christmas 1881 police

Pleasure boat and more serious vessels on the Clyde.

had to be sent to the Broomielaw to control crowds awaiting the arrival of a giant cheese from the US. Lipton had placed sovereigns in the cheese and the entire 1,375 lbs (625 kg) was sold in less than two hours.

The *P.S.Waverley*, the world's last ocean-going paddle steamer, has its berth at **Anderston Quay** on the far side of the Kingston Bridge over which the Ring Road passes. During the summer the *Waverley*, with its two distinctive red raking funnels – the very last of the "doon the watter" ships – still sails to such places as Greenock, Largs, Dunoon and the islands of Bute and Arran.

Further along (and seen before it is reached) is the massive **Finnieston Crane** (it carries the logo CLYDEPORT), an industrial monument which, on occasions, is still brought into use. Built in 1932, this hammerhead crane was once the largest in Europe and hoisted to new levels of fame not only locomotives but also the Glasgow which built them. Glasgow was then the most important loco-

motive city in Europe; steam locomotives built in the Springburn district were brought on loaders to this crane to be placed on ships which steamed off to India, Egypt and Russia.

The round building in the lee of the crane was formerly the entrance to and the exit from the now defunct Harbour Tunnel; it opened in 1895 and which was closed to vehicular traffic in 1940. However, until 1980, pedestrians could descend the 138 steps and walk, if not *on* water, then at least *under* water. The **North Bank rotunda** is now a restaurant, while its twin on the south bank is a **Dome of Discovery**, a hands-on science and technology exhibition which will delight children of all ages.

Another half-a-mile leads to **Stobcross Quay** and the former **Queen's Dock** which has been filled in and where now stands the **Scottish Exhibition and Conference Centre**. A wide variety of events, including exhibitions, conferences and pop concerts, are held here in several halls.

Fun and games at the Scottish Exhibition and Conference Centre.

THE MERCHANT CITY

As the city grew and prospered during the 18th century, largely as a result of trade in tobacco, sugar and cotton with the Americas, it spread westwards from High Street. The area which was colonised was largely flat and extended from the Trongate and Argyle Street in the south to George Street in the north. Large homes and warehouses belonging to merchants were built here rather than lowly tenements for the hoi polloi.

However, the merchants soon abandoned these homes and moved westwards and their former abodes became banks and warehouses. By the end of the century the **New Town** or **Merchant City** had taken shape and, during the ensuing Industrial Revolution, went on growing.

Expensive execution: At about this time, that part of the city between Trongate and George Street was described as being "occupied by a succession of beautiful streets intersecting each other at right angles... Wilson Street, Great Glassford Street, Millar Street, Queen Street, Buchanan Street, and Ingram Street. Besides these are Cochran Street, John Street, Glassford Street, George Square, Gordon Street, and Camperdown Place: in all of which the buildings vie with each other in the expensive and elegant manner in which they have been executed." All these streets, except the last, can be visited.

When, after World War II, Glasgow and the Clyde went into a steep and almost terminal decline, so too did the Merchant City, but, since about 1980, there has been a renaissance, a rejuvenation and a recycling of buildings in the Merchant City. The result is that yuppies and others are now moving into gentrified buildings, many of which were formerly warehouses. Nearly every month sees the opening of a new restaurant, a brasserie, a wine bar or an up-market pub. Those who were members

of the Presbyterian **John Street Church** would turn in their graves if they knew that, after 30 years of desuetude, it is now the vine rather than Jesus which is worshipped within its rusticated plinth.

Purists might say that the Merchant City stops at the eastern side of George Square but, for practical reasons this, the heart of the city, will be included in this chapter. And, one building just outside the eastern perimeter of the Merchant City will also be included.

The **Martyrs' Public School** is one of the first buildings to show the imprint of Charles Rennie Mackintosh and will be on the list of all who are on his trail. (It stands at the top of **Castle Street**, separated from the Royal Infirmary by a tangle of motorways and reached from the main Infirmary entrance by an overhead bridge.) The doors, the windows and the stairways all announce Macintosh. The **Forum Arts Society Trust** hope to make this building their HQ.

About 1 mile (1.5 km) from here is **Candleriggs** and the **City Hall** which,

after a fire in St Andrews Hall in 1962 (*see page 157*) and until the opening of the International Concert Hall in 1990, was the city's principal concert hall. Scarcely a beautiful building – this is partly due to its cramped quarters – the hall has excellent accoustics. Until quite recently the basement and rear of the building were occupied by the city's fruit and vegetable market and the entire region was thronged with hawkers. Now, the hawkers are confined to the rear section of the building which becomes a market on Fridays, Saturdays and Sundays.

Mungo's miracle: Closing the vista at the northern end of Candleriggs (they did make candles here until the 17th century) is the **Ramshorn** or **St Paul's and St David's Parish Church** which derives its name from the legend that here St Mungo performed the miracle of turning a stolen ram's head into stone. Or was it because of "a furious battle waged one night by rams against rams, at a time when it was customary to fold

sheep in considerable numbers upon the grounds"? Nowadays, further miracles are enacted here by thespians rather than by theologians, the church having been converted into a theatre for the University of Strathclyde. The initials R.F. and A.F. inscribed on the pavement to the right of the church entrance mark the graves of the Foulis brothers who were famous University of Glasgow printers and founders of Glasgow's first School of Art.

Two hundred yards further along **Ingram Street** a delicate, white square building from 1805 with a clock face steeple beckons. The figures in the two alcoves at the front of **Hutchesons' Hall** were made in 1649 and occupied a previous building of the same name. They are of the philanthropists George and Thomas Hutcheson who donated the building as an institutional headquarters and meeting hall. The original building was a hospice built by George in 1639 to take care of "aged decrepit men of the age above 50 years" and

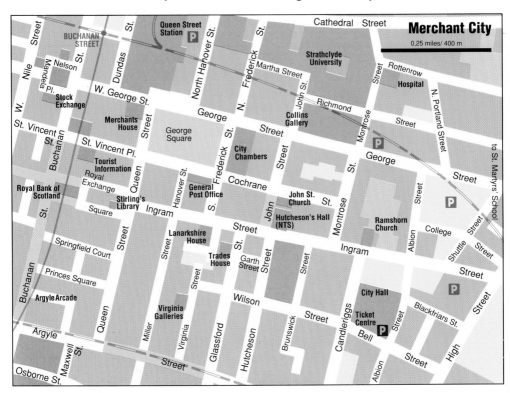

then, with a bequest from Thomas, "to also attend to the needs of eleven orphan boys". By the 1870s the orphans had become the nucleus of a new school in the Hutchesontown district of the Gorbals. This school would become Hutchesons' Grammar school, now a co-educational fee-paying school in a south side suburb and one of the most renowned schools in Glasgow. The Ingram Street building is now occupied by the West Regional offices of the **National Trust for Scotland**. A shop occupies the ground floor and an elegant, richly decorated hall with handsome pedimented doorways (open for viewing) is upstairs.

One of the portraits in the hall is of Sir William Smith who, in Glasgow, in 1883, long before Lord Baden Powell had dreamt up the Boy Scouts, founded the **Boys' Brigade**, an organisation with a religious framework and one which has branches in several Commonwealth countries, the USA and Scandinavia. An off-shoot is the **Jewish Lads and Girls Brigade**, whose Glasgow unit boasts the only Jewish pipe-band in the world.

The back of a massive neo-classical building, originally the County Chambers and later the Sheriff Court, stands empty directly opposite Hutchesons' Hall in what is sometimes erroneously referred to as Ingram Square. Soon, it will become a **Museum of Costume**. At the front of the building, a hexastyle Ionic colonnade stands atop a giant plinth on which is carved a rather tired relief frieze showing the course and the functions of justice. Then, in the middle of the west flank – the building grew like Topsy, being altered five times in the first 50 years after it was built in 1844 – a hexastyle Corinthian colonnade flanked on either side by a pair of Corinthian pilasters rises from a balustrade and suppports a massive corbel table on which stand giant urns. After this, the mansard roof becomes somewhat incongruous.

Look westwards from the colonnade

Below, today's merchants – of fashion. Right, Hutcheson's Hall spire, with the City Chambers steeple in the background.

along **Garth Street** and the view is of the **Trades House** which is the home of the 14 Glasgow trade guilds (open to the public). This, the second oldest building in the city still serving its original function (the oldest is the Cathedral), is from the drawing board of Robert Adam, the great Scottish architect, and was built in 1794. A rusticated ground floor supports a heavily pedimented first floor while the upper floor is topped by a balustrade with a central frieze above which sits Brittania flanking the Glasgow coat of arms. Behind this is a modest, green dome.

A few years ago good taste – although not necessarily astute financial acumen – prevailed, albeit nearly 150 years after the publication of a broadsheet which stated: "We cannot conclude this brief notice without condemning the parsimony which induces those connected with the Trades House to let the apartments in the lower storey for huxters' shops which detracts considerably from the appearance of the building."

Those who cannot list the guilds – Hammermen, Tailors, Cordiners, Maltmen, Weavers, Bakers and the like – when they enter the building will certainly be able to do so on leaving. Stained glass windows, chairs, the cupola of the dome and walls all carry the coats of arms of the individual guilds as well as the Glasgow coat of arms but with one subtle difference. Although the familiar bell, fish and bird are all here the words "Let Glasgow Flourish" are replaced by "Union is Strength".

A 30-ft (9-metre) oak bench, divided into seven sections by heavily carved arms with figure tops, stands on the right of the entrance hall. The coats of arms of the 14 guilds, of various Scottish towns and of various Belgian cities are embossed on the bench which was carved by Belgian wood carvers who were refugees in Glasgow during the 1914–18 war. From here a double flight of steps – Adam lovers should not look for anything comparable to Culzean or Mellerstain – ascends to the first floor and a magnificent banqueting hall whose carved wooden ceiling and cupola are especially attractive. A wide, fawn-coloured, silk frieze around the walls pays tribute to the workers of all the trades and mahogany mortification panels tell of bequests.

Next door is the Saloon with more craft crests and more mahogany mortification panels. (Since its inception one of the objectives of the Trades House is to provide hospitals for the sick, pensions for the elderly and to succour the needy.) Worthy of a glance is the Almshouse Bell of 1635.

Proceed up **Glassford Street** and immediately turn left back into Ingram Street. Here is **Lanarkshire House** whose three storeys are topped by a massive corbel table below which stand six figures which are, from left to right, Britannia, Wealth, Justice, Peace, Industry and Glasgow. Walk through **Virginia Place** at the side of this building to the rear and you will find a pretty, red sandstone building topped by a delicate

The Trades House, designed by Robert Adam.

green dome and with carvings of cherubs in the window pediments.

This stands at the top of **Virginia Street**. To pass the **Virginia Galleries** at number 33 with their black and white Corinthian pilasters would be to ignore one of the most valuable heirlooms of the city's great trading tradition. Enter through the handsome wrought iron gate into a high galleried hall. This was the tobacco or the sugar exchange, probably only one of a number of such exchanges where trading was carried out in the city. The ground floor is not original but the columns on the first floor date to 1819 and give lie to the statement "they don't make things today like they used to". They are merely hollow pieces of wood. The former exchange and the adjoining building are now occupied by antique shops and stores selling alternative life-style items. How well the tobacco lords lived can be judged from the magnificent, well-preserved three storey building which faces the Virginia Galleries.

Miller Street, a relatively quiet street in terms of pedestrian and vehicular traffic, is situated to the west of and parallel to Virginia Street. It was first developed in 1761 when Mr Miller, a Maltman and Glasgow Bailie, decided to extend "a street of Gentleman's Houses" through the garden behind his house. Number 42 still stands and, although in rundown condition, exhibits the strict requirements which Miller laid down for the development of houses on this street: "each house to consist of a half sunk and two square storeys, no gables, chimney or *corbie steps* facing the street and to be entered by a front door and flight of steps projected on the intended pavement". Apart from the mansard, the pedimented house with its Corinthian pilastered door looks much as it would have when built more than 200 years ago.

An adjacent building (number 46) with a rusticated ground floor, canopied windows on the first floor and blind oblong windows above this still shows

The Merchant City stops for tea.

some of its past glory. Note the Scottish thistles in the decoration of the facade.

The north end of Miller Street debouches into **George Square** which is the city centre. It was built in 1787 on a piece of marshland and for long was the prime showpiece of the New Town. Sheep grazed in the square until well into the 19th century and were prevented from straying by a 4-ft (1-metre) high railing. Later, the square became the main hotel centre of the city and then, in the 19th century, the Municipal Chambers and the **General Post Office** were moved to here from Glasgow Cross and the Briggait respectively. One of the old hotels much changed and now called the **Copthorne**, still occupies part of the north side of the Square and the Post Office still stands on the south side. Originally, the west side was occupied by a symmetrical Italianate building but this symmetry was destroyed in 1907 when additonal storeys were added to the north corner.

Scattered about the Square are statues

of 11 persons who appear to have been selected as the result of a lottery. In the centre, looking down on all, with his plaid, as was his wont, thrown over his left, rather than right, shoulder, is Sir Walter Scott standing atop an 80-ft (24-meter) slender Doric column. This was the first memorial in the land to be erected in honour of Scott, an Edinburgh man, whose connections with Glasgow are at best tenuous. Who said Glaswegians are parochial?

Royal disgrace: George III, after whom the square was named when it was laid out in 1781, should occupy the spot where Scott stands but losing the American colonies cost the Glasgow tobacco lords dearly and cost George III, if not his head, at least his position in Glasgow's George Square. However, royalty are represented by statues of Queen Victoria and of Prince Albert.

Robert Burns and James Watt, whose statues stand in the southwest corner of the Square, will be known to all, as will William Gladstone and Robert Peel, but who on earth was Thomas Campbell? He was the most famous of Glasgow's men-of-letters, at least in his time (1777–1844), and was three times elected Lord Rector of the University of Glasgow, on one occasion defeating Scott who now towers over him. Gladstone and Peel also held this title. The other statues are of Sir John Moore, hero of Corunna; Lord Clyde (Colin Campbell), a field marshal who crushed the Indian mutiny (does Glasgow's not inconsiderable Indian community know he stands here?); Thomas Graham, the "father of colloid chemistry" and James Oswald, a minor parlimentarian – Glaswegians all. Finally, dominating the east side of the Square is the **Cenotaph**, a powerful memorial to Glasgow's dead in the two world wars.

Behind the cenotaph, the entire east side of the square is occupied by the massive **City Chambers**. They were opened in 1888 by Queen Victoria who, in her only other visit 39 years previously, had not liked the city and said that

Glasgow-born Lulu at a New Year's party in George Square.

she would prefer not to return. The style, typical of the time, is Italian Renaissance, although the 216-ft (65-metre) tower, capped by a domed cupola, owes little to the Mediterranean. Each corner carries a domed cupola.

The facade is covered with innumerable bas-relief tableaux and sculptural groups. The tableau in the main pediment commemorates the Jubilee Year of Queen Victoria who sits on her throne atop a flight of steps with the lion at her feet and figures representing England, Scotland, Ireland and Wales supporting her. At the side of these are other figures representing the then many British colonies. The figures, 8 ft high (more than 2 metres), are larger than those in the Elgin Marbles and appear life-sized when viewed from the street. In a smaller pediment above the entrance which contains symbolic figures depicting Religion, Virtue and Knowledge, is the city's motto "Let Glasgow Flourish". This, an abbreviated version of the text written on the bell of the Tron Church cast in 1631, reads: "Lord, let Glasgow flourish through the preaching of Thy word and praising Thy name".

Enter the building (morning and afternoon tours) and the triumphal announcement, loud and clear, is of success, wealth and confidence. Let there be no doubt that this is the home not only of Scotland's premier city but of the second largest and second most important city of the far-flung British Empire. (Both statements were valid when the Chambers were opened.)

Rich red coupled columns which look like marble but which are actually cut from Peterhead granite and which are said to be the most beautiful pieces of granite ever quarried in Scotland stand atop grey slabs of Aberdeen granite and are topped by dark green Italian marble capitals. The vaulted ceiling and dome dazzle with brilliant Venetian mosaics while other mosaics cover the floor. The visitor can well imagine that he has entered an Italian basilica although forced to wonder if the four enormous

Bird's-eye view of George Square.

caryatids came in via the backdoor. Leave the entrance hall and enter an Italian Renaissance palace.

Two stairways lead to the upper floors. One can do no better than quote William Young, the architect: "the view from the first landing is really magnificent. Tier upon tier of pillars, arches and cornices, the whole height of the stair, three lofty storeys in various coloured marbles – purple Brescia, veined Carrara and red transparent alabaster surmounted by a vast conical ceiling in richly ornamental plasterwork and a cupola filled with tinted glass."

Visit, among other rooms, the Council Hall, the "Municipal Drawing Room", the Octagonal Room, the Mahogany Salon and the Banqueting Hall. The craftsmanship is terrific, the attention to detail meticulous; but remember that not all the artisans were Scots: some were from France and Italy. The superbly carved Spanish mahogany in the Council Hall evokes memories of skilled medieval artisans and would have thrilled Tilman Riemenschneider. Above the wood is a freize of wheat-coloured Tynecastle tapestry, a mixture of leather and papier-mâché.

Dining out: However, the *pièce de résistance* is the huge Banqueting Hall – 110 ft (33 metres) long, 48 ft (14 metres) wide and 52 ft (16 metres) high – with its glorious arched ceiling, leaded glass windows and paintings depicting scenes from the history of the city. The south wall is covered by three large murals which are the work of members of the Glasgow School (*see page 79*). Alexander Roche's painting is of the incident when a ring was found in a salmon caught in the Clyde. The king of Strathclyde believed that Languoreth, his queen, was having an affair with one of his knights and, indeed, she had given the fellow her ring. And so, when the knight was asleep the king stole this ring, hurled it into the Clyde, and ordered the queen to wear it that evening. Languoreth appealed to St Mungo who dispatched a monk to fish in the river

Victorian ornateness: the City Chambers.

and to bring to him the first fish which he caught. The salmon had the ring in its mouth. Honour was saved and that is why the fish appears on the Glasgow coat of arms.

Edward Walton's mural is of the "Glasgow Fair" on Glasgow Green *circa* 1500. Walton used a rare technique, at least among British artists, of mixing his paints with sand resulting in a dramatic almost 3-D effect. The third mural which shows the busy River Clyde towards the middle of the 19th century is by Sir John Lavery. The three large gracious chandeliers in this room are the originals for, even although the Chambers were built in 1885, they were illuminated by electricity.

The building at the northern corner of the west side of the square is the **Merchants' House** (open to the public) whose original members were relatively wealthy wholesalers, exporters and importers. The exterior is remarkable, among other details, for its corner oriel windows supported by corbels in the shape of Amazons. Atop the domed tower is a sailing ship similar to the one atop the Briggait Steeple. Notable in the Banqueting Hall with its Corinthian engaged columns and pilasters are the mortification boards commemorating bequests made by wealthy members of the House. The Directors' room is also richly furbished and its walls are lined with Tynecastle silk. One of the occupants of the building is the Glasgow Chamber of Commerce, the oldest chamber of commerce in Britain.

Exiting from George Square at its southwest corner leads to **Queen Street** and, after a few steps to **Royal Exchange Square**. The heart of the square is occupied by the **Royal Exchange Building**, inside which is the **Gallery of Modern Art**, a recently-opened building celebrating the Glasgow Festival of Visual Arts 1996. It showcases the work of both Scottish and international painters, photographers and sculptors. The display space on all four floors each represents the four natural elements:

Below, piping up in the City Chambers. Right, a city officer on guard.

fire, water, air and earth. Also on show are various interactive displays through which visitors, if they are feeling especially creative, can make their own art.

Although this classic building is now extending its tentacles into the abstract realm of modern art, it started life in 1780 as the most imposing tobacco lord's mansion in the city. It belonged to William Cunninghame who made an enormous fortune at the time of the American War of Independence by buying up all stocks of Virginia tobacco held by nervous merchants and reselling it later at a 700 percent profit. In 1827, Cunninghame's home became the Royal Exchange and David Hamilton added the impressive portico of 12 giant fluted columns atop a modest pedestal. The sides of the building are pilastered with, towards their western end, colonnades while the rear of the building has considerably smaller engaged columns and pilasters. All are of the Corinthian order. Hamilton also added the lantern, a handsome affair whose upper part is supported by more Corinthian elements, but one whose texture is somewhat at odds with the rest of the building.

Enter through an oval foyer with a spiral staircase into what was formerly the main hall of the Royal Exchange where city merchants would deal in cotton, sugar, rum and other commodities and where some would first learn of the loss of argosies. Today, this stunning Byzantine basilica with a superbly decorated lofty and arched roof and divided in three by two rows of massive fluted Corinthian columns is filled with shelves of books. Madder brown is the dominant colour.

The **Royal Bank of Scotland**, to the rear of the library, is fronted by an impressive raised Ionic hexastyle portico atop a flight of steps. Two handsome arches flanked by coupled Ionic columns attempt to prevent the bank linking Exchange Square and Buchanan Street. Sadly, the bank and the library are scarcely matched by other buildings in the Square.

On the roof of Merchants' House.

136

It is not too surprising on the streets just strolled to encounter groups of elderly Glaswegians seriously talking with young Asians about information technology and video productions. All are students at Glasgow's second university – and the term second is used in a temporal rather than in an academic sense – the **University of Strathclyde** which occupies most of the buildings on the north side of **George Street** and many buildings in neighbouring streets.

The elderly indigenes are mature students enrolled in a "Learning in Later Life" programme while the younger Asian students are some of the more than 1,300 students from 93 countries attending the University. A glance at the examination pass lists in engineering reveal that many of these students are from Malaysia, Singapore, China and Hong Kong.

The University of Strathclyde began life in 1796 as the Andersonian Institution, a technical school which was the brain-child of "Jolly Jack Phosphorus" Anderson, an irascible professor at the University of Glasgow who was "the enemy of lucre-loving professors". In 1912 it became the Royal Technical College and, later, the Royal College of Science and Technology or, to all Glaswegians, simply the "Tech". In 1964 university status was obtained and Strathclyde became the first of Scotland's post-World War II universities. Today, almost 8,000 students, of whom about 20 percent are postgraduates, study in the four faculties – engineering, arts and social studies, science, and the Strathclyde business school – of Scotland's third largest university.

The University, which for long has had strong ties with industry, has abandoned the classical three-semester structure of most British universities in favour of a modular system which permits flexi-courses and flexi-examinations with the opportunity for such intriguing study programmes as psychology and law or modern languages and marketing. Basically, Strathclyde is still a red-

brick, technically oriented, city university with most of the students being youngsters who commute daily from in and around Glasgow.

Yet it is not parochial. Scientists from all the world comes here to garner knowledge at the University's National Centre for Prosthetics and Orthotics (aids for physically disabled) and its business school is the largest and, academically, one of the top five in Europe.

Over the past quarter of a century the university has grown and grown and grown but its heart remains the large red Italianate building on George Street which was built at the beginning of this century. Behind this, on Richmond Street, is the **Collins Gallery** where excellent art exhibitions are mounted. In 1989 the University took over two churches, the Barony and the Ramshorn, and just to show that they are a technical university in the 20th century, the churches have been successfully converted into "Solar Residences". Who says the sun never shines in Glasgow?

Proof that the sun does sometimes shine.

THE CITY CENTRE

As the years passed, the city moved further west and began to build on the characteristic Glasgow drumlins. In the main, commercial and public buildings rather than homes were constructed. Today, the major shopping streets – some of which have been pedestrianised, although sometimes not too successfully – are in this part of town. However, as in other large cities, vast enclosed shopping complexes are now part of the scene, both in the city centre and the suburbs.

This is the part of the city where among – although not next door to – tatty shops can be found such renowned names as Christie's and Sotheby's, Burberry and Mappin & Webb. An affluent society has spawned some streets rich in picture framers and galleries, others in bookshops and brasseries. This, too, is the area with most of the surviving theatres and cinemas – and with more Mackintosh and "Greek" Thomson buildings than can be seen anywhere else in the world. This part of the city is where the visitor, when not window-shopping, should remember the exhortation "Eyes Up", not because chimney pots are tumbling downwards but rather to view the glorious tarradiddles which decorate many buildings.

Indicative of the shopping trend is the vast glass-covered **St Enoch Centre** in the square of that name. Complete with ice-rink and occupying the site of a former railway terminal, this is Europe's largest glassed-in area. (The name St Enoch is derived from Thennach or Thenew, mother of St Mungo.) The pretty, red, Jacobean building with turrets at its four corners which stands in the middle of the square, looking for all the world like a castle which has fled from the Scottish Highlands, houses the **Travel Centre**.

From St Enoch's, enter **Buchanan Street** which was once, and possibly still is, Glasgow's premier shopping street. It is now pedestrianised but strollers are advised to keep a wary eye for vehicles even while admiring the grand array of Victorian facades which line much of the street. **Argyle Arcade** on the east side – it has another entrance on Argyle Street – is a delightful early 19th-century glassed-in L-shaped complex. It was Glasgow's answer to Milan's renowned Galleria and in the same way that the latter links the Piazza Duomo and the Piazza Scala so the Argyle Arcade joins Argyle Street and Buchanan Street. The arcade, which is lined mainly by jewellers, is about 160 yards long and has a right-angle turn at its midpoint. Among the jewellers and other shops is Sloan's restaurant, which lays claim to being the oldest restaurant in the city.

Immediately beyond this lies the **Princes Square** shopping mall, which is sheer magic. Formerly an open loading area, it has been converted with great imagination and élan into a centre

Preceding pages: motorways came to Glasgow in a big way. Left, St Enoch Centre, a lofty glasshouse. Right, Salvador Dali on the sidewalk.

worth visiting even for those who do not shop, do not eat and who are in all ways fully paid-up misanthropes.

Still standing in this part of the city, although not now used for their original purpose, are two buildings with which Mackintosh's name is associated. Each was once occupied by a major Glasgow newspaper. The **Glasgow Herald Building** on Mitchell Street was constructed in 1893–95 when Mackintosh was a draughtsman rather than an architect but authorities claim that the fenestration, the positioning of the octagonal corner tower and the carved stone and wrought-iron ornamentation all announce his distinctive combination of art nouveau and Scottish baronial styles. (Incidentally, the *Herald* claims to be the oldest daily newspaper in the English-speaking world, having been established in 1783.)

The nearby former **Daily Record Building** (1901) on **Renfield Lane** also has many Mackintosh hallmarks, including glazed green-and-white brickwork patterned with a triangular tree motif and a row of steeply battered dormer windows. Admiring these and other delightful touches incurs a stiff neck: Renfield Lane is very narrow.

On the way back to Buchanan Street stop and admire the **Ca'd'oro** (corner of Gordon and Union Streets), another glorious building which has a facade of glass and cast-iron and which is Glasgow's answer to Venice's 15th-century Golden House. Giant romanesque masonry arches sitting on top of Doric pilasters enclose vast expanses of glass and above this is a row of circular attic windows. Here is a rare example of shops not detracting from the beauty of the building. The marriage of commerce and art is helped by the fact that the entire ground floor is occupied by one of the several bookshops found in this part of town. One of these shops, John Smith (not to be confused with W.H. Smith & Son, the large nationwide chain), was established in 1756 and is Scotland's oldest bookshop.

142

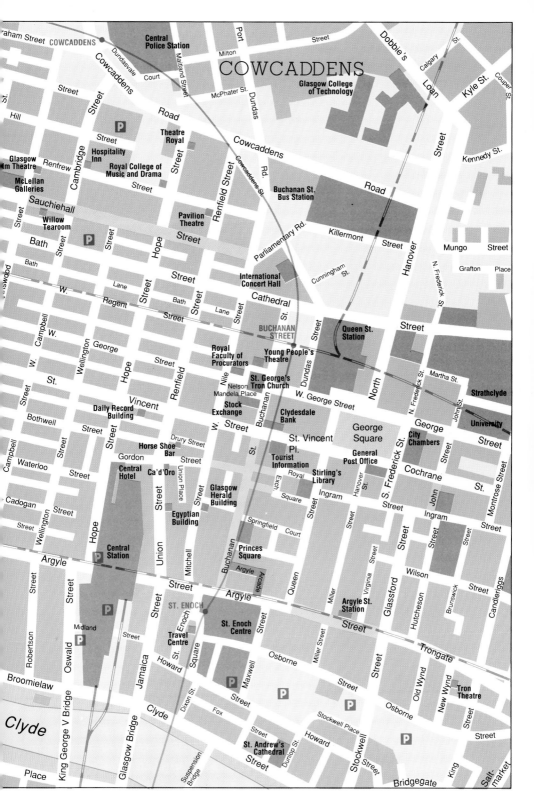

Almost next to the Ca'd'oro on Union Street is another, less obvious, cast-iron framed building. The **Egyptian Halls** are from the drawing-board of Alexander "Greek" Thomson (1817–75) a major figure in European architecture. Especially unusual in this linear building are the dumpy, Egyptian-like columns found on the upper floor; they practically form a colonnade or an eaves gallery. Observe, too, the wide decorative bands of moulding between the different floors.

Sadly, Thomson, who was a predecessor of Mackintosh (he was awarded a Thomson Travelling Fellowship to Europe), has failed to receive the adulation, even in his native city, that is now bestowed upon Mackintosh. A not inconsiderable number of his bold buildings still stand, but few in Glasgow can point at them and say: Greek Thomson.

What Mackintosh thought of Thomson's work can be assumed from a speech that he (Mackintosh) made to the Glasgow Architectural Association: "It is absurd to think it is the duty of the modern architect to make believe that he is living five, six hundred, or even a thousand years ago." Thomson is reported to have said, although not in riposte, that "architecture of the present ought to be the summation of the *principles* of the architecture of its past, not the imitation of its *forms*."

Time for a "refreshment". Enter the **Horse Shoe Bar** at 17 Drury Street: it is reputed to have the longest continuous bar in all Europe. Three hundred yards to the east of here, past John Smith's bookshop, is **St Vincent's Place**, which is nothing more than a widening, on the south side, of the street of that name. Magnificent Victorian Renaissance buildings, mostly banks and insurance companies, line both sides of the Place, with the vista to the east being closed by the City Chambers.

The **Greater Glasgow Tourist Board and Convention Bureau** occupies premises here; but rather than visiting the Bureau de Change in their office,

Former ticket office for St Enoch station, now a fanciful tourist information centre.

cross the road and be dazzled by the **Clydesdale Bank**. The modest foyer scarcely prepares the visitor for what is beyond the next glass doors. The black, gold and russet banking hall is arcaded in the Venetian manner and topped by an elliptical cupola. Fanciful wrought-iron designs fill the coffers (not the tills but the lacunae in the ceiling) and permit light to enter the hall which is decorated with black engaged columns with pseudo-Ionic capitals decorated with laurel leaves. Around the top of the walls are the heads of 30 Roman emperors and empresses.

A little further up Buchanan Street is **Nelson Mandela Place**. Formerly, this was **St George's Place** – as it still is to many older Glaswegians – but in 1986 the city council, yielding to pressure, changed the name. (Incidentally, although, apart from a few hiccups, the city has had a Labour council for more than 50 years, this is by no means a "looney left" administration, even if their rhetoric can suggest it.)

Dominating the centre of the square and evocative of Wren is **St George's Tron Church** (1807) with a tower topped by an obelisk thrusting heavenwards. The four obelisks at the level of the clocks are poor substitutes for the four evangelists.

The **Stock Exchange** (open to the public), that glorious icing cake at the southeast corner of the square, positively shrieks Venice and it is unfortunate that its beauty should be marred by incongruous stores at ground level – incongruous not so much for their contents of wool and food as for their facades. On the walls of the building are carvings symbolising Building, Engineering and Mining (Mandela Place side) and Science and Art (Buchanan Street side).

Diagonally opposite is the lavish, two-storey Venetian **Royal Faculty of Procurators** (1854), the lower floor rusticated and each floor topped by a balustrade. Features of this building are the handsome keystones which are suppos-

edly the heads of distinguished members of the legal profession, the frieze where lions sit among foliage, and the decorated window frames. The Palladian ensemble on the West Nile Street side is especially attractive. The adjacent building with figures of Purcell (music), Flaxman (sculpture), Wren (architecture) and Reynolds (painting) standing on a ledge supported by four Ionic columns was, when constructed in 1886, the Athenaeum and then became the College of Dramatic Art. Now, it is once again buzzing with thespians, having been converted into a **Young People's Theatre** in 1990.

Six hundred yards west of Mandela Place, on the crest of a drumlin on **St Vincent Street**, stands a church of that name whose podium would make a perfect stage for a performance of *Aïda*. This quintessential "Greek" Thomson building has antecedents, as do so many of his buildings, not only in Greece but in other eastern countries.

The site, on a steep hillside, is particularly awkward, but Thomson overcame this by designing an enormous podium with Egyptian-like doors. On top stands the main church hall fronted by an Ionic portico; its sides, however, are more Egyptian than Greek and its tower would not have been out of place in India during the Raj. Inside, the colours and designs recall classical Egypt and a delightful anthemion frieze echoes a frieze on the exterior of the building.

From Thomson's renowned church, it's just a short steep climb to **Blythswood Square** (1823–29), which is possibly the most perfect square in the city: it occupies a spirit-level flat piece of ground on top of a drumlin, is perfectly square and is planted with grass and flowers. The late classical, three-storey, grey buildings on all four sides, each with three Ionic porches and lintels above the windows of the middle range, were residences but are now clubs, restaurants and offices. The immaculate **Royal Scottish Automobile Club** building occupies all of the eastern side.

Left, Glaswegians love to shop. Below, to locate the Willow Tearoom, look for a jeweller's.

The magnet here for Mackintosh lovers is the doorway at No. 5 on the north side which he designed for the former occupants, the Glasgow Society of Lady Artists. No. 7, next door, was the home of Madeleine Smith, the defendant in one of Scotland's most notorious murder trials. In 1857, she was accused of poisoning her lover. The jury, to rapturous applause, brought in a verdict of "not proven", which in Scots law can be construed to mean "go away and don't do it again".

Leave the northern side of the square, stroll the 100 yards to **Sauchiehall Street** and turn right for morning coffee or afternoon tea at the readily recognisable, light-coloured, light-hearted, small building bearing the sign Hendersons the Jewellers. The ground floor of this store does sell jewellery but venture upstairs to the **Willow Tearoom** (Sauchiehall is Scots for the Meadow of Willow Trees) and be delighted, for this is an exact reconstruction of one of the four tearooms which Kate Cranston employed Mackintosh to decorate. What's more, it is the only one of the four for which Mackintosh was both architect and interior decorator.

Mackintosh believed in total design and the furniture (reproduction), the cutlery, menu-cards and fittings – leaded mirror glass doors and similarly treated windows – are original Mackintosh or the work of his wife Margaret. Note how the windows in this, the Room de Luxe of the original tearoom, arch across the facade, allowing waves of diffused daylight to flicker in and around the furnishings.

If it is raining on leaving the tearoom, then those carrying their mackintosh should give thanks to Glasgow. Another Macintosh from Glasgow, who was also christened Charles but who lived 100 years before the artist, was the inventor of the process which permitted the making of waterproof clothing.

The bust of a young Queen Victoria occupies an alcove below the Glasgow coat of arms above the entrance to the

Inside the Willow Tearoom, designed by Charles Rennie Mackintosh.

CHARLES RENNIE MACKINTOSH

Charles Rennie Mackintosh, Glasgow born and educated, was the toast of avant-garde architects and designers in Europe, who even referred to a sophisticated style prevalent at the beginning of this century as "Mackintosh-ismus". Yet, in his own country, he was a prophet ignored. Budapest, Munich, Dresden, Turin, Venice and Moscow toasted: "To our master Mackintosh, the greatest since the Gothic" – but in Glasgow the vast majority scoffed.

How could such frivolity be taken seriously? The reactions from "the saner seven-eighths of mankind", especially to his School of Art and to Miss Cranston's tearooms, were hilarity, bewilderment and revulsion. Only with the re-awakening of interest in art nouveau in the 1950s did his furniture and architecture begin to exert any influence on designers and, to a lesser extent, on architects in Britain. Today, Mackintosh is a cult figure of international renown, with a reputation built on a remarkably small opus, executed over scarcely more than 20 years.

He was born in 1868 and, although neither his parents nor his 10 siblings showed much interest in the arts, he became an architect, finding his inspiration, as did so many others, in the vernacular buildings of the countryside. This is evident in his *magnum opus*, the Glasgow School of Art. His simple geometrical manipulation of space based on combinations of straight line and gentle curves, with the former predominating, was a harbinger of later purist work. His was an eclectic mixture, part utilitarian and modernistic, part artistic and traditional.

Contemporary with Mackintosh at art school were several talented designers, artists and craftworkers who constituted a group which created the Glasgow Style. Mackintosh insisted that he was not part of that school and never its leader. Yet, in many respects, the Chinese and Cloister rooms which he designed for Miss Cranston's Ingram Street tea-rooms are the ultimate statement of the Glasgow Style.

At art school, Mackintosh and his friend Herbert McNair met the women whom they would marry: the artist sisters Margaret and Frances Macdonald. "The Four", influenced by both Pre-Raphaelitism and Aestheticism, were dedicated to the search for a distinctive modern style and collaborated on designs for furniture, metalwork and illustration.

Mackintosh's furniture – chairs have tall attenuated backs and tables have spindly supports – has an aesthetic quality which contrasts with the lush opulence and exaggerated sensuality of French art nouveau. He favoured woodwork painted white or with neutral colours and sparsely decorated with intricate flower patterns reminiscent of Japanese motifs and elaborated and entwined by a Celtic manuscript illuminator. The atmosphere of his complete rooms was created by few furnishings which helped create a muted ambience and which led to these rooms being called *chambres garnies pour belles âmes*.

Mackintosh's concept of the total integration of architecture and interior design and his insistence on complete control of every detail made commissions few and far between. He could not bear to compromise, with the result that, on occasions, he lost both his temper and his commission.

He was fortunate to find an ideal client in Kate Cranston. Not only was she an astute businesswoman but she also shared his vision of bringing art into every aspect of daily life and within everyone's reach. When Mackintosh could not obtain any work in Glasgow, she was always willing to support his most innovative designs. Between them, they raised the tea-room business from mere commerce into an art form.

By 1913, with his talent eroded by both a drinking problem and a lack of confidence, he and Margaret abandoned "philistine" Glasgow and went to live in Suffolk where he intended to take up painting seriously. A year later they moved to Chelsea where he attempted to resume his work as an architect and designer.

However, by 1923, Mackintosh had abandoned all hope and emigrated to the south of France to devote himself to water-colour painting. In 1928 he died in London, in a Hampstead nursing home, from cancer of the tongue. ∎

McLellan Galleries building (immediately to the West of the Willow Tearooms at the corner of Sauchiehall and Rose Streets). Archibald McLellan, a coach-maker, was an art buff who bequeathed to the city his not inconsiderable collection, which was especially strong in 16th and 17th century Italian masters, and the building in which it was housed.

Unfortunately, as with the Burrell collection, there were problems with the legacy and it was only after McLellan's numerous debtors had been satisfied that Glasgow was able to receive the bequest which became the basis for the collection in the Kelvingrove Art Gallery. This classical, three-storey building, with a dome at its corner and windows topped by triangular or curved pediments or lintels supported by brackets, was beautifully restored in 1990 after a fire – does Glasgow have more than its fair share of conflagrations? – and now houses one of *the* galleries in the city.

The **Cosmo Cinema** or the **Glasgow Film Theatre**, on the other side of **Rose Street**, a 1930s building in *Moderne* Scandinavian style, is one of the city's few remaining cinemas and the closest thing it has to an art cinema. Not too many years ago Glasgow, with more than 130 silver screens, was dubbed Britain's "Cinema City" and had, it was claimed, more picture palaces per head of population than any city outside America. One of these, Green's Playhouse, was, until its gallery was removed in the 1960s, Europe's largest cinema, seating 4,400.

Mackintosh's monument: And so to **Renfrew Street** and a steep climb of 100 yards to that building in Glasgow which attracts most visitors: the **Glasgow School of Art**. (To determine visiting times, telephone 353 4500.) Built in 1897–99 and with a wing added in 1907–09, this is Charles Rennie Mackintosh's *magnum opus*, a work which was the harbinger of a new movement in Europe and one which would influence

The Art School, inside and outside.

the Continent rather than the homeland. Mention must be made of Francis ("Fra") Newbery, who was the director of the school at the time of the competition for a new building and who insisted that Mackintosh's entry should win.

The design of the building was a challenge, not only because of the paucity of funds available (that is why it was constructed in two parts) but because it is built between two of the steepest hills in the city. It is not too long since a parked lorry hurtled down Garnet Street, to the west of the school, flew across Sauchiehall Street and, with loss of life, destroyed the buildings on the far side of that street.

The entrance on Renfrew Street is startlingly asymmetrical and the gentle curvature of the stone stairway contrasts with the linearity of this facade, which is dominated by enormous windows. These, some of which are embellished with fanciful wrought-iron, permit north light to enter the studios. Although the great proportion of glass to

stone in this facade reversed the trend in Victorian buildings, it was not without precedent in Glasgow. (Compare Gardener's building (*see page 120*) and the Ca'd'oro (*see page 142*). The east wall is more evocative of an ancient Scottish castle, rough and powerful, and it has been suggested that the Governors accepted this startling design with its lack of ornamentation only because it would be inexpensive to build. (The windows at the northern end of this facade were later additions through which live animals from an adjacent circus were brought in for life classes.)

On the west facade, grille-covered oriel windows soar upwards for three storeys, forming an irregular pattern which is at its most magnificent when illuminated by the setting sun. The back of the building, which looks down on Sauchiehall Street and is difficult to see, is a powerful mass composed of Scottish baronial details.

The interior, with its magnificent use of timber, has been described as a "warren of discovery" which was the result, at least in part, of the building being constructed in two stages. The most celebrated and the most exciting room is the two-storey galleried library, sombre yet light, severe yet a soufflé. Here, Mackintosh's use of primary colours, which became a hallmark of his work, is well demonstrated. So, too, is the great attention which he paid to detail not only for the convenience, but also for the delight, of those who would work in the building. A collection of architectural drawings, watercolours and furniture from several of Mackintosh's other commissions can be found in the Mackintosh Room and the Furniture Gallery.

Continue westwards along Renfrew Street for about 300 yards to **Garnethill Synagogue**, the principal and oldest Jewish house of worship in Glasgow. Just beyond this, Renfrew Street ends in a modest belvedere from where remarkably splendid views of the towers of the Park Conservation scheme and of the University of Glasgow can be savoured.

Art School students are much sought after.

150

War and peace: Two quite different small museums can be reached from here. Descend the steep drumlin to the north to reach the **Tenement House** at 145 Buccleuch Street or descend the equally steep drumlin to the south to the **Royal Highland Fusiliers Museum** at 518 Sauchiehall Street. The latter contains 300 years of military memorabilia of the regiment whose name it bears and which has the greatest number of battle honours of any British regiment.

Time is frozen in the fully furnished Tenement House. Built in 1892, it gives an insight into life in Glasgow between 1911 and 1965 when a Miss Agnes Toward, who could not bear to throw away a scrap of paper, lived here. Most Glaswegians lived in tenement houses, some few grander than this, many not so grand. Enter the flat and enter a time capsule of the gas-lit era with a coal bunker, china tea service and the yellow glow of gas mantles over the black-leaded cooking range.

Although these two places – the Milit-

ary Museum and the Tenement House – are entirely different, they have a tenuous link. It was the male occupants of these tenements who voluntarily rushed in their thousands to the defence of their country in both world wars. Many never returned. Who knows if Miss Toward would have remained a spinster saving all these *lares* and *penates* had these wars not been fought!

Still on Sauchiehall Street, a few yards to the east of the Military Museum are the **Grecian Chambers**. This work by "Greek" Thomson has marked similarities, especially in the free-standing row of squat columns which form an eaves gallery, to the Egyptian Halls in Union Street *(see page 144)*. The **Centre for Contemporary Arts (CCA)**, which occupies one of the ground-floor shops here, was, when opened in the mid-1980s as the Third Eye, Glasgow's first contemporary arts centre. It has successfully kept up with the times and now boasts a studio-style theatre, two exhibition galleries, a wholefood cafe-

It's yesterday once more at Tenement House Museum.

teria and bar, and a shop which stocks recherché books.

A few steps to the west of the Military Museum is the spectacular curve of the five-storyed, red sandstone **Charing Cross Mansions**. This château-like building, which would hardly be out of place in the French countryside, is a Glasgow tenement – not of the kind formerly found in the Gorbals, but nevertheless, a tenement. The oriel windows, steep attic roof and three-bay centre-piece with a clock and galleried cupola are altogether a truly splendid sight to behold.

Oldest school: Across the road from here, on the east side of **Elmbank Street**, stands a handsome classical building with statues atop four columns which flank the entrance. It is now occupied by the Strathclyde Regional Council but was formerly the home of the Glasgow High School for Boys which was founded even before Glasgow University (1451) and which might be the oldest school in Britain.

Three of the oldest and largest theatres in the city can be found in this part of town. The **King's**, at Charing Cross, with a rich red-and-gold Edwardian interior, stages musicals and the occasional play from London's West End; although grand and large, it is also rented out at modest sums to amateur groups. Then, close to the junction of Renfield and Sauchiehall Streets is the **Pavilion**, a music hall whose boards have been trod by many of Scotland's great comedians and which now presents rock and pop concerts as well as shows for the family.

Nearby is the **Royal**, undoubtedly Scotland's most prestigious theatre, which, as befits the home of Scottish Opera, is a beautiful jewel box where opera and ballet usually occupy the stage. Across the road is the relatively new modern brick building of the **Royal College of Music and Drama**. Then, 300 yards to the east is the new **Concert Hall**, purpose-built in 1990; its main auditorium seats 2,500.

Left, the King's Theatre. Below, the Centre for Contemporary Arts.

GLASGOW CHIC

I f Edinburgh has poise, Glasgow has swagger. Edinburgh was born easily out of quiet, un-assailed prosperity; Glasgow was a love-child, the impudent offspring of a shotgun marriage between stubbornness and deprivation.

Men in the rag trade always used to claim that girls in Glasgow had bigger breasts than elsewhere in Britain – shorter legs but bigger breasts, giving them a look that was simultaneously wholesome and sexy. Today the felicitous bosom is still the life and soul of Glasgow's party, but the legs are longer than those of a generation ago, thanks to a better diet and a keep-fit culture.

Part of Glasgow's physical swank, of course, is derived from its large Italian and Irish communities which have rarely been burdened by any puritan guilt about dressing up. "Glaswegians love to put on the style" says a leading chain-store director. "In fact, in terms of fashion and hairdressing, I would say this is the most alert city outside London."

That said, Glasgow still thinks like an individual in matters of fashion. Determined to break free of the straitjacket imposed by multiple deprivation, the city, well before its present renaissance, has always been willing to give anything a whirl. Whether outsiders bothered to notice or not, here was a population that reacted to its hopeless reputation by cultivating a strong, personal identity, salving a threatened ego with panache.

Out of the city's defiant vitality, a new aspect of Glasgow style has emerged as a generation of home-grown young artists, designers and craftsmen learn the hard, commercial lessons of how to sell innovation and élan. At the heart of such activities there usually lies a training gained at Glasgow School of Art, internationally regarded for the vigorous and original quality of its design education. Stretching from graphics to ceramics, from furniture to jewellery, textiles and industrial products, exhibitions of students' work are seen regularly at the School and annually in London.

Often unpredictable in its individualism, Glasgow, with its long commitment to the Labour Party, is the most interesting example of designer-friendly socialism in a Conservative Britain. The purists may dismiss its rebirth now as shop-window politics, but no-one who really cares about the city would suggest for a minute that building restoration and a Euro party hat are sufficient to banish the nightmare quality of its remaining dismal housing schemes, or the ashen faces of the enduring unemployed.

Certainly Glasgow believes that it is the most vital and vibrating city in Britain, but is it chic? It is too full of jagged energy for that. What many outsiders appreciate is, indeed, its lack of over-whelming middle-class gentility. The resilience that underpins its folk memory of hardship has also taught how to get by on outrageous friendliness and laughs. One visiting American claims that it has the same sort of vibrancy as parts of New York and Chicago.

"This town shakes with activity," says John Mauceri, stylish New Yorker and Scottish Opera's musical director. When he is away from his brownstone on West 20th Street, he regards Glasgow as being as close as he can get to the pace and disputatious cheek of Manhattan. "The reason I feel so comfortable here is because Glasgow in temperament is so much more like New York than London, Paris or Rome. It has a grit to it and an ethnic exhibitionism which makes the place buzz."

In a taxi queue outside Central Station, an old hoofer, choral with cheap sherry, is winking at a group of boulevardiers in their dreamy designer numbers as he passes round the hat. "See me, pals, I fought for you in the last war. I died for you, so give generously..." As much as anything, it is this mix of inconsequence and outrage which defines the 40-mile (64-km) culture gap between Glasgow and Edinburgh. In Glasgow, self-admiration is permitted only if accompanied by mockery. In Edinburgh, it resides unchallenged by civic provincialism and notions of good taste.

But then Glasgow seeks no shrine status, like Edinburgh, Venice, London or Paris. It is – and always has been – essentially its people, equipped with merry anarchy and enterprise, heroic forbearance, quick-on-the-uptake daftness, and a grand, effusive ability to dress up, hit the town, and have a great time. ∎

THE UNIVERSITY AREA

Beyond Charing Cross is the west end with the University of Glasgow and several of the city's best galleries and museums. Here, too, are many of those buildings which led John Betjeman, who was an architectural enthusiast as well as Britain's Poet Laureate, to describe Glasgow as the "Greatest Victorian city in Europe".

The solid, copper-domed Renaissance building on North Street, on the west side of the ring road at Charing Cross, is the place to visit in order to learn more about Glasgow. The **Mitchell Library** was founded in 1877 by Stephen Mitchell, a tobacco baron, and moved to its present site in 1911. A visit is mandatory in order to admire the sumptious, yet comfortable, fittings of this, one of the largest public reference libraries in Europe. Collections are devoted to Glasgow, Robert Burns and rare books.

The **Burns Room** contains the largest collection of first editions of the poet as well as a host of Burnsiana. The first editions, of which there are more than 4,000, are in 32 languages, which range from Bohemian to Welsh and even include English. Pride of joy in the **Rare Book** collection are the four folio volumes of *Audubon's Birds of America* and two Kilmarnock editions of the works of Burns.

The rear of the building, on **Granville Street**, boasts one of the most powerful facades of any Glasgow building and is the entrance to the **Mitchell Theatre**. Observe the eight caryatids at the upper level and, below, inscribed on the cornice, the names of Mozart, Beethoven, Bach, Michelangelo and Raphael. The musicians' names give the clue to the fact that, until a fire in 1962, this was St Andrew's Hall, home of the Royal Scottish National Orchestra.

Name changes: The first buildings of the **Park Conservation Area** are just north of the Mitchell, on the other side of Sauchiehall Street. These buildings, which occupy the gentle slopes of Woodlands Hill, have resulted in the statement that Glasgow is the "finest piece of architectural planning of the mid-19th century". All the buildings in this part of town are three-storey, yellow, sandstone terraces: mansards have been added to some. All were originally private homes but now nearly all are offices. (Incidentally, those looking for an actual address may well be frustrated: names here change and then re-appear frequently and the same name can describe street, place, terrace, circus and crescent.)

It all began in 1831 with **Woodside Crescent**, which starts at right angles to Sauchiehall Street. Today, this is scarcely a homogeneous terrace with both stone and iron balconies and only some of the entrances being fronted by porticoes. However, this soon curves gently into Woodside Terrace, which parallels **Woodlands Place** below and from which it is separated by a private green park 50 yards wide.

Doric porticoes reached by flights of stairs with metal banisters punctuate **Woodside Terrace** where the windows are supported by consoles. In best New Town style, the porticoes at the ends of the terrace form pavilions and are topped by a balcony. The entire facade has a balustrade, raised at each end.

Woodside Terrace is bissected by a short stretch of **Claremont Place**, at the north end of which a broad flights of stairs leads to a massive square Gothic tower to the left and three taller Lombard towers to the right. The former belonged to the **Park Church** and has now been recyled into offices. The latter were part of the **Trinity College and Church** and now house delightful apartments. Collectively, from a distance, these towers evoke images of a sunkissed Italian hill town – San Gimigano, perhaps? – rather than of a mist-shrouded Scottish metropolis.

This leads after a few yards, via **Lynedoch Place** and **Park Circus Place**, to **Park Circus**, which is not quite circular despite its name but rather a flat centrepiece with curving quadrants. This is the highest point of Woodlands Hill. Several of the buildings on Park Circus are University of Glasgow halls of residence.

From here, exit on to a belvedere above **Kelvingrove Park** and marvel at the glorious vistas. Immediately ahead, across the valley of the park, stands the university: to the left is the River Clyde with the cranes of those few shipyards which still function; to the right are the northern suburbs of the city and the Campsie Fells. The bronze **equestrian statue**, surrounded by weeping willows, which enjoys these vistas every day, is of Field Marshall Lord Roberts of Pretoria and Waterford, the hero of the Crimean War.

The belvedere is backed by **Park Quadrant** to the northeast and **Park Terrace** to the southwest. These are probably the most magnificent of all the terraces in the Park Conservation Area. The architecture of the quadrant and the

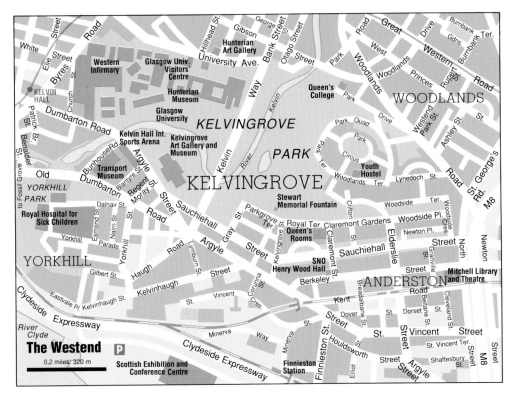

terrace is more or less identical and the north-facing parts of each with doors and windows with consoles and carved heads on the facade resemble French châteaux. Now the visitor can fully appreciate why this part of Glasgow has been called "the grandest town planning exercise in mid-Victorian Britain".

From Park Terrace, descend a flight of steps to **Park Gardens**, one of the most handsome and homogeneous terraces on the hill. This leads to almost as beautiful **Claremont Terrace** which ends at the junction of **Claremont Gardens** and Woodside Place. Turn right along the former to **Claremont Street**; a left turn then leads back to Sauchiehall Street. Some buildings have bay windows; others have basements protected by wrought-iron rails; still others have wrought-iron rails fronting balconies; this one has that falderal, that one another. All have grandeur, style.

The **Queen's Rooms**, an ashlar, pedimented, temple-like box, solid rather than columned, with a broad, deep frieze, stands at the corner of Claremont Gardens and Claremont Street. The frieze on the east wall illustrates the progress of civilisation while that on the north shows Minerva distributing gifts to representatives of the arts and sciences. Minerva, it was claimed, is a "fair portrait" of Mrs Bell, the wife of the original owner of the building: also seen are Mr Bell and Charles Wilson, the architect, holding the building plans.

The medallion carvings between the frieze and the rounded windows on the east side are of Watt (science), Hamilton (architecture), Reynolds (painting), Flaxman (sculpture), Handel (music), Peel (politics) and Burns (poetry). Originally this building was a concert hall: today, it is a **Christian Science Church**.

Architects and builders did not neglect Sauchiehall Street and a series of terraces was built on both sides of this thoroughfare. Can it be that, lacking the rarified atmosphere of Woodlands Hill, these enclaves are, in the main, not so elegant nor so well maintained as those

on the hill? One exception is **Royal Crescent**, which is possibly the most eclectic stretch in this part of the city. Claremont Street, which bisects Sauchiehall Street between Fitzroy and Sandyford Places, leads to the tall spire of the former **Trinity Church**, which is now the Royal Scottish National Orchestra's **Henry Wood Concert Hall**. The building is used as a rehearsal hall for the RSNO and as a concert hall for other groups who perform on a stage backed by pretty stained-glass windows.

From here, the **Scottish Exhibition and Conference Centre** is just a mile to the south. En route, stop at **St Vincent Crescent**, the most outstanding late classical terrace to be built in all Scotland. This terrace, unlike those just visited on Woodlands Hill, contains flats rather than three-storey homes. Some of the flats in this imposing 700-yard sweep of three-storey tenements with balustrated eaves and solid Doric porchs, had as many as 10 rooms.

Proceed from here along **Argyle Street** for about 1,000 yards, to just past its intersection with Sauchiehall Street (about 300 yards). Handsome red sandstone buildings stand on either side of the road. That on the left is the the **Kelvin Hall International Sports Arena**, which boasts that it is Britain's most comprehensive indoor sports complex. Students of the University of Glasgow are fortunate in having access to its facilities.

Another part of this building, with an entrance around the corner, is the **Museum of Transport**, rated by many as the UK's best transport museum. Glasgow and the Clyde not only built ships and steam locomotives but also, at one time or another, aeroplanes and airships, motorcars and motorcyles, and their fleet of tramcars was the envy of the world. On display are examples of many of these forms of transport, as well as bicycles, horse-drawn vehicles, steam rollers and fire engines.

Automobile enthusiasts will delight in those cars made in the early 1900s by

Kelvin Hall.

Scottish automobile companies, long since gone out of business, such as Argyll, Albion and Arrol-Johnston. Then there is a gorgeous black Rolls-Royce Phantom II which was a gift to Sir William Burrell from his wife, an equally gorgeous blue 1935 Lagonda tourer and a 1934 green Bentley.

Tramcars were a familiar sight on Glasgow streets for 90 years and the trams on display range from horse-drawn vehicles to the elegant, green-and-yellow double-decker Coronation trams. In their heyday the Glasgow trams were unequalled anywhere in the world for their cheapness, comfort and colour: different coloured panels around the upper deck designated different routes and so were readily identifable from a distance.

The city's love of these vehicles was strikingly demonstrated on 5 September 1962, a rain-soaked day, when 250,000 people turned out to cheer one last procession of 20 trams from Dalmarnock depot, in the northeast of the city, to Coplaw depot (now the Tramway Theatre) on the southside. Every tenement along the 3-mile (5-km) route was occupied by *hingers'oot*.

Springburn, in the northeast of the city, was once the world's largest centre of locomotive manufacture; four great works built steam locomotives which were exported to more than 60 countries. Among the engines on display is No. 123-4-2-2 (Scottish locomotives were seldom provided with nameplates) which exceeded speeds of 70 miles (110 km) an hour in a famous London to Edinburgh race in 1888.

The **Clyde Room** on the first floor is magic for all. Here are more than 200 model ships (this represents only about one-third of the total collection) which can be enjoyed not only for their historical value but also for the skill and artistry which have gone into their construction. As if to show that Glasgow is not parochial, a few models are of ships which were not built on Clydeside. Most models are built to the traditional 0.25

Queens of the sea in the Museum of Transport.

inch = 1 ft scale, being 1:48 (or approximately one-fiftieth full-size). Some models are 18 ft (more than 5 metres) long and in all instances enormous attention has been paid to detail.

Pride of place must surely go to that case which contains large models of the *Queen Mary* and of the two *Queen Elizabeths*: the hulls of both the *Queen Mary* and the *Queen Elizabeth* are those which were used in the tank test of the liners. Other models (and all mentioned here are Clyde-built) range from the tiny *Comet*, the first steam-driven passenger vessel in Europe, to the giant battleship *Hood* which was sunk in World War II. Look out for the *Sirius*, a wooden paddle steamer which was the first ship to cross the Atlantic under continuous steam power (1838); the *Cutty Sark,* which broke the China Clippers' record in the 1870s; the *Livadia*, a fantastic, almost circular yacht built for the Czar (1880); Glasgow's own Clyde paddle-steamers including the *Columba*, "the most perfect of all the Clyde steamers",

which gave immense pleasure to millions of Glaswegians for almost 60 years, and the royal yacht *Britannia.*

Then there is *Le Stanley*, built for the journalist and explorer of the same name to use on his Central African explorations and the *Nepaul,* a paddle steamer built for the Irrawadday Flotilla in Burma. Both craft, although launched about 100 years ago, were prefabs which were constructed in sections to be reassembled later.

Sadly, Glasgow's pioneering efforts in flying are not exhibited in the museum. The R34, the first airship to cross the Atlantic, was built near Renfrew by Beardmore. Nor is Percy Pilcher's glider on display. In 1895, Pilcher, a member of the Naval Architecture staff at the University of Glasgow made the first flight in Great Britain of any piloted heavier-than-air aircraft. Four years later, when experimenting with a petrol engine attached to his glider, he was killed. Had it not been for that accident, the honour of the world's first powered flight might have fallen to Britain and not – several years later – to the Wright Brothers in America.

Nor is there any remembrance in the museum of the world's first monorail which George Bennie, a Glaswegian, built and ran on a half-mile track at Bearsden, in what is now Greater Glasgow, in the 1920s. Also not mentioned is the fact that J.B. Dunlop was the first man to make a really practical pneumatic tyre (1887), without which the development of planes and cars as we now know them could probably not have occurred.

Cross the road to the most imposing **Art Gallery and Museum** which is topped by a veritable forest of spires, turrets and towers. Visitors might wonder why they enter from the rear rather from the front: they do not. During the construction of the building the location of the main road was altered so that it now passes the rear of the building. It is malicious rumour – nothing more – that the architects "got it wrong" and that

Final stop at the Museum of Transport.

one of them committed suicide by leaping from the top floor.

A bronze statue of St Mungo, who is depicted as protector of art and music, guards the entrance to a soaring atrium with a black, white and straw-coloured marble floor, red sandstone arches and an organ. (Evening concerts are not infrequently given in the Gallery.) The names of various Incorporated Trades of the city – barbers and bonnetmakers, masons and maltmen, wrights and weavers and the like – are carved in the spandrels of the first-floor arches and, on a frieze above these are the names of famous composers including Wagner, Mendelsohn, Listz, Gluck and lesser luminaries. (The Wallace mentioned is not the fiery national hero but rather a 19th/20th century Greenock composer.)

The ground floor is devoted mainly to natural history and archaeology (Egyptian as well as local) and, above all, to an outstanding collection of armour. Scottish weapons and militaria form an intriguing background for this collection but the most valuable items are the Gothic Milanese field armour (1450), probably the earliest and most complete plate armour in Britain, and the "richly graven and gilded" Greenwich field armour for man and horse (*circa* 1550-58). Both items are part of the collection donated to the museum by Robert Lyons Scott, yet another local shipbuilder – well, not just any shipbuilder: his company, now part of Scott Lithgow, is possibly the oldest shipbuilding company in the world.

Renowned tearoom: Also on the ground floor is a reconstruction of a part of Miss Cranston's Tearoom in Ingram Street which was decorated by Rennie Mackintosh. The theme is Chinese. The tearoom, with its startlingly blue decor, considered the ultimate statement of the style, is part of a Glasgow Style (1890–1920) exhibit. This contains works – bookbinding, stained glass, ceramic decorations, metalworks, enamels and other arts and crafts – of Mackintosh's contemporaries.

Kelvingrove Art Gallery.

These include his wife Margaret, her sister Frances and her husband Herbert MacNair (the two couples were known as "The Four") and others such as Salmon, Talwin Morris and George Walton. None of these was part of a Mackintosh movement – he insisted there was no such thing – but rather, like Mackintosh, were students, friends and colleagues of Francis Henry Newbery, the inspirational director of the Glasgow School of Art, and his wife Jessie.

The galleries situated on the upper floor, devoted to paintings and sculpture, were re-organised in 1990. Those in the West Wing display permanent exhibits which are arranged, not according to school, but according to a theme (e.g. classical, religious, etc.) with paintings, ceramics, glass and other art forms exhibited as an ensemble. The galleries in the East Wing contain temporary exhibitions of Kelvingrove's own and of visiting collections.

The Scots believe that there is *guid gear in sma' bulk* (good quality in small size) but at Kelvingrove there is *guid gear* in great quantity. The Fine Art collection consists of more than 3,000 oil paintings, 12,500 prints and drawings and 300 pieces of sculpture. After a visit to Kelvingrove, visitors will not leave Glasgow in the belief that Sir William Burrell was the only Glasgow ship-owner to leave his art collecction to the city.

Mention has already been made of Lyon Scott. William McInnes (1868–1944) was another Glasgow shipowner who bequested his paintings, prints, drawings, silver, ceramics and glass to the city. This gift included 33 French works by such artists as Monet, Degas, Renoir, van Gogh, Cézanne and Picasso, while British works included canvasses of the Glasgow Boys and the Scottish Colourists, of whom McInnes was a regular patron.

Dali attraction: Undoubtedly, the Museum's most renowned painting is Salvador Dali's *Christ Upon the Cross.* Rembrandt's *The Man in Armour* and

Lost for words at Kelvingrove **Art Gallery.**

Rubens' *Nature Adorned by the Graces* are just two of the canvasses in the rich display of the 17th-century Dutch school. Early French artists are not that well represented but the museum is well endowed with works of later periods ranging from Corbot to Picasso. The Italian collection, although modest, exhibits most of the main currents in that country's art with canvasses by, among others, Giovanni Bellini, Filippino Lippi, Sandro Boticelli and Salvator Rosa.

Paintings by Scottish artists predominate in the British collections. However, especially in the period before 1850, sufficient characteristic works by their English contemporaries permit the viewer to study the development of Scottish painting within the British school. Many consider that the most important British painting on display – albeit the work of an American – is Whistler's *Arrangement in Grey and Black no. 2: Portrait of Thomas Carlyle*, the first Whistler to be hung in a British gallery. (Whistler was proud of his Scottish back-

Rembrandt's The Man in Armour.

ground announced by his name: James A. McNeil.)

The Scottish School is, as one would expect, well represented with large canvasses of, among others, the Glasgow Boys. This school consisted of a group of painters who banded together in the 1880s and who, it is suggested, even assisted one another in painting cavasses, over a period of 20 years. They joined together, not so much to promote a style of painting, but to fight the Royal Academy in London and the Scottish Royal Academy in Edinburgh, both of whom ostracised them. Glaswegians often believe – and sometimes with justification – that they are ignored by the establishment in both Edinburgh and in London.

Also on view are the works of the Scottish Colourists – Peploe, Cadell, Hunter and Fergusson. The term Colourist was first coined in 1948 when three of them were already dead and simply announced their love of colour – nothing more. One hundred years after the first Scottish School, a second which

includes Steven Campbell, Peter Howson and Ken Currie, all graduates of the Glasgow School of Art, appeared and has gained a reputation far beyond Glasgow.

The Print collection, which is frequently changed, is mainly of British artists, with Scots such as Strang, McBey, Cameron and Muirhead Bone featuring strongly. In addition, there are European prints from the 18th century to the present and a few old masters. Most of the watercolours and drawings are 19th and 20th-century, and British.

The sculpture collection covers the period from the late 18th century to the present and is predominantly of the British school with works of Flaxman, Benno Schotz (a Glasgow man and Scotland's most prominent 20th-century sculptor), Caro and Paolozzi. The Continent is represented by, among others, Degas, Renoir and Rodin.

The balconies on this floor house Decorative Art, including glass (especially strong in items from Spain), silver

(much of it donated by Victor J. Cumming, not a shipowner but one of the managers of a shipping line), metalwork and ceramics. Here, too, are the yachting trophies of Sir Thomas Lipton, including the cup which the Americans awarded to him as "Gamest Loser in the World of Sport".

A most unusual, indeed unique, permanent exhibition is the Seton Murray Thomson collection which is devoted entirely to horses. On display are more than 400 quadrupeds from 19 different countries and from three-and-a-half millennia and made of more than 30 materials ranging from amber to wax by way of mother-of-pearl, papier-mâché and ivory.

Seat of learning: From the gallery's entrance, a massive Victorian Gothic pile, touched with an infusion of Franco-Scottish baronial style, can be seen on a ridge on top of a tree-covered slope. This is the main building of **the University of Glasgow**. It can be reached by either strolling through **Kelvingrove Park**, through which the River Kelvin flows, or by walking along Kelvin Way for about 600 yards and then turning left on to **University Avenue**.

Take the latter route and, just after the bridge, turn right for a short detour into the park and a glance at the richly sculptured **Stewart Memorial Fountain**. The bronze figure of *The Lady of the Lake* atop the fountain is the clue to the fact that this structure honours a former Lord Provost (= mayor) of Glasgow during whose term of office Loch Katrine's water was first piped to the city. Note the birds (are they cormorants, sea-eagles?), one of them with a fish in its mouth, on the fountain's rim.

Great physicist: Back on the main road, an even shorter detour to the left leads to the statues of Lord Lister and then Lord Kelvin, two of the most distinguished figures associated with the University of Glasgow. William Thomson, Lord Kelvin, was probably the Victorian era's greatest applied scientist and certainly the greatest physicist. He was professor

The Stewart Memorial Fountain in Kelvingrove Park.

of natural philosophy at Glasgow for 50 years and thrice declined the prestigious Cavendish Chair at Cambridge. He was also one of those most responsible, in 1871, for the University being moved from High Street to its present site.

Pearce Lodge at the foot of University Avenue is one of the oldest parts of the university, having been transferred in 1870 to its present location from the Old College on High Street. It now houses computing services. Rather than entering through the gates at Pearce Lodge, proceed to the crest of **University Avenue**. The university is all around: some of the buildings are old, some are modern; some are former terrace houses, some are purpose-built. The whole is an outdoor architectural museum which illustrates building in Glasgow over the past 150 years.

Enter the university through the gates, at the top of University Avenue, which bear the names of 28 distinguished alumni or former faculty, including Lister, Kelvin, Watt and Adam Smith.

The gates were erected in 1951 to commemorate the founding of the University by a Papal Bull issued in 1451. The University of Glasgow is the fourth oldest university in Britain. Enter through these gates and facing, on the ground floor of the main building, is a **Visitor Centre**.

From here, ascend the stairway and visit the east and west quadrangles and, between them, the **Cloisters** (or Undercroft) which support the **Bute Hall**, possibly Britain's most glorious Victorian Gothic hall. The columns are of wrought iron, the arches are severely pointed, fleur-de-lys and rosettes are common themes and four sets of handsome stained-glass windows pay tribute to 32 world figures. Behind the wooden screen at the back of the hall is the smaller Randolph Hall which has portraits of William Hunter by Reynolds and of Joseph Black by Raeburn. On occasions, both rooms may be visited.

Next, make for the flag-pole vista point in front of the 300-ft (90-metre)

The River Kelvin by the university.

tower whose spire is not that designed by G.G. Scott, the original architect but that of his son, John Oldrid Scott. All considered Scott senior's spire to be top-heavy and preferred the present delicate tracery. Excellent as are the views from the base of the flag-pole, they are nothing compared to those obtained from the Tower which can be ascended. (tel: 339 8855, ext. 4271 to determine the opening hours).

Lion and unicorn: Back on *terra firma*, visit the adjacent **Professors' Square** which was built for those gentlemen and where the Principal still lives (No. l2). The lamps around the square are original and a VR (Victoria Regina) mailbox is still in use. The **Memorial Chapel** (1926), on the left, (open to the public) is entered by the **Lion and Unicorn Stairway** which was constructed in 1690 and which was brought here in 1872 from the Old College.

About half the undergraduates, who represent five out of six of the university's 13,000 students, are locals who commute from home. On the other hand, half of the graduate students are from overseas: they come from countries ranging from Austria to Zimbabwe, with the largest numbers being from Algeria, Iraq, Malaysia, Hong Kong, Singapore and Norway. Most Asian students are in the engineering faculty, which is the oldest engineering faculty in the world. Largest of the seven faculties is arts and social sciences and the medical faculty is, in terms of undergraduates, the largest in Europe. Other faculties are social sciences, law and financial studies, veterinary medicine, divinity and science.

Average would best describe the efforts of Gilmorehill students in extracurricular activies although, in the tradition of Clydeside, they excel in debating and University of Glasgow debating teams invariably command leading places in world competitions. As at most British universities, most students are apolitical; although the left is vociferous, it is a small minority.

Few of these students – they are too

Scrolls of success on graduation day.

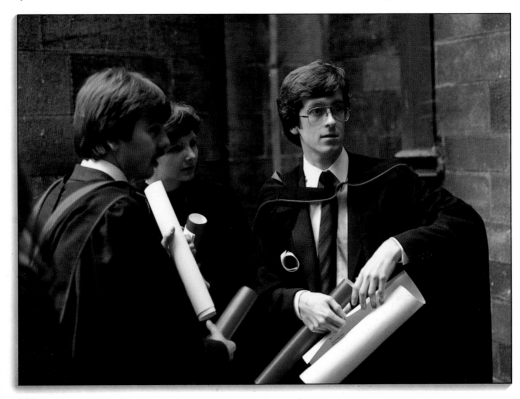

busy studying – will be found in the **Hunterian Museum**, which is adjacent to the Bute Hall. When opened in 1807, it was Scotland's first public Museum and the basis of its contents – and of that of the Hunterian Gallery which occupies another part of the campus – are private collections of William Hunter, a magpie of a collector and one with the most catholic of tastes. Hunter was a student at Glasgow in the 18th century. He subsequently achieved fame and fortune in London, first as an anatomist and pathologist, then as a medical teacher and finally as an obstretician – he delivered Queen Charlotte of her children. Yet, for all this, he remained true his to *alma mater*, to which he bequeated his enormous and varied collection.

The emphasis in the museum is on geology, ethnography and archaeology and there is also an outstanding numismatic collection with more than 30,000 coins, most of which belonged to Hunter. The museum's extravagant wrought-iron supports are extremely attractive and, if the university tower is closed, then excellent panoramas of the north of Glasgow can be enjoyed from the museum's mezzanine floor.

The **Hunterian Gallery** is on the other side of University Avenue. The Main Gallery, entered through handsome cast-aluminium doors by Eduardo Paolozzi, houses a splendid, although scarcely large, collection of European paintings, including canvasses of Rembrandt, Ramsay and Reynolds. Fergusson, Guthrie, Peploe, Earley and McTaggart, some of Scotland's best 19th and 20th-century painters, are also represented. Essentially, however, one visits this gallery to admire the paintings of Whistler, a collection rivalled only by that in the Freer Museum in Washington. Not only are the artist's paintings displayed but one can also see his painting equipment and the furniture, silver and porcelain he collected.

The Gallery's print collection, the largest in Scotland, includes works of Durer, Picasso and Hockney as well as

Kelvingrove Park in winter.

Whistler and Mackintosh. Exhibitions are mounted in the Print Gallery and the entire collection can be viewed, on request, by serious scholars. A number of pieces of contemporary sculpture are displayed in the Sculpture Courtyard.

A longitudinal mail box in a white door on the outside of the Gallery suggests Mackintosh and indeed that door is part of a reconstruction of three levels of the nearby home in which the Mackintoshes lived for eight years. The interior decoration, where cool colours predominate, duplicates the original and contains more than 60 pieces of Mackintosh furniture.

Hunter's contributions to his *alma mater* did not stop with those items seen in the Museum and the Gallery. The **University Library**, adjacent to the Gallery, contains Hunter's library of more than 10,000 books, one-quarter of which are from the 16th century and 650 beautifully and intricately decorated manuscripts including the York psalter dating from 1170.

The starkness of the towers of the library – no turrets or spires here – might appear to be an attempt to make amends for the frivolity of those falderals atop both the main building and the Kelvingrove Art Gallery and Museum. The circular **Reading Room** with, like the Pantheon, a rectangular entrance, immediately to the southeast of the library, predates it by 30 years and was to be part of a grand complex which, unfortunately, was never completed.

Next to the reading room is the **Wellington Church** which, with its splendid Corinthian portico atop an enormous stylobate, looks as if it could have come from the drawing board of "Greek" Thomson but rather is by Thomas Watson of a later generation. It is most unusual in that the Corinthian colonnades on the north and south side are not tetrastyle nor hexastyle but consist of five columns.

From here, a stroll down University Avenue leads to **Byres Road**, with its pubs, restaurants and bookshops. One thing that must be pointed out about this seasonal hub of Glasgow's west end is that its population fluctuates widely as the University students come and go. For instance, throughout the autumn, winter and spring – the months when students are busying away in their lectures and tutorials – the entire street is packed with hordes and hordes of chattering scholars, descending from their studies onto more leisurely pursuits. However, during the summer the street is, in comparison, deserted, allowing you to enjoy its offerings at a more relaxed pace.

Join **Dumbarton Road** at the south of Byres Road and travel westwards for 1½ miles (2 km) to **Victoria Park**. The **Fossil Grove** at the western end of this park was uncovered during road construction in 1887 and contains fossilised tree stumps which are more than 300 million years old. The fossils are not petrified wood but casts formed by mud which penetrated into the trees and set while the bark retained its shape.

Below, Peploe's *Still Life, White Roses* in the Kelvingrove Gallery. Right, a Mackintosh bedroom at the Hunterian Museum.

TO THE NORTHWEST

St George's Cross, at the northwest of the city centre, is now nothing but a memory and has been replaced by a spaghetti junction dominated by the ring road. **Great Western Road**, which begins here, is probably the longest absolutely straight road in Glasgow and, were it not for a couple of drumlins, then Anniesland Cross, 2½ miles (4 km) to the northwest, would be visible. This road was projected in the 1830s to provide a grand new approach to the city, thus avoiding the squalor which had accompanied the rise of Glasgow as a manufacturing and trading centre.

Glorious result: Decimus Burton, the most eminent English suburban planner of the day, was commissioned to and prepared a plan of crescents and terraces which would line the thoroughfare. Behind these would be detached houses. It is fortunate that the glorious result still stands for when, in the late 1960s, the city fathers were determined to make Glasgow "the most modern city in Europe", ring roads and radial motorways were all the rage. Great Western Road was to become one of the latter; but, in the nick of time, sanity prevailed, and the road remains, little changed after a century.

Here, when the sun shines (it does sometimes) the flowers bloom and the birds twitter, one can imagine being on a continental boulevard – alas, without the sidewalk cafés. And, indeed, during Victorian times this was the place for the *passeggiaro*. Today's visitors can be excused for doubting this panegyric as they set off along the road but very soon the soaring spires of two churches beckon and the plaudits for this great avenue begin to be justified.

St Mary's Episcopal Cathedral and **Landsdowne Church** both stand on the north side of the road about half-a-mile from St George's Cross. The architecture of both is Early English. The steeple of the cathedral, which is the first of the two edifices but almost 50 years younger than the church, is not quite as tall as that of its neighbour; this difference is accentuated by the slimness of the latter, one of the city's most attractive Gothic churches. In the church the well-to-do have individual pews with private doors: the hoi-polloi know their place upstairs!

Just after this comes **Kelvin Bridge**, backed on the north side by the solid Glasgow Academy, one of several fee-paying schools in this part of the city. Now comes the crest of the first drumlin and here, still on the north side and slightly raised from the level of the road, is **Ruskin Terrace**, built in 1858. It is a harbinger of better things to come.

One mile past St George's Cross is the busy intersection with **Byres Road** to the south and **Queen Margaret Drive** to the north. The enormous spread of glass visible just beyond the entrance to the Botanic Gardens, which occupies the northwest corner of this intersec-

Preceding pages: wedding group in the Botanic Gardens. Left, inside the Botanic Gardens. Right, Kirklee Terrace.

tion, is **Kibble Palace**, one of the largest and most spectacular glasshouses in Britain.

The Crystal Palace, as it was originally called, did not always occupy this site. Rather it graced the estate on Loch Long of John Kibble, an eccentric engineer for whom it was built in 1863. Ten years later Kibble decided to take his Crystal Palace to town and had it brought up the River Clyde on a raft towed by a puffer (a small, locally built tramp-steamer). However, he retained the use of the palace and for the ensuing 21 years it was used for concerts and other entertainments and became the focus of social life in the west end.

The heat must have been more intense than usual on those occasions when Disraeli (1871) and later Gladstone (1877) gave their rectorial addresses here. Unfortunately, enthusiastic revellers destroyed both the peace of the neighbourhood and the plants of the Gardens, and John Kibble was forced to turn over his palace to the directors of the latter. (Rector is a peculiar office unique to Scottish universities. Different student factions nominate candidates who are all, in one way or another, famous or infamous. Glasgow students, unlike those at other Scottish universities, tend to be somewhat restrained in their choice of rectors: not for them stars of stage and screen and sport but rather, in most cases, politicians; the last incumbent was Winny Mandela, who defeated the candidacy of Yasser Arafat. Installation of the rector is a boisterous and rambunctious affair.)

Kibble Palace, to which a glass entrance aisle and transept were added, now houses a wide selection of ferns from temperate lands, mainly Australasia. Nothing can be more pleasant on a grey day than to sit here nudged by ferns through which peeps one of the statues which grace the conservatory. The British National collection of begonias and a gorgeous array of orchids can be enjoyed in the neighbouring and more conventional range of glasshouses,

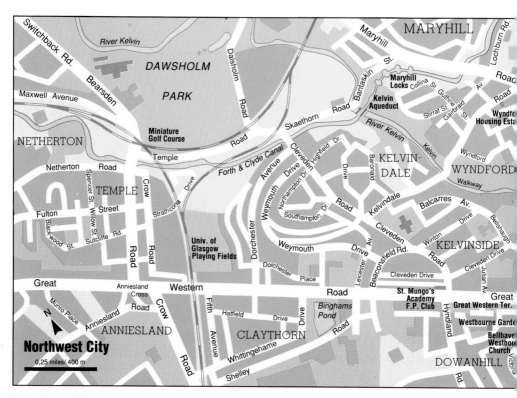

each of which houses a particular speciality. Around, and stretching away from, the glasshouses are a constantly changing kaleidoscopic variety of blooms in the rock garden, the herb garden and the systematic garden.

The long march: Those still in search of nature will make for the **River Kelvin** at the northern side of the park and stroll along the **Kelvin Walkway**. Citywards, it proceeds in a rather circuitous manner to Kelvin Bridge: westwards, it ultimately joins the West Highland Way which stretches to Fort William and beyond: *that* is a safari to be tackled only by the intrepid.

Urban ramblers will exit from the Botanic Gardens immediately to the north of where they entered and find themselves on **Queen Mary Avenue**. Facing is an architectural hotch-potch which is home to the British Broadcasting Corporation in Glasgow. The core building, which is now a tiny part of the entire complex, is the richly renaissance Northrop House; it was built in 1869 to house the art collection of the Bell brothers, who owned the Glasgow Pottery at Port Dundas, Scotland's largest pottery.

One of the two brothers was an avowed recluse and misogynist. How he must have turned in his grave when, in 1883, the building was sold and, in honour of King Malcolm Canmore's wife, was named Queen Margaret College and became a centre of higher education for women. Before this, professors from the university had given "Occasional Lectures for Women". By 1892 the University admitted women to its classes on equal terms with men, one of the first in Britain to do so.

Back on Great Western Road, the first terrace to be encountered is on the south side. **Grosvenor Terrace** (1855) which faces the Botanic Gardens, is reminiscent of a Venetian renaissance palazzo. Repetitiveness is the theme and individuality absent from this glorious 200-yard stretch of three equal storeys, each with round-headed windows which are separated by the slivers of classical

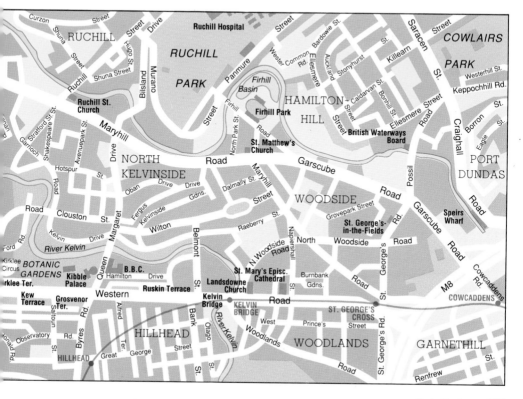

ons. Looks deceive; the terrace is ...ly not a homogeneous entity. In 1978 a fire gutted the Grosvenor Hotel at the east end: this proved to be a blessing in disguise and the entire terrace was restored to its former glory.

Grosvenor Terrace is followed by unremarkable **Kew Terrace** (1849) which possesses a discrete, dignified air and then, across the road, immediately beyond the Gardens, is **Kirklee Terrace**, another grand Italianate palace with each house having a projecting porch. This, somewhat raised above the level of the main road, was the first of the glorious Great Western Road terraces to be built (1845).

Back across the road, and also somewhat raised, stands the great *oeuvre* of "Greek" Thomson which is simply called **Great Western Terrace** (1869). Two three-storey pavilions interrupt the long two-storey facade and the balanced ensemble announces a splendid dignity. This, possibly the greatest of Thomson's terraces, bears his unmistakeable Greek imprint. Sir William Burrell, of the acclaimed Burrell collection, lived here at number eight.

Immediately to the rear of Great Western Terrace is **Westbourne Gardens** whose architecture is not as distinguished as that seen in some of the Great Western Road terraces and yet which forms a unified triangle with a pretty park in the centre and which has, at its northwest extremity, the most unusual – at least for Glasgow – **Bellhaven Westbourne Church**. This classical twostorey Italian renaissance building, the lower windows being enclosed by Ionic columns, the upper by Corinthian columns, would surely appear perfectly at home in Italy.

Terraces now stop and are replaced by villas, modern apartments and the playing fields of **Glasgow University** and several of the city's fee-paying schools. One school, which does not have playing fields here, is **St Mungo's Academy**, but it does own, as a clubhouse for its former pupils, a magnifi-

West End antique shop.

/ BOTHWELL LANE   9:30 AM.
                   5:30 PM

cent free-standing Victorian palazzo which formerly belonged to a Victorian ironfounder and which, had it been seen by Decimus Burton, would have reminded him of his Athenaeum in London, built half a century earlier.

Anniesland Cross is reached 2½ miles (3 km) after leaving St. George's Cross. Great Western Road does not stop here but continues, albeit not so straight, for several more miles, passing little boxes, diminutive boxes rather than elegant terraces until it disappears beyond the city boundary towards the Kilpatrick Hills. Rather than following this, turn right at Anniesland Cross into **Bearsden Avenue** and, about half-a-mile later, cross a bridge and turning right into Temple Road arrive at the **Forth and Clyde Canal**.

From sea to sea: This somewhat inconspicuous ribbon of water is part of what was dubbed Scotland's Grand Canal when it opened in 1790. This was Britain's first sea-to-sea waterway and linked the Firth of Clyde on the west

coast with the Firth of Forth on the east. The west terminal was at Bowling and the east at Grangemouth, a distance of 35 miles (56 km). In addition, there was a 4-mile (6-km) Glasgow branch. The absence of fixed bridges enabled masted vessels to voyage between the Atlantic and the North Sea.

In 1963, in an act of bureaucratic vandalism, the canal was closed for navigation. However, a current multimillion dollar project will, it is hoped, result in the re-opening of 12 miles (20 km) of canal from slightly further west of this point to Kirkintilloch in the east. This will include the Glasgow branch and will permit boats to pass once again through the city.

Stroll eastwards along the canal for about half-a-mile and arrive at the impressive aqueduct which carries the canal across the River Kelvin. When the **Kelvin Aqueduct** was opened in 1790 it was the largest structure of its kind in Britain. It is 70 ft (21 metres) high and its four 50-ft (15-metre) arches with

Great Western Terrace in winter.

arched spandrels supported by massive buttressed piers carry the canal for 135 yards (122 metres). To appreciate better the glory of this massive structure, which so impressed the populace that odes were written in its honour, stroll down to the Kelvin Walkway (five minutes). Unfortunately, even from here, the grandeur of the aqueduct is partially masked by trees.

Return to the canal and the **Maryhill Locks** which are linked by oval basins, are immediately reached. Locally, this group of five locks is known as "The Botany Locks" because of the many people from this area who emigrated to Botany Bay in Australia. These locks and the Kelvin Aqueduct are now listed as scheduled ancient monuments.

Difficult to believe that puffers – including the world's first – were built in the Kelvin Dock Boatyard, between Locks 22 and 23, until 1949. Puffers were cargo boats which derived their name from the fact that the exhaust of the early puffers was turned up through the funnel and produced a puffing noise. On average, they were about 60 ft (18 metres) long and 15 ft (4.5 metres) wide and had a 6-ft (2-metre) draught.

No Glaswegian, no Scot, worth his salt is not familiar with puffers as a result of the writings of Neil Munro and the screening of these writings on television. *Para Handy* was the inimitable captain of the *Vital Spark*, a puffer which, like most of these craft, plied the Clyde and its estuary rather than the canal.

More Mackintosh: Leave the canal at this point and enter **Maryhill**, a blend of 19th- and 20th-century tenements which survived the wholesale demolition of the 1950s. Proceed towards the city on **Maryhill Road** passing on the right **Wyndford Housing Estate**, one of the city's earliest and most successful post-World War II public housing schemes. After about three-quarters of a mile (1 km) turn left in **Ruchill Street** and immediately observe the red sandstone Ruchill Parish church. Much more renowned, although less conspicuous, is the adjacent grey sandstone **Church Hall** which was built in 1898 and which is from the drawing board of Charles Rennie Mackintosh.

It has been suggested that Mackintosh was not chosen as church architect because of his extravagant style although little of this is evident in this hall. Still, seven years elapsed between the building of the hall and the church, a period during which his idiosyncratic style evolved.

Actually, there was no need to await this evolution because, 1,000 yards further down Maryhill Road, at **Queen's Cross**, stands Mackintosh's only church. It is contemporary with the Ruchill church hall. Both the exterior and the interior of this 1898 building loudly announce the involvement of the esteemed Charles Rennie Mackintosh.

When **St Matthew's Church** was built, Queen's Cross was, unlike now, a cramped area and Mackintosh was restrained by space. However, urban clearance means that the church, with its

A handy lamp-post in Maryhill.

unusual, truncuated, slightly tilted, Gothic *art nouveau* tower, can now be seen at its best. Within, Mackintosh's innovative ideas are exemplified by the use of giant steel ties which cross the nave. The spaciousness is enhanced by a high arched wooden ceiling which is identical, even to the extent of caulking, with the inverted hull of a wooden boat.

The church was vacated in 1976 and is now the headquarters of the **Charles Rennie Mackintosh Society** which has been involved in a massive restoration. The church has a Mackintosh reference library and a small exhibition.

Behind the church is **Firhill Stadium**, home of Partick Thistle, another of Glasgow's major soccer clubs where, on most occasions, the number on the field exceeds the number of spectators. A flight of stairs at the city side of the stadium ascends to the Glasgow Branch of the **Forth and Clyde Canal**. This branch was described by the *Edinburgh Courant* in 1797 as "a ditch, a gutter, a mere puddle". At the top of the steps,

turn left and stroll a short distance to the **Firhill Basin** in which timber was once seasoned and where now youngsters revel in water sports. A right, rather than a left, turn leads towards the city on a towpath bordering water where mallards and moorhens, heron and swans, enjoy their leisure. Some ditch! Some gutter! Some puddle!

After about half-a-mile a bascule bridge (such bridges work on the see-saw principle) crosses the canal and leads to the new Scottish headquarters of the **British Waterways Board**. Near here, Sir William Burrell, he of the art collection, had a small shipyard. Continue past the bridge for a few hundred yards, admiring the superb vistas of the city with the prominent towers of the Park Conservation area and the University of Glasgow.

The canal now makes an acute right turn. Dominating the opposite bank is a magnificent range of five- and six-storey Victorian buildings which are among the best surviving buildings from old

Below, the church that Mackintosh designed. Right, detail from a Maryhill tenement.

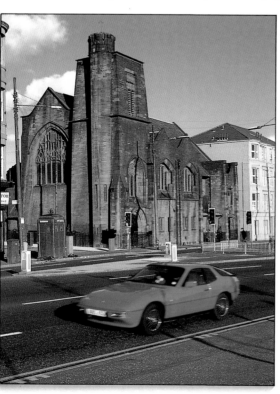

industrial Glasgow. Originally, these were grain mills and then were used as a whisky bond. Recently, they have been lovingly recycled to become luxury apartments.

A handsome two-storey Georgian building at the city end of **Speirs Wharf** has also been recycled and is now a small hotel with restaurants. Formerly, the business of the canal was conducted from this building and passengers boats, the *Swifts*, which could carry 60 people, left from here for Falkirk and, when the Union Canal (the Edinburgh branch of the Forth and Clyde) was opened in 1822, for Edinburgh. These boats offered a comfort which the stagecoaches could not equal.

From here, too, would leave cargo vessels preferring these non-tidal waters to the as yet undredged River Clyde. Between 1893 and 1939 pleasure steamers, the *Queens* – the *Fairy*, the *May* and the *Gipsy* – which could carry as many as 200 passengers, departed from here for trips on the canal.

A wee dram: This marks the end of the Glasgow branch of the canal. The heady aroma which fills the air here is from the neighbouring **Port Dundas** distillery which produces 8½ million gallons (39 million litres) of whisky a year. Some of this is matured *in situ* while most is sent to other distilleries where it is used in some of the best-known blended Scottish whiskies.

The ring road passes here and below, a couple of hundred yards to the south, is **St George's Road** which, after 400 yards, leads to St George's Cross. En route, spare a glance for the building of **St-George's-in-the-Fields** which represents the flowering of classical revival in Glasgow. Standing in splendid isolation, this thoroughly classical basilica, which has now been converted into apartments, has a raised Ionic portico carrying a carving of Christ feeding the multitude in the tympanum of the pediment.

<u>Right</u>, from Maryhill and proud of it.

JUNK Shop
REGULAR MUSIC FESTIVALS PRESENT
SIMPLE MINDS
WITH
TEXAS
THE SILENCERS
BHUNDU BOYS
EDINBURGH
MEADOWBANK
SATURDAY
12th AUGUST
GLASGOW ROCK CLUB
at the Saints & Sinners
St. Vincent Street, Glasgow
SAT 8th JULY
METRAUX
+ SUPPORT
SAT 15th JULY
SAT 22nd
Enjoy
STRONG LAGER
BATCAVE
HENRY AFRIKAS

EAST OF THE CROSS

Immediately east of Glasgow Cross and occupying an area between the **Gallowgate** and **London Road** is the **Barras** (Barrows), an open-air market which derives its name from the fact that goods were – and to some extent still are – sold from barrows. The Barras is not just any open-air market but a Glasgow institution where the Barra boys with their quick-fire patter and jokes, many of which are even beyond the comprehension of those Glaswegians who are not Eastenders, are not only determined salesmen but also first-rate comedians.

The time to visit the Barras, where you can buy everything from second-hand furniture and used clothing to fresh fruit and vegetables, is at weekends. Part of the complex is **Barrowland** which, between the wars, attracted Eastenders and others who loved to tango, to Charleston and to foxtrot. Glasgow at, that time was dance-crazy and in 1937 the city boasted more than 200 halls licensed for public dancing.

Exhausted by shopping and laughing at the Barras, stop for a "refreshment" at the unpretentious **Old Barns** which occupies the same spot at the comer of **Ross Street** and London Road as did the Burnt Barns Tavern, established in 1679 and said to be Glasgow's oldest licensed public house. Before continuing along London Road, venture south for a couple of hundred yards to **Greenview School** and Greenhead Road.

This sparkling grey building is readily recognisable because of the larger than life-size stone figure of a winsome urchin sitting on a gable with a slate in his lap. The building originally belonged to cotton merchants but, in the 1850s, was purchased by the Clan Buchanan who established an orphanage for boys of their clan. Today, it is a school for disturbed primary students.

Back on the London Road, proceed eastward for about three-quarters of a mile (1 km) to **Bridgeton Cross** where an apparently infinite number of roads intersect and form a veritable maze. Standing in splendid isolation in the midst of this confusion is the 115-year-old "Umbrella", an elegant cast-iron gazebo whose roof is supported by 10 slender columns. Above the roof is a clock-tower with four faces below which are four Glasgow coats of arms.

The **Olympia**, a large red building at the comer of **Orr Street**, is now a bingo hall; it was formerly a cinema and, before that, a music hall. However, its claim to fame is that here, after World War I, charismatic Jimmy Maxton, a "Red Clydesider" if ever there was one, made his fiery speeches which led to his being elected to parliament in 1922 and to Bridgeton having the strongest Independent Labour Party (ILP) in Scotland. (The ILP was a party well to the left of mainstream Labour.) Sir Winston Churchill, who often crossed words with Maxton, said that he "was the greatest gentleman in the House of Commons".

Left, the poster advertises a local pop group who made it big. **Right**, looking for bargains at the Barras market.

The word gentlemen could scarcely be used to describe the Billy Boys, a gang who frequented Bridgeton Cross in the 1930s and who were allegedly the prototype for the main gang in *No Mean City,* that infamous novel about Glasgow. They could be heard singing their theme song "Hello, hello, we are the Billy Boys" to the tune of *Marching through Georgia* even before they could be seen.

From Bridgeton Cross, proceed along London Road. After about a mile, "Paradise" for many Glaswegians – and for others – comes into view. **Celtic Park**, readily recognisable by its towering pylons, is the home of the green and white, the Celtic Football Club, one of Glasgow's two great rival soccer teams. (Tours of the stadium are possible: telephone 556 2611.)

Soon after this, turn left into **Springfield Road** and observe, on the left, the large, undistinguished modern red factory. This is the home of Barr's, Britain's largest soft drinks manufacturers and, much more importantly, the makers of Scotland's "other national drink", Irn Bru, the drink "made from girders". A common soft drink for many Glaswegians, this orange-coloured tonic is said to have powerful qualities when consumed, primarily the ability to lift cars, lorries, buses and the like – a clear advantage over the less fortunate members of the public who insist on buying "inferior" soft drinks.

Glass pyramids: It is apt that the drink "made from girders" should have its home here for, just to the north, on **Duke Street**, stood the Parkhead Forge, a huge ironworks "which by day enshrouded the city in clouds of smoke, by night in shafts of fire". Now, where Hector, Priam and Achilles, and Samson and Goliath (the names given to steam-hammers) once rocked Parkhead to its core, stand elegant glass pyramids which enclose a large shopping complex.

Parkhead Cross, other than Glasgow Cross, the best survivor of the inroad of ring roads, stands between the

Sincere sales pitch at the Barras.

Parkhead Forge and Barr's at the intersection of five roads. Here are spectacular turn-of-the-century red sandstone buildings with turrets, towers and battlements. Unfortunately, because the buildings are crammed together, the parts are greater than the whole. Bas-reliefs are carved on the exterior walls of some buildings.

During the summer months, enthusiastic horticulturists should proceed from Parkhead Cross along **Tolicross Road** for about 1,000 yards (1 km) to the entrance to **Tollcross Park**. The hillside to the right of the entrance is ablaze with roses in a recently constructed rose garden which, each summer, wins major British awards.

From here, it is about 2 miles (3 km) through the districts of Shettleston and Springboig to pleasantly landscaped **Auchinlea Park** at the eastern extremity of the city. The entrance on Auchinlea Road immediately leads to pretty **Provan Hall**, possibly the most perfect example in all Scotland of a pre-Refor-

mation house. The small, round tower and delicate crow-stepped gable of this two-storey, 15th-century house, which was the country abode of the prebend (canon), are especially attractive.

Return to the motorway, head back towards the city, exit at interchange I I and travel northwards through fairly open countryside to **Robroyston** at the northeastern limits of the city. Here, alongside a farm at the side of the northern and narrow part of **Robroyston Road**, a 20-ft (6-metre) granite cross marks the spot where William Wallace was captured by the English in 1305 and taken to London where he was accused of treason and done to death.

The cross, which incorporates the double-handed sword always associated with Wallace, was restored in 1986 with the aid of donations from members of the Clan Wallace in the United States. The donors were unimpressed by historians who believe that such swords were not known to have been used by knights until the late 15th century.

That's got it licked.

THE GORBALS AND THE SOUTHEAST

A good place to start an exploration of the **Gorbals** and the southeast of the city is **Carlton Place**, situated on the south bank of the river, linked to the city by the elegant **Carlton Suspension Bridge**. Carlton Place is backed by a 400-yard-long stately Georgian terrace, built at the beginning of the 19th century at the behest of the Laurie brothers, David and James, who took up residence in the house with the rounded portico at the eastern end of the terrace. The interior of this house boasts exquisite plaster work which is believed to have been executed by Italian artists employed by George IV to decorate Windsor Castle.

Carlton Place is neatly bisected by broad **South Portland Street**, which was intended as a continuation of Buchanan Street, albeit interrupted by St Enoch Square and the Carlton Suspension Bridge, and which would reflect the elegance of that street. It was intended as the linchpin of the distinguished district of Laurieston whose showpiece would be a great academy which would provide education for all men – sons of the middle-class during the day and craftsmen and apprentices in the evening.

End of the dream: The Laurie dream was never realised and Carlton Place turned out to be little more than an architectural folly, although it and other Gorbals streets still carry the names of aristocracy and royalty such as Carlton and Cumberland, Cavendish and Oxford, Bedford and Norfolk. The absence of civic control permitted ironworks and railways to destroy the dreams and Laurieston ended as "a slum annexe to the Gorbals; a useful overflow district with large homes capable of subdivisions into warrens housing 150 people under one roof".

The Gorbals was torn apart after World War II in order to improve living conditions – although those who occupy the high-rise blocks in the district do not believe this was achieved. As a result, South Portland Street was truncated to just 150 yards and the late, lamented **Gorbals Cross**, whose centrepiece was a gentleman's public lavatory, disappeared from the face of the earth. Yet a few handsome buildings, often ecclesiastical, have survived and some new interesting, if scarcely handsome, buildings have appeared.

Among the latter, immediately east of Carlton Place, is the forbidding, heavy, totalitarian **Sheriff Court**, the second largest such building in Europe and one of the most expensive buildings ever erected in Glasgow. Prettier by far is the salmon-coloured **Strathclyde Police Training Centre**, crowned by a gigantic white coat-of-arms, immediately to the southwest.

The **Citizens' Theatre**, to the east of this Kremlin-Pentagon, is another relatively modern Gorbals landmark and is pleasant, in spite of its exterior of bath-

Preceding pages: time for reflection in the Gorbals. Left, the re-born Gorbals. Right, Glasgow Central Mosque.

THE CITIZENS' THEATRE

The window was flung open and the housewife shouted: "Poofter, what's playing tonight?" The man so addressed looked up and said "*Hamlet*", to which the response was: "Ah dinny think al come: that's nae for me". The place was the Gorbals: the man was an actor in the Citizens' Theatre Company and the interlocuter a working woman exhibiting that Glasgow characteristic of affectionate name-calling. She probably would have thoroughly enjoyed the *Hamlet* for the three co-directors of the Citizens' (the Cits, as it is colloquially known) believe that theatre should be fun and lively and any Cits production is dazzling, even outrageous. It is this élan which has given the theatre an international name and which leads to it being invited to perform all over the world.

The first production of Giles Havergal, Philip Prowse and Robert David MacDonald when they took control in 1970 was an outré *Hamlet* which rocked Glasgow and beyond and which terrified the then conservative Labour District Council which threatened to withdraw its grant to the company. Since then, the Cits has developed an idiosyncratic non-naturalistic style, a part of which is that the actors remember at all times that they are acting. The directors – and the presence of three directors makes it difficult for outside directors to get a look-in – remember at all times that they are running a theatre: no money men for them – they are involved in everything from the cost of a seat to the price of a bottle of beer at the bar.

Brilliant Cits successes still talked about include the *The Painter's Palace of Pleasure*, *The Good Humoured Ladies*, *Chinchilla*, *Venice Preserv'd* and *A Waste of Time*, the last being based on Proust's *Remembrance of Things Past*. It is not part of the Cits' policy to stage sure winners to finance more controversial works or to run a subscription season to attract people to plays they might not otherwise have attended.

This is all a far cry from the original Citizens' Theatre which was founded in the middle of World War II, in 1943, by James Bridie and Tom Honeyman. Their avowed aim was the development of a Scottish theatre – which did not mean a theatre in Scotland but a theatre with Scottish actors performing the works of Scottish playwrights. Many plays presented were by Scottish writers – including Bridie, who was a dramatist of international stature – but by the late 1950s the works of foreigners were being performed.

However, Scottish actors including international names such as Molly Urquhart, Alastair Sim and Duncan Macrae still trod the boards. All agree that it was the inspiration of Bridie and Honeyman and their Glasgow Citizens' Theatre which led to the Scottish political and working-class theatre which is now so popular in Glasgow.

When the present directors arrived on the scene in 1970, all this changed. What was of concern was quality and equality and since then the theatre has staged the works of Balzac and Brecht, Genet and Goethe, Albee and Arrabal. (Before coming to the theatre, MacDonald was a translator for the United Nations.) Their productions are stylish, visual – Philip Prose can make silk purses out of sows' ears – and full of blood and thunder. Prissy, never!

Equality is enforced on both sides of the proscenium arch. All the actors, the majority of whom have been with the company since the triumvarate took over, receive the same pay and all seats are the same low price. (Compare this to Glasgow's working-class theatres, the 7:84 and the Wildcat, where seat prices depend on location.) Pensioners and the unemployed are admitted free. Formerly, The Close, a small experimental Club theatre, was part of the Citizens' but when it burned down in 1973 the present directors refused to be involved with its resurrection: because it was a club, it smacked of elitism.

Havergal believes that classical drama must always be popular drama. He is fascinated by the Elizabethan idea of a theatre to which everybody came: not just a specific audience pre-selected by class or income or occupation. The location of the Citizens' is perfect for this ideal: it is enclosed within the Gorbals and 400 yards to the north is the Merchant City with its young and affluent population. If Havergal had his way, all seats at the Cits would be free: his is a utopian world. ∎

room-like tiles – is it attempting to commemorate the lost gentlemen's lavatory? Enter the foyer under statues of the Four Muses and be greeted by larger than life-size statues of Robert Burns and William Shakespeare and then pass into the auditorium through doors flanked by gilded elephants. All these figures are part of Glasgow's theatrical heritage and were rescued from city theatres now destroyed.

The **Glasgow Central Mosque and Islamic Centre**, immediately to the north of the theatre, is instantly recognisable because of its minaret and relatively unpretentious multi-faceted glass dome. The Gorbals has always been the magnet for new immigrant groups. The Irish made it their Erin and then the Jews found that it was the Promised Land. They, in turn, were followed by the Pakistanis who had found Paradise.

Nothing remains of the Great Synagogue or of the many other Jewish buildings but the **St Francis' Roman Catholic Church and Friary** still stand on that part of **Cumberland Street** which is about 400 yards southeast of the mosque. This 1880 building, incorporating stones from the first Franciscan complex in Glasgow which was dedicated in 1477, is a delightful example of early decorated style. The interior, whose beauty matches that of the exterior, has excellent acoustics.

No-go area: Spirit of a different kind is distilled a couple of hundred yards to the north at the **Strathclyde Distillery** (look for its distinctive tall chimney). Regrettably, this building, in which 7 million gallons (32 million litres) of the *guid stuff* is distilled each year, is not open to the public.

From here, travel westwards for about a mile along **Caledonia Road**, towards a beacon-like square tower which rises from alongside a raised Ionic colonnade and clearly bearing the imprint of "Greek" Thomson. The **Caledonia Road Church** dates from 1856–57 and when functional had, in sharp contrast

The Clyde at night.

to most of its contemporaries, a bright and colourful interior. This, Thomson's first church and one of the great 19th-century Scottish buildings, was burnt to a shell in 1965 and its future is in doubt. Possibly it is best left, as has been suggested, as it is: a work in picturesque decay like the Acropolis from which Thomson sought his inspiration.

Turn south along **Pollokshaws Road** and in half-a-mile **St Andrew's Cross** (invariably referred to as **Eglinton Toll**) and the exit to the Gorbals is reached. Eglinton Toll, a major intersection of five roads, was, in years gone by, bathed in the hellish orange glow of the open-top blast furnaces of **Dixon's Blazes** – or, to give them their more correct name, the **Govan Colliery and Iron Works** – which were a major source of employment for inhabitants of the Gorbals. It is said of the great blast furnaces that "the bright glare cheers the long winter night, and at the same time does the work of a score of policemen, by scaring away the rogues and vagabonds who so plenti-fully infest other and darker parts of the city." Nothing remains.

From Eglinton Toll, a wide, straight-as-a-die, mile-long, handsome, suburban thoroughfare runs south to the gates of Queen's Park, the first of the city's green lungs south of the river. However, before proceeding along **Victoria Road**, make a short detour from Eglinton Toll to **Pollokshaws Road**, the other southbound artery. Here, at the corner of **Albert Drive**, stands the **Tramway**; it owes its name to the fact that its home is the former tramway sheds which, when opened in 1893, housed 385 tram-cars and 4,000 horses. The cavernous Tramway is ideal for experimental, imaginative and inventive theatre and the first production mounted here was the première of Peter Brook's spectacular epic *The Mahabharata*.

A broad flight of granite steps stretches from the main entrance to **Queen's Park** to the summit where stands a 209-ft (64-metre) flagpole. Magnificent views can be enjoyed to the north, across the city

Playing bowls at Queen's Park.

to the Campsie Fells and, on a clear day, beyond to Ben Lomond, somewhat to the west.

Within the park are **Camphill House** and, at the northeast corner, **Langside Public Hall**. The former is a pleasant two-storey building with an Ionic porch, which was built in 1815 and which now houses a small **Museum of Costumes**. The latter, built about 30 years later, is a strikingly handsome renaissance building with keystone heads over the lower openings representing the rivers Clyde, Thames, Shannon and Wye. Atop the cornice stand the royal coat-of-arms flanked by Britannia and Plenty; the base of the building is marred by ghastly green wooden doors. This edifice started life as the National Bank when it stood in Queen Street in the very heart of the city. It was uprooted and transported to its present site at the beginning of this century.

The reason for the park's name can be found immediately outside its western extremity which is about the same altitude as the flagpole. Here stands the **Langside** (or **Battlefield**) **Monument**, an uncomplicated 60-ft (18-metre) column with four eagles perched at the base and topped by a couchant lion. This marks the site of the **Battle of Langside** where Mary Queen of Scots was defeated. Eleven days before the battle, Mary had escaped from imprisonment on Loch Leven and had made her way to Hamilton. Here, she attracted an army of 6,000 under the leadership of the Earl of Argyll and planned to make her way to the River Clyde at Renfrew, ford the river and then make for the security of Dumbarton Castle.

The enemy, which was led by the Regent Murray, Mary's half-brother, learnt of these plans and took up position at Langside. Mary's troops, who were superior in numbers and who had the support of powerful families including the Maxwells of Pollok and of Haggs, gained ascendancy during the first part of the one-hour battle but then – some claim because of internal strife, others

say because of the incompetence or illness of Argyll – were soundly defeated. Mary fled to England in such terror that she did not stop or dismount until she reached Sanquar, 60 miles (100 km) to the south. She was never to return to Scotland.

Mary is believed to have watched the defeat of her troops and, at one point, even to have ridden forward in a vain attempt to encourage their flagging spirits, from **Queen's Know** which is about 2 miles (3 km) to the southeast of where the battle was enacted. The spot, reached via Battlefield and in the northeast corner of **Linn Park**, is marked by a plaque, the original of which is in the People's Palace.

Old Castle Road cuts through the park, whose attractive mixture of woodlands and riverside (the **White Cart Water** flows through here) attracts many birds. On the other side of Old Castle Road are the sparse, ivy-covered ruins of 15th-century **Cathcart Castle**. The paucity of these ruins prompted an in-

dignant and proud Glaswegian to exclaim: "If it had been somewhere in Edinburgh, they would have protected and floodlit it".

Immediately to the southwest of these vestigial remains is the charming Snuff-Mill bridge. Alongside this stands a former snuff-mill now converted into luxury apartments. The date 1624 is inscribed on the eastern outer wall of the bridge and Burns is said to have crossed these very stones. Justification for the claim is that, at the time of Burns, this was the main stage-coach route between Ayr and Glasgow.

Another lost cause stands immediately to the west of the Langside monument. The vandalised two-storey **Langside Free church** with its imposing Ionic facade suggests the drawing board of "Greek" Thomson. However, both it and the Monument are the work of Alexander Skirving, for many years his chief draughtsman. The tympanum of the church pediment was intended to hold a sculpture of John Knox exhorting

Memorial by Cathcart Castle to Mary Queen of Scots.

Queen Mary, with the Regent Moray as onlooker. However, the congregants were too canny to spend the money.

Not to worry if a most enormous roar is heard while travelling between the Monument and Linn Park: Scotland must have scored a goal at soccer. The route passes close to **Hampden Park**, Scotland's national stadium and home of Queen's Park, the only amateur club in a major British soccer league.

Back on **Clarkston Road**, go south for about 2 miles (3 km) to **Clarkston Toll** and then travel along the **Mearns Road** for a similar distance to Greenbank Gardens which are set in pleasant farmland. (The estate is also reached from Eastwood Toll, close to the southeast corner of Rouken Glen.) **Greenbank Gardens** has a handsome two-storey, modest-sized home dated 1763. The style immediately suggests the Adam Brothers, but it is too soon for Robert and too light for William.

The house is not open to the public (the interior decor is simple) but the

grounds are most attractive; they include woodlands and a splendid walled garden (this serves as a demonstration and advice centre) with more than 2,000 perennials. Several highland cattle from the prize-winning City of Glasgow herd adorn the landscape.

Return to Clarkston Toll, take the **Busby Road** and, immediately after passing under the Busby railway bridge, turn left for the attractive village of **Carmunnock** (2 miles/3 km); here some 18th-century houses still stand in the lee of the church. After Carmunnock, continue for a further mile on the B759 to the crest of the hill atop which stands a television tower. This is **Queen Mary's Seat**, the highest point (600 ft/180 metres) of **Cathkin Braes Park** and, with immense vistas. It must be the best view point in Glasgow.

The inevitable game of golf is being played immediately below. Beyond that are all those places which have already been visited and all those still to be visited. Then, from west to east, are

Paisley and Gleniffer Braes, the Campsies, Arthur's Seat and the Pentland Hills. Beyond this are Ben Lomond, Ben Ledi and the Cobbler and even Goatfell on the island of Arran.

Continue on the B759 and then turn left and travel north for about 3 miles (5 km) following the "Rutherglen" signposts. Small but busy **Rutherglen** is Scotland's oldest burgh, having gained that honour half-a-millennium before Glasgow, and resents now being a part of the City of Glasgow. (Its status as a burgh gave a town or a community rights and privileges of administration and trading within a defined area.) Parliament sat in Rutherglen in 1300 and tradition suggests that here Sir John Menteith agreed to betray William Wallace to the English.

Both events are believed to have occurred in the **Parish Church**; it is entered from **Main Street** by the **Kirk Port**, which was built in 1663 with fines paid by those who profaned the sabbath. Within, and on either side of, the Port stand stone alcoves where church elders collected offerings from the congregants before services. These sentry boxes were also used, it is believed, by church officers on the lookout for body-snatchers whose target was the graves in the cemetery surrounding the church.

The church windows, even the upper ones, are protected with mesh against vandalism by today's violent youth. Yet, already in the 17th century the town council had passed legislation which stated "considering the brakeing of the glass windowes in the kirk... Under the payne of fyve pounds money and the parents to be lyable and answerable for their children": *plus ça change, plus c'est la même chose.* The free-standing steeple in the cemetery dates from about 1500 and was a bell tower for both the church and town. Situated next to the church is the striking baronial **Town Hall** (1862) with its sun-seeking tower and turreted frontage. The centre of Glasgow is about 4 miles (6 km) north of here.

Subtle tastes in the suburbs.

THE GHOST OF GLASGOW PAST

The Merchant City, where the Glasgow renaissance first kicked off, is situated where the old slums were. Areas such as Townhead, Calton and Dovehill – as well as the fabled Gorbals – were dank slums of Dickensian dimensions. Now, some areas whose level of deprivation would recently have recalled the Third World are splendid districts and models of imaginative planning. Indeed, with an extra dash of social mix, Glasgow will probably come to be seen as one of the most successful re-designed cities of Europe.

It is not, therefore, the old districts which shame the city now. It is the areas which were built a quarter of a century ago and in particular the peripheral housing estates which in Scotland became known as the "Schemes". These housing "schemes" were to be the dawn of a new social democratic day. Houses would have inside toilets and baths. There would be lots of grass on which children, released from the back streets, could romp safely.

Glasgow was one of the first municipal authorities to attempt such housing developments and the early "schemes" worked well; indeed, many still do in a quiet way. Inter-war areas such as Mosspark and Knightswood are decent enough. It was the post-1945 experiments which went horribly wrong. Nitshill, Pollok, Drumchapel, Easterhouse, Castlemilk, estates built on the outskirts of the city, all became nightmares. It is on such estates that the city's rousing claim "Glasgow's Miles Better" has failed to fulfil its promise.

Easterhouse, for instance, became the home of thousands of families, yet it had no schools, shops, pubs, libraries, theatres, cinemas or hospitals. For years, it lacked any social focus, and public transport was deplorable. Glasgow has been suffering from this brave experiment in municipal idiocy ever since.

Huge areas of these peripheral estates have remained no-go areas for every social service. Before a doctor makes a home visit, he may ask the police to check out the enquiry in case it is a trap set by addicts lying in wait to separate the doctor from the drugs in his medical bag. Police often accompany doctors on their rounds. Firemen are sometimes stoned by the locals when they come to the scene of a blaze – a curious reaction, given that Glasgow until recently boasted the highest fire fatality rate of any comparable community in the world except for Soweto – and *that* township's rate was only higher because of the "necklace murders" where rubber tyres were placed around victims' necks and set alight. Glasgow's fires are almost all related to alcohol abuse.

In the city's schemes, as many as three out of four babies are born out of wedlock and infant mortality is higher than in Naples. Crime is endemic, and unemployment among young males approaches 100 percent. A descending spiral goes on as "decent" people, to their dismay, find their children becoming as *lumpen* as those of their neighbours.

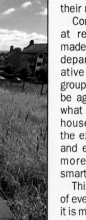

Considerable attempts at renewal have been made by the city housing department, an imaginative and sympathetic group, but the odds may be against them for it is what goes on *inside* a house that determines the exterior. Employment and education are much more important than smart exteriors.

This is true, of course, of every city in Britain; but it is more true of Glasgow, where a culture of deprivation, with a large underclass, has developed. However, the casual visitor to the city is unlikely to see anything of this dispiriting situation, for the underclass sticks to its own.

Naturally, not all the schemes are like this and most of the inhabitants, even of the worst schemes, are decent, hard-working people angered enough on occasions to display a flash of resentment at the goings-on of the well-heeled in the West End and the Merchant City.

What they resent is that they can only too rarely take part in it all, for they also enjoy bright lights and excitement and relish the vibrant nightlife of Glasgow. Young unemployed youths and girls save up their meagre dole money for a monthly bash in the lurid and expensive nightclubs and bars of the city centre. Such outings never come cheap. They save seriously for the smart, designer outfits – for Glaswegians, like gypsies, love smart and brightly coloured raiments. ∎

FROM GOVAN TO
THE BURRELL

Govan, on the south side of the river, is one of Glasgow's oldest suburbs and was once one of the most famous. Today, however, its economic importance has largely disappeared but urban renewal has been less drastic here than in other parts of the city.

This might be the place to enjoy Glasgow's "Clockwork Orange", the affectionate sobriquet bestowed upon the subway or, as it is now called, the **Underground**. This charming and extremely efficient system – dare it, because of its size, be called "toy"? – consists of two 6½-mile (10.5-km) circular tracks, one within the other, on 4-ft (1-metre) gauge. One line runs clockwise, the other counter-clockwise, through separate 11-ft (3-metre) diameter tunnels and both serve the same 15 stations. An entire circuit takes just 25 minutes.

The system opened in 1896 and was originally cable-driven. It was electrified in 1935 and modernised in 1979. Be warned: at most stations only one platform, which is about 10 ft (3 metres) wide, serves both lines. During the rush hour it can get quite crowded.

The **Govan Old Parish church**, the site of which has been in ecclesiastical use longer than any other in Scotland, stands next to Pierce Hall and hides one of Glasgow's best-kept secrets. Within the church, which is usually locked but whose keys – and many are required to gain entry – can be obtained in the Pierce Hall, is the most remarkable and the largest collection of **Celtic crosses** in the country. These 26 stones represent the best of 46 stones which were uncovered in the churchyard in the 19th century.

It is believed that the stones originally formed a Druid Circle but when Christianity came the stones were inscribed with Celtic crosses. However, the initials on them are of a much later date and some were used by Govanites as tombstones. The most unusual stones are five hog-backed ones; they resemble sea animals and were possibly originally erected above the graves of Viking chiefs. Within the chancel church is a delicately decorated sarcophagus which contained the relics of St Constantine, the 6th-century founder of this very handsome church.

Greatest-ever liners: A few towering cranes stand on the riverside just beyond the churchyard. They are part of the **Kvaerner Shipyard**, the last great yard on the Clyde. In years gone by, it boasted 40 yards and, at one time, launched nearly two out of every three ships built in the world. Some of the greatest-ever liners were launched from this site, which was known first as the Govan Shipyard, then as Fairfields, and is now Norwegian-owned.

When the Grand Duke Alexis of Russia came to this yard in 1880 for the launch of his turbot-shaped yacht *Livadia*, he spoke of Glasgow as "the cen-

Preceding pages: Pollok House. Left, inspired by on-the-wall art. Right, cranes at Clydebank.

tre of intelligence of England". Who dared to dissent!

Board the Underground at **Govan station** and alight at the next stop, **Cessnock**. Immediately next to the station is run-down **Walmer Crescent**, one of the more monumental works of "Greek" Thomson. Stark simplicity is the theme here, although it is slightly relieved by the grouping together of projecting bow windows.

Ibrox Park, the home of Glasgow Rangers, one of the city's two most famous soccer clubs, stands a few hundred metres to the west. None, not even followers of Celtic, their traditional rivals, will deny that this is Glasgow's most luxurious soccer stadium. Tours are possible.

Travel two further stops on the Underground to **Shields Road**. Across the road from this station stands the **Scotland Street School**, now a **Museum of Education**. It is the work of Charles Rennie Mackintosh and not, as some might suppose, an early oeuvre but one from the start of this century. The north facade is dominated by stairway bays, constructed almost entirely of glass, while the rear of the building displays some pretty art deco touches with, in parts, the rich red sandstone offset by delicate green tiles.

Return to the Govan Underground station. From here, a drive of about a mile on **Broomloan Road** leads to **Dumbreck Avenue** (immediately after the Ring Road) where, on a slight incline on the left, stands a sign **Craigie Hall**. This glorious villa, surrounded by other equally beautiful villas in what was (and still is to some extent) Glasgow's most elegant residential district, is now a business centre.

Neglect and vandalism had brought the villa to the verge of extinction when a Glasgow engineer and businessman, Graham Roxburgh, purchased and refurbished it, following the original schemes as much as possible. The house had been built in 1873 according to the plans of John Honeyman and, 20 years

later, his junior partner, assisted by recently recruited Rennie Mackintosh, extended it and made internal improvements. Mackintosh's imprint is seen in the hall and the library fittings and in the organ which is said to be the only extant Mackintosh musical design.

Special award: Quintessential Mackintosh can be enjoyed in **Bellahouston Park**, just across the road from Craigie Hall. The **House for the Art Lover** was built in 1990 from plans Mackintosh had submitted in 1901 for a competition sponsored by *Zeitschrift fur Innen-Dekoration*, a German magazine. He failed to win the prize – one reason given is that he submitted fewer than the required number of plans – but he received a special award. The judges commented that "the design especially stands out because of its pronounced personal quality, its novel and austere form, and the unified configuration of interior and exterior".

The plans sat gathering dust until Mr Roxburgh (of Craigie Hall) decided to

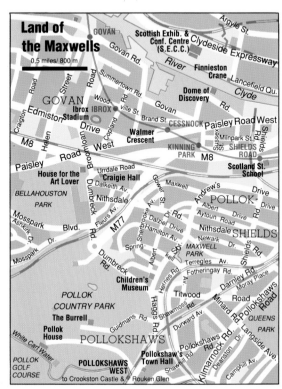

build a genuine Mackintosh, almost a century after it was designed and 62 years after the architect's death. In an act of generosity, the city fathers agreed to sacrifice a tiny part of their beloved parks for the building of this house which is quintessential in that it was not built to satisfy a client but to satisfy the architect. It is one of only three domestic buildings designed by Mackintosh.

From here, a practically uninterrupted green belt of both parks and golf courses – of which only the last, **Deaconsbank**, is public – stretches for 5 miles (8 km) to the south. Continue along **Dumbreck Road** and, after about 2 miles (3 km) a roundabout is reached where there is a non-vehicular entrance to Pollok Estate and a road to St Andrew's Drive.

The former is a delightful way to enter the Estate for those who wish to enjoy nature; those whose interests are man-made rather than natural and who are driving rather than walking should enter Pollok from Pollokshaws Road.

Haggs Castle, at 100 St Andrew's Drive, is a baronial edifice rather than a fortified castle and is now a **Children's Museum**. It was built in 1685 and occupied, as was nearly all of this part of Glasgow, by the Maxwell family. Covenanters met here in the 17th century after which the castle fell into disuse. It was restored during the 19th century when the north wing and spiral staircase were added.

Today, the castle's past is brought to life. Upstairs, Sir John and Lady Maxwell are in their bedroom preparing for dinner and the Victorian nursery is filled with toys. Downstairs, the kitchen has been restored and is fully equipped with a quern stone, cauldron, spit and cooking utensils. Children are encouraged to touch and are given the opportunity to make butter and cheese, oatcakes and sweets and to learn weaving and sewing. Croquet and archery can be enjoyed in the garden. Displays based on historical themes are mounted in the exhibition rooms.

Return to the roundabout and follow

Old-time learning at Haggs Castle.

Haggs Road to the **Pollokshaws** entrance to Pollok Estate (about 1 mile) which is immediately opposite the charming **Pollokshaws Town Hall** with its crow-stepped gables (1897). Those without transport can board buses into the park at this entrance.

Pollok Estate is something of a rarity: a country park complete with rangers in the heart of the city. Enter through its gates and the city, which is just a few yards away, has vanished. Yet rurality does not exclude urbanity. **Pollok Country Park** offers Italian earthenware as well as earthworms; tapestries as well as playing fields; glorious autumn paintings (Sisley's *The Bell Tower at Noisy-le-Roi*) as well as glorious autumn days. Here at Pollok there is something for everyone.

Violent game: There is fishing in the **White Cart Water** and, when the weather is clement, swimming in the waters below the weir. One can watch shinty, a violent Scottish field game which is a cross between mayhem and murder, or applaud as Fruin and Fraz, Czar and Haig go through their paces. They are among the 70 German shepherds, golden labradors and English springer spaniels at the Strathclyde Police Dog Training centre. (Demonstrations are often held on Tuesday mornings between 10 and 11am.) Then there are nature walks and garden walks and the opportunity to gaze at shy roe deer and at brilliant kingfishers, at dragonflies over the pond and at culture vultures in and around Pollok House and the Burrell Collection. For Pollok Country Estate is the home of two magnificent art collections.

Pollok House which was designed in the middle of the 18th century by William Adam and completed by his more famous son John, houses a superb art collection, assembled around 1850 by Sir William Stirling Maxwell, an authority on Spanish art. The collection includes works by Goya, El Greco, Murillo and outstanding prints of William Blake, as well as a collection of

Pristine collection at Pollok House.

exquisite oriental furniture, silver, porcelain and Spanish glass. Some will wish to visit the basement kitchens to see how, not that long ago, the oh-so-rich were taken care of.

Always competing for the visitor's attention are the magnificent vistas which can be seen through the tall glass windows. How splendid to look past an El Greco to the fields where Caitin and Unadubh, Magaidh and Maili graze, their ruminations disturbed only by a hooked golf ball from the nearby golf course. Caitin and friends belong to the Pollok Fold, a herd of about 70 prize-winning Highland beasts which belong to the city of Glasgow. Aye, and beasts they are, with their long, shaggy, brown hair covering their eyes. Yet, despite that ferocious look (the result of their long horns), they are the most gentle of all cattle.

The formal gardens at the rear of the house, which is more attractive than the front, are at their glorious best in summer. Immediately east of this is the **Woodland Garden** which is planted mainly with shrubs and rare trees. Rhododendrons are a special attraction. Many of the cultivars, including *Jock, Glasgow Glow* and *Scarlet Lady,* were originally produced by Sir John and his head gardener, "Jock" McTavish. Just south of this is the demonstration garden and the gardeners' bothy (a land-worker's cottage) in what was originally the estate's **Walled Garden**. The bothy shows just how life was for a gardener working here at the turn of the century.

Remarkable hoard: And so to the **Burrell Collection**, which for many is the *pièce de résistance* not only of the Park but of Glasgow and even of Scotland. Sir William Burrell, a Glasgow ship-owner, was a compulsive collector. When other youngsters were buying cricket balls with their pocket money, he was buying prints. And so, for 80 years, with good sense and good taste, he built up a remarkable art collection which rivals those of such great Ameri-

The Burrell Collection.

can collectors as Frick, Mellon or Rockefeller. On one occasion, Burrell bought from William Randolph Hearst, another compulsive collector, a 12th-century stone archway. Hearst had shipped it from France to California, and Burrell was able to buy it for one-tenth of what Hearst had paid.

On his death in 1958, Burrell left his collection to the city of Glasgow. However, there were provisos which could not be fulfilled and the collection lay in storage – small sections were occasionally exhibited – for many years. Then, in 1966, Mrs Anne Maxwell Macdonald gifted Pollok Estate to the city. A custom-built prize-winning museum to house the impressive collection was added in 1983.

Honeymooners' retreat: Back on Pollokshaws Road, turn right and travel for about half-a-mile to a large roundabout. Turn right onto the **Barrhead Road** and journey between golf courses for 2½ miles (3 km), after which a right turn on to **Crookston Road** leads, after another mile, to **Crookston Castle**. The castle, the first property in Scotland to come under the aegis of the National Trust (1931), stands amongst trees on top of a mound in the middle of a low-rise housing estate. The black-stone castle, which stands three storeys high in parts, owes its fame to the fact that Mary Queen of Scots and her cousin Henry Stuart (Lord Darnley) spent a few days here in 1565 after their marriage.

From here **Rouken Glen** lies about 5 miles (8 km) to the southeast. The principal formal attractions in this glorious estate, much of which has been left in its natural state and through which flows a waterfall, are the **Walled Garden** and the **Butterfly Kingdom**. In the hothouses of the latter, the visitor can enthuse over *Common Jezebels* and *Red Admirals* which spread their wings among orange trees, bougainvillea and passion flowers. Somewhat less colourful and more deadly are the scorpions and tarantulas and myriad other insects in the Insectarium.

Sir William Burrell assembled an exotic collection of objects.

PUTTING THE BURRELL IN PERSPECTIVE

The Burrell Gallery's opening, which the Queen performed in 1983, was perhaps the very first thrust of the new Glasgow. It had been 40 years in the making and nobody in the city had expected it would ever happen at all. Sir William Burrell, a shipbuilding magnate who had helped make Clydeside a byword for ships, craftsmanship and untrammelled capitalism, left Glasgow his vast and erratic collection of treasures. In a final insult to the city, he insisted that his collection of bric-a-brac – which admittedly did include some very impressive things – be shown as a complete exhibit within the bounds of the city.

It was an eccentric bequest and one which Glasgow, strapped for cash as it characteristically was, could not meet. In fact the city broke the legality of the bequest by showing a lot of the Burrell pieces in its own municipal gallery at Kelvingrove. Eventually, however, the city fathers decided to meet the demands of the bequest and purpose-built the Burrell Museum.

Situated in Pollok Country Park, minutes away from a mansion they already owned, the Burrell was bright, modern, imaginative – and cost £20.6 million. Overnight, it became a major tourist draw, topping Scotland's league table of most visited sites

and winning just about every major architectural award. The critics liked it because it was the first modern public building to be erected in Glasgow for years; the public were impressed by a level of hype more usually associated with a Barry Manilow concert. The Glasgow media basked in its glow and spread the word.

Today the hype has died down somewhat and the old Kelvingrove Gallery and Museum has regained its position as the city's most visited building. Indeed, the number of visitors to the Kelvingrove, (officially the Glasgow Art Gallery and Museum) exceeds the figures for the Burrell by a ratio of five to three.

So why did the Burrell become the icon it did in the early days of the Glasgow renaissance? Some would answer that, looked at coolly, much of the Burrell collection is over-priced tat, a collection of junk foisted on the ageing Sir William by every charlatan in the art-dealer world. Despite the amount of money spent on housing it, they point out, some items in the collection of carpets betrays the prolonged attention of moths, and the bits of old wooden furniture on show might well be Tudor or Elizabethan but wouldn't look out of place in a department store. But others are fascinated by the very pot-pourri nature of the collection and argue that a major attraction is the exhibit's pleasant surroundings.

As it happens, Burrell, for once well advised, also assembled a rather fine group of French Impressionist paintings, including two superb and world-class Degas, and a superb Cézanne, *A rainy landscape at Arles*. But, until recently, the lighting of this little set of paintings was so appalling as to render the exhibition something of a visual disappointment.

Many visitors forget that across from the Burrell is a fine Adam building, Pollok House, once the property of the Stirling-Maxwells. It has a marvellous collection of Spanish paintings by Goya, El Greco and Raeburn. And across the River Clyde is the Kelvingrove Museum. Not many people know that this museum is Britain's second most visited art gallery, bowing only to the Tate in London.

Despite criticism that Glasgow Art Gallery does little to assist contemporary painting in Scotland itself – and this is not entirely true either – the fact remains that Glasgow has the finest collection of paintings anywhere in the country save London and that the museum itself can lay claim to being among the most vibrant in Europe. Its modern collection may have been depleted by the issue of Impressionists to the Burrell on the south side of the city, but it is still a grand collection. More than that: the Glasgow Kelvingrove Museum is a fun place, great to take the children to, and Glaswegians visit it in droves.

The Burrell – almost mandatory on the tourist circuit – was a valuable harbinger of Glasgow's new cultural sensibility and is still, without doubt, well worth the trip to Pollok Country Park. But there are many other museums in Glasgow, and the Burrell doesn't really deserve to overshadow them as it once did. ∎

GREATER GLASGOW

The realignment of boundaries in 1973 resulted in Glasgow simultaneously shrinking and expanding. This apparent anomaly was the result of the boundaries of the actual city being drawn back while new outlying districts were included. Today, Greater Glasgow consists of the districts of Renfrew, Inverclyde, Strathkelvin, Cumbernauld and Kilsyth, and Monklands. It stretches in the west to Wemyss Bay, in the east past Airdrie, in the north past Lennoxtown and in the south past Lochwinnoch. The east-west axis is 40 miles (64 km) long and the north-south axis about half that.

Visitors to solid, sensible **Paisley**, in the **Renfrew District**, can be excused if confused about the exhortation "Keep your eye on Paisley". When Benjamin Disraeli gave this advice, which was to become a catch-phrase to politicians who had enquired how they might gauge the tide of national opinon, Paisley was a craft-based (mainly weaving), money-making burgh eager to mind its own business. Paisley has fallen on lean times since these halcyon days and it is only lately that urban renewal has begun to gain momentum.

To reach Paisley, with a population of 100,000 the largest town not only in Renfrew District but in Scotland, either travel west on the M8 and leave at exit 27, a total distance of about 7 miles (11 km) or take the A737 from Glasgow city centre. Alternatively, there are four trains an hour from Central Station: the journey takes about 15 minutes.

Smack in the heart of town, on the banks of the tiny **White Cart Water** – incidentally, the first US troops to set foot on British soil in World War II did so just one mile from here – stand the **Abbey** and the **Town Hall**, as solid a pair of buildings as one would wish to see. The latter, which houses the tourist information office, is in classical Victorian style with hexastyle colonnades –

Corinthian to the east and Ionic to the west – on top of a high *piano nobile*. Two dissimilar towers – the taller, to the north, more slender and with clock faces – complete the picture.

The abbey was founded in 1163 as a monastery of the Cluniac order by Walter Fitz Alan, who was the first hereditary high steward of Scotland and a founder of the Royal House of Stewart. It was largely destroyed by Edward I in 1307 in response to its monks assisting William Wallace but was rebuilt during the 14th and 15th centuries.

The exterior of the abbey belies a much more attractive interior. Worth observing are the choir with its stone vaulted roof and stained-glass windows and St Mirin's chapel which occupies the place of the south transept and where a series of 12th-century panels depict episodes, of doubtful authenticity, from the life of Mirin, the town's patron saint.

Also in this chapel is a recumbent effigy of Marjory Bruce, daughter of the Scottish hero Robert Bruce. Standing at

the eastern end of the north aisle is the 11-ft (3.4-metre) weathered, 10th-century Celtic Cross of St Barochan. Attached to the south of the abbey is the **Place of Paisley**, which was converted to secular use in the 16th century.

A stroll to the west and to the hilly north of the abbey along **New** and **Shuttle Streets** and then across **High Street** and up **Church Hill** to **Oakshaw Street** – the entire distance is only about 1,000 yards (1 km) – reveals a surprising number of churches and several statues and buildings bearing the name Coats. The Coats family were the pre-eminent merchants of Paisley and generous in their gifts to the town in which they made their fortunes. Statues of Thomas and Sir Peter, the two principal benefactors, stand just to the west of the Town Hall, across the river.

Acrobatic angels: The large number of churches reflects the fact that the weavers, who formed the main corpus of Paisley's workers, had much time to contemplate, not so much the number of angels who could stand on one of their pins, but rather about the relationship between church and state. Secession was very much the in-word, followed by excommunication and, by the 18th century, the town had its Burgher and anti-Burgher churches, the East Relief and the West Relief churches, Primitive, United and Congregational Methodist churches. As if all these were not enough, one group of weavers, the Pen Folk, founded their own church.

Some churches are now secular and so, at the corner of **Shuttle** and **New Streets** stand the unprepossessing Laigh Kirk (Low Parish Church) which is now an **Arts Centre** and, opposite it, the even less prepossessing Free Gaelic Church which is now part of the **University of Paisley**. Here, too, are the **Sma' Shot Cottages**, restored artisans' houses from the Victorian era with various photographs and artefacts of local interest. (The "small shot" was a hidden linking thread in cloth which was being woven.)

Much more impressive is the **High Church** whose steeple, which rises in five stages to support an obelisk spire, dominates the Paisley skyline. It is reached by a long flight of stairs: in this respect, and in no other, it recalls Rome's Trinita dei Monti and the Spanish steps. A much wider and more elegant flights of steps leads to the majestic, cruciform, red sandstone **Thomas Coats Memorial Church**, more a cathedral than a mere kirk. The marble and alabaster interior of this Baptist church, one of the most splendid in the land, is just as handsome as the exterior.

Immediately east of this church is the **Paisley Museum and Art Gallery**, a gift of Peter Coats, which has sections devoted to local history, natural history, art and, most importantly, Paisley shawls. These shawls and their accompanying patterns were introduced to Britain in the early 1700s by members of the East India Company who had visited Kashmir. Although several motifs existed, it was the tear drop (or

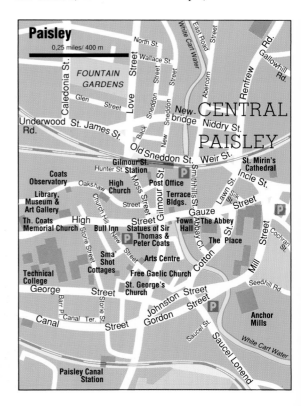

tadpole, or comma or pine cone) which caught the imagination. These were originally filled with an abstract mosaic of colours but were later replaced by buds, stalks and leaves.

Paisley pattern: It says much for Paisley that it was able to imprint its name on these colourful designs, for they were executed not only in Paisley but in other weaving centres such as Edinburgh and Norwich, Paris and Lyons and Vienna. Both Edinburgh and Norwich were making "Paisley" pattern shawls 20 years before they were produced in Paisley. Yet shoppers invariably asked to be shown "Paisleys".

This marketing success was made possible by a combination of hard work and low costs; by pirating Norwich designs (the government introduced patenting of designs only in 1842); and by using the mechanical French Jacquare loom which was able to produce a smooth curved line and which required only one, rather than the two, operators needed for the traditional and slower

drawloom. By the middle of the 19th century, Paisley shawls were booming; but by the end of the century interest had waned. However, by then Paisley had become the world's premier centre for the production of cotton thread.

Behind and above the Museum and open to members of the public is the **Coats Observatory** (the benefactor was Thomas), readily recognisable because of its observation drum below which runs a lovely Doric frieze and cornice supporting a baslustrade. Astronomical and meteorological data have been recorded in this, one of the best equipped observatories in the country, since the late 19th century.

On the way back to the town centre the visitor might stop for a refreshment at the **Bull Inn** on New Street where art nouveau glass and woodwork from the 1920s is joined by juke boxes and slot machines. Then, back in the centre of town observe the former glory of Paisley by looking at the **Terrace Buildings**, a glorious three-storey Italianate

Punks at Paisley Abbey.

confection with pedimented windows held up by brackets and a corbel table supporting a balustrade on top of which are festooned urns.

Leave Paisley for the southwest on the A737 and, after 3 miles (5 km), at the far end of the village of **Elderslie**, a monument marks the birthplace of William Wallace. Turn right on the B789 and after a mile turn left on the A761 for a further mile to reach the former weaving village of **Kilbarchan**. Weaving demonstrations are given in a small 1723 cottage which houses the last of the village's 800 looms.

Water sports: Backtrack to the A737 and, passing through delightful rolling country, turn right after 5 miles (8 km) on to the A760 and enter a landscape which shelters several lakes and which provides enormous pleasure for ornithologists and water sports enthusiasts and which has some interesting sights for antiquarians and historians.

After about 800 yards, a Norwegian spruce building with a tower is the head-quarters of the **Lochwinnoch Nature Reserve**, a habitat for more than 150 species of birds and extremely popular with winter migrant wildfowl. (Lochwinnoch Railway Station is just opposite the reserve: one train an hour from Glasgow makes the journey in 15 minutes.) Soon after this, a right turn at the garage leads through the main street (B786) of the village of **Lochwinnoch** to **Castle Semple Loch**, where sailing, fishing and rowing are available.

A 2-mile (3-km) stroll along the loch leads to an early 16th-century **Collegiate Church** while beyond that – and better reached from the village of **Howarth** – is **The Temple**, a folly, from where crippled Lady Semple could watch the hunt. Besotted antiquarians will also visit **The Peel** and **Barr Castle**, scanty remains of which are located near Lochwinnoch.

About a mile north of Lochwinnoch, a single-track takes off to the left and leads to **Muirshiel**, at an altitude of more than 1,000 ft (330 metres), in the

Cooper at Lochwinnoch making barrels for a distillery.

heart of the **Regional Park** of that name. Over a distance of 4 miles (6 km) the scenery has changed from a neat domestic landscape to a grand valley leading into open moor. (Muirshiel Regional Park covers a superb stretch of countryside and extends for 16 miles (26 km) to the northwest.)

Lochwinnoch is almost at the southwest extremity of Greater Glasgow. From here one can return directly on the A737 to Glasgow (17 miles/25 km) or travel further to the southwest on the A737 (19 miles/30 kms) to Irvine (*see page 241*) or on the A760 (15 miles/24 km) via Kilbirnie to Largs.

To visit the **Inverclyde District**, travel west on the M8 from Glasgow. Pass Glasgow Airport and 16 miles (26 km) after leaving the city centre take an acute left turn. This leads on to the A8 and, after about a mile, turn right onto the B789 on which, after about another mile, stands **Formakin House** in the estate of that name in **Bishopton**. (Bishopton and Langbank, the next place

visited, are both in the Renfrew rather than the Inverclyde district but for convenience are included here.) The design of the house – which was never completed, although all the ancillary buildings were – is pure Scottish baronial. The house is called the **Monkey House** because of stone monkeys which clamber all over the exterior and the interior – on the eaves, on mantlepieces. Another whimsical touch are the initials D.L. (*Damned Lie)* above the entrance to the stable courtyard.

This was to be not only a home but a museum to house the not inconsiderable collection of John Holms which included Chinese porcelain, oriental rugs, English silver plate and furniture. The entire collection was sold at auction in 1936 and some pieces were purchased by Sir William Burrell and are now exhibits in the Burrell collection in Glasgow. The house stands in 160 acres (64 hectares) of extremely attractive grounds which are home to an excellent collection of rare farm animals.

Fenwick Church, a centre for militant 17th-century Covenanters.

Travel westwards along the A8, which parallels the River Clyde, for less than 2 miles (3 km) to **Langbank** and, just within the Renfrew-Inverclyde boundary, observe the entry to **Finlayson House**. This large, somewhat rambling building, the oldest parts of which date from the 14th century, is the home of MacMillan, chief of the clan of that name. He and his wife make visitors very welcome; they will point out the ewe tree under which John Knox is said to have sat and the exact spot where Robert Burns scratched his name on a window-pane.

Burns considered the then Laird of Finlayson as his only true patron but a problem exists. The date etched on the window pane below the signature is 1772, at which time Burns would have been a mere stripling and patronage would scarcely have entered his head. The matter is resolved by suggesting that the date represents the year of the bottle of wine which Burns quaffed when he visited Finlayson. The grounds are delightful. One of the rooms contains an extensive doll collection.

Continue for about 4 miles (6 km) along the A8 until the Port Glasgow roundabout is reached. To the right, on the shores of the river, in stark contrast to the neighbouring shipyard stands, the solid, symmetrical 16th and 17th-century **Newark Castle** (not to be confused with the 18th-century castle of the same name at Selkirk in the Borders), yet another mansion of the Maxwells. With crow steps and gabled windows, turrets and 15th-century tower, this is a good example of Scottish baronial.

There is little to attract the visitor to **Port Glasgow** other than an excellent replica of the *Comet*, the first commercial steamship in Europe. Continue along the shores of the Clyde. The cranes of Scott Lithgow, one of the few remaining functioning shipyards on the Clyde, soar into view and are soon replaced by the splendid skyline of the churches and the town hall of Greenock, 23 miles (37 km) from Glasgow.

James Watt remembered at Greenock.

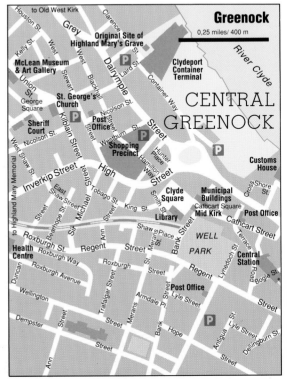

Greenock, which today has a population of 65,000, was an imporant shipbuilding and indudstrial town in the 18th and 19th centuries. The oldest dock on the Clyde was built here in 1711 and in 1859 the last great wooden ship was launched. Down on the waterfront stands the massive, classically correct, renovated **Customs House Building**, considered to be the most splendid such building in Britain.

The focal point for the visitor is **Cathcart Square** with the impressive **Municipal Buildings** and the soaring 245-ft (74-metre) **Victoria Tower**, which is from a previous building. When built, it was said of the municipal buildings that they "had every beauty but the beauty of economy". The elevation is incomplete at the east end because the owner of the property refused to sell. Opposite is the **Mid Kirk**, built in 1761, with a pedimented Ionic portico.

James Watt, inventor of the steam engine, was born in Greenock in 1736 and the **McLean Museum and Art Gallery** houses items relating to his career as well as an art collection which features the works of several Scottish artists alongside canvasses of Boudin and Corbin. The tombstone of Robert Burns' beloved *Highland Mary,* who died in 1798, can be seen in the local churchyard.

Most interesting of the city's several churches is the **Old West Kirk** which, in 1920, was removed to the east end of the esplanade which runs west from town. This was the first church built after the Reformation (1591) and the first Presbyterian church confirmed by Parliament. Its windows have stained glass by the pre-Raphaelites, Morris, Rossetti and Burne Jones.

On the way out of Greenock, turn left on **Lyle Road** and ascend to **Lyle Hill** where a large granite Cross of Lorraine commemorates the Free French who were based here in World War II. This is *the* great viewpoint of the region, and the views of the Clyde and its estuary and the lochs and mountains of the High-

A quiet afternoon at Greenock.

lands are breathtaking. Rather than retracing the same route to the main road, continue along Lyle Hill to join the A78 which, after 2 miles (3 km) arrives at **Inverkip**, with possibly the best marina on the Clyde.

Continue for a further 5 miles (8 km) to **Wemyss Bay** from where the ferry leaves for the **Isle of Bute** and **Rothesay**. The main attraction in Wemyss Bay is its magnificent railway station, light and airy and featuring wrought iron and with the reputation of being Scotland's most beautiful railway station. To arrive at Wemyss Bay is to know that one is on vacation.

On the return trip from Wemyss Bay to Glasgow, a distance of 31 miles (50 km), take the coast road after Inverkip, the A770, and drive past the grassy shore of **Lunderston Bay** (this is the western extremity of the Muirshiel Country Park) and stop at the **Cloch Lighthouse**. From here, there are delightful views of the Firth of Clyde.

Proceed onwards to the rather peaceful seaside resort of **Gourock**, from where car ferries leave frequently for **Dunoon** and passenger ferries for **Kilcreggan**, near Helensburgh (*see page 229*). In Gourock visit **Granny Kempcock**: seven times round this ancient monolith weathered to almost human shape is said to bring good fortune to sailors and fishermen, brides and grooms. Continue to Glasgow on the A770, which becomes the A8, which in turn joins with the M8.

Walks and views: The main attractions in the **Strathkelvin District**, which is to the north of the city, are the **Campsies** and restored sections of the **Forth and Clyde Canal**. The former offers superb hill-walking and splendid views of Glasgow. Leave the city by the A803 and, after about 5 miles (8 km) cross the canal. A little beyond this take the left arm of a Y-junction (the A807) for a mile and then turn right on the B822 which, after 3 miles (5 km) reachs **Lennoxtown**. After a further 2 miles (3 km), a large parking lot tells the visitor that this is the place to enjoy magnificent views and to start walking.

One or two pleasure craft (including cruising restaurants) are based on the Forth and Clyde Canal at **Bishopbriggs**, **Kirkintilloch** and **Kilsyth**, which are respectively 3, 5 and 10 miles (5, 8 and 16 km) east of Glasgow. **Colzium House** in Kilsyth, a splendid Victorian mansion, houses an art gallery and local museum. Near Kilsyth are two **Antonine Wall** sites: **Bar Hill** has a fort, rampart and ditch and **Croy Hill** a ditch and beacon platforms. The Wall was built by the Romans *circa* AD 143 to keep back marauding Scots.

The major attraction in the **Cumbernauld and Kilsyth District**, to the northeast of the city, is Glasgow's satellite town of **Cumbernauld**, one of Britain's most successful new towns. (Leave the M8 at exit 12 and drive for 11 miles/ 18 km on the A80.) **Cumbernauld**, after 35 years scarcely "new", has its headquarters at **Cumbernauld House**, built by William Adam in 1731. The enormous clock in the town shopping centre was retrieved from St Enoch Station in Glasgow when it was demolished. Contemporary art and sculpture are dotted about the town centre.

Visit in the **Monklands District**, due east of the city, the **Summerlee Heritage Park** which shows how Glasgow and Scotland earned the title the "Workshop of the World". This living industrial museum reverberates to the sound of steam and also has reconstructed Victorian buildings. A tramcar runs round the 25-acre (10-hectare) site and a branch of James Watt's 18th-century Monklands Canal has been reopened.

The Park is near **Coatbridge**, formerly the iron and steel capital of Scotland, and can be reached by driving to the end of the M8, then joining the A89 for 3 miles (5 km) and then turning south for a mile on the B804. The eastern end of the M8 also links with the A74 where, after a mile, one finds the **Glasgow Zoological Gardens**, a fairly modest affair.

Right, a mother and child sculpture at Cumbernauld.

DAY TRIPS

Glasgow may have destroyed much of its heritage in its headlong rush to have the best ring-road system of any city in Europe but, on the positive side, it is now a superb place to get out of. Incidentally, "a superb place to get out of" is not a criticism of the city's facilities and sights but rather refers to its topography. The Campsies, Loch Lomond, the Trossachs, the Burns country, the Clyde Valley are all on the city's doorstep.

Then there is the traditional "**Doon the Watter**" trip – a visit by paddle steamer to the seaside resorts of the west coast and some of the islands, such as **Arran** and **Bute**, in the Firth of Clyde. Even **Edinburgh** can be reached in 50 minutes by road or rail: trains depart every 30 minutes. (Bus companies run half- and full-day tours to all the places mentioned here, and many more.) The country around the city is well served by theme and day parks, innumerable golf courses, waters which can be fished for brown trout, pike and perch, and race-tracks at Ayr, Hamilton and Lanark which hold flat and hurdle programmes at irregular intervals.

Roman remains: Those who cannot bear to tear themselves away from Glasgow even for a half-a-day may be able to spare a couple of hours for a visit to the **Campsie Fells**, the hills immediately north of the city. A bonus is the opportunity to visit a distillery. Exit from the city on the A809 at **Anniesland Cross** and **Milngavie** (pronounced *Mull Guy*) is reached after 3 miles (5 km). Turn left on the A810 for **Bearsden** which is reached after about 2 miles (3 kms). A right turn at **Bearsden Cross** on to **Roman Road** leads to Roman Court, a superior housing development whose residents can boast of the ruins in their front yard of a **Roman Bath House**, built in the 1st century. This bath house,

<u>Preceding pages:</u> across the sea to Ailsa Craig.

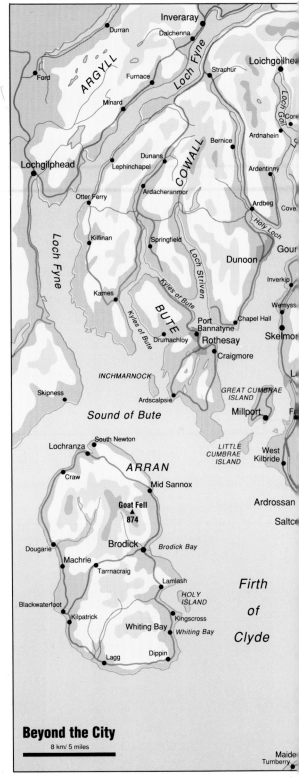

Beyond the City

8 km/ 5 miles

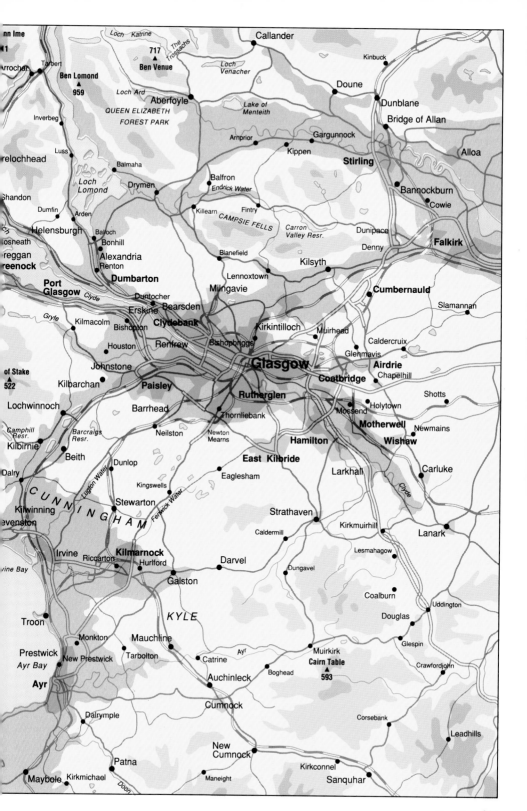

used by soldiers stationed in the adjacent **Antonine Wall** fort, is Scotland's best surviving visible Roman building. A further mile east and, in the **New Kilpatrick Cemetery**, are two not very upstanding, yet very important, sections of the **Roman Wall** which was built in order to keep out the wild Scots.

Return to Bearsden Cross and travel north on the A809 for 7 miles (11 km) to **Queen's View** (Auchineden Hill, 1,711 ft/351 metres) where today's visitor can still enjoy, as did Queen Victoria in 1869, a first glimpse of **Loch Lomond** and the mountains to the north. Turn south on the A809 for 2 miles (3 km) and then left for 3 miles (5 km) for the village of **Strathblane**; it sits in the lee of **Earl's Seat** which, at 1,896 ft (569 metres), is the highest point of the Campsies.

Head north on the A81 for 4 miles (6 km) to **Glengoyne Distillery** where visitors are graciously (on payment of a fee) received, given a tour of the distillery and fortified with a dram or two of the Highland malt which is distilled here. Proceed for a further 4 miles (6 km) on the A81 to **Killearn**. From here it is 6 miles (10 km) on the A875 and then the B818 to the village of **Fintry**, the northernmost point of this outing.

One mile from Fintry on the B818 leads to the B822 which ascends and descends across the moors of Campsie Fells to **Lennoxtown** (7 miles/11 km). Stop at the summit (1,000 ft/300 metres) which is on the Greater Glasgow boundary for spectacular views of the Clyde Valley. Glasgow can be seen to the west. At Lennoxtown join the A891 and immediately turn right on the B822 for **Torrance** from where it is a further 5 miles (8 km) to the city centre.

An outing to the Campsies can be combined with a visit to Loch Lomond or a trip to Stirling. In either case, travel northwards from Fintry on the B822 and journey for 7 miles (11 km) to the pleasant village of **Kippen** with its attractive relatively modern church and a splendid old dovecot. Much more re-

Loch Lomond.

SCOTCH WHISKY

The variety of malt whiskies on sale in Glasgow astounds visitors familiar with only a few heavily marketed brands such as Glenfiddich and The Macallan. But is the diversity an illusion fostered by advertising? Isn't the liquid behind the labels pretty much the same?

Certainly not, the experienced Scotch drinker will argue. The practised tongue can easily differentiate between Highland malts, Lowland malts, Campbeltown malts and Islay malts, and there's no mistaking the bouquet of a drink such as Laphroaig, often described as tasting of iodine or seaweed. The sheer variety of Scotch, in fact, far surpasses that of brandy.

But which is best? Whole evenings can be whiled away debating and researching the question, with no firm conclusions being reached. It all comes down in the end to individual taste.

The one point of agreement is that a whisky made from a good single malt (the product of one distillery) should not be drunk with a mixer such as soda or lemonade, which would destroy the subtle flavour – though ice and water *can* be added. After dinner, malts are best drunk neat, as a liqueur. The well-known brands of blends (such as Bell's, Teacher's, Dewar's and Johnnie Walker) contain tiny amounts of as many as 30 or 40 malts mixed

with grain whisky containing unmalted barley and maize. A typical blend for a popular brand is 60 percent grain whisky to 40 percent malt.

In contrast with the upmarket images conferred on Scotch today, the drink's origins were lowly. In the 18th century it was drunk as freely as the spring water from which it was made, by peasants and aristocrats alike. A spoonful was given to newborn babies in the Highlands, and even respectable gentlewomen might start the day with "a wee dram". The poorest crofter could offer his guest a drink, thanks to the ubiquity of home-made stills which manufactured millions of gallons of "mountain dew" in the remote glens of the Highlands.

Yet something as easy to make cannot be made authentically outside Scotland. Many have tried, and the Japanese in particular have thrown the

most modern technology at the problem; but the combination of damp climate and soft water flowing through the peat cannot be replicated elsewhere. Indeed, no-one – not even the most experienced professional taster – can agree on what elements create the best whisky. Is the water better if it runs off granite through peat, or if it runs through peat on to granite? Does the secret lie in the peat used to dry the malt in a distillery's kiln? Or the soft air that permeates the wooden casks of whisky as the liquid matures for between three and 10 years? The arguments are endless.

Two grain whiskies are produced in Glasgow itself (Strathclyde and Port Dundas) and several Lowland malts (such as Auchentoshan and Inverleven) are distilled within easy reach. However, so automated have Scotland's 100 or so distilleries become that visitors to establishments such as Glengoyne (*see facing page*) which run guided tours are left with only the haziest idea of what goes on inside the beautifully proportioned onion-shaped copper stills. What happens is this. To make malt whisky, plump and dry barley (which, unlike the water, doesn't have to be local) is soaked in large tanks of water for two or three days. It is then spread out on a concrete floor or placed in large cylindrical drums and allowed to germinate for between eight and 12 days. Next it is dried in a kiln, preferably heated by a peat fire. The dried malt is ground and mixed with hot water in a huge circular vat called a mash tun.

A sugary liquid, "wort", is drawn off from the porridge-like result, leaving the solids to be sold as cattle food. The wort is fed into massive vessels containing up to 45,000 litres of liquid, where living yeast is stirred into the mix to convert the sugar in the wort into crude alcohol. It's a bit like mixing cement.

After 48 hours, the "wash" (a clear liquid containing weak alcohol) is transferred to the copper stills and heated to the point where alcohol turns to vapour. The vapour rises up the still, to be condensed by a cooling plant into distilled alcohol, which is then passed through a second still. The trick is to know precisely when the whisky has distilled sufficiently. It is then poured into porous oak casks and left to mellow for at least three years – and sometimes 10 or 15. ∎

markable, considering the weather, was a vine which grew here until 1964 when it was removed in the name of progress. It produced 2,000 bunches of grapes annually and was said to be the largest in the world.

Immediately beyond Kippen the B822 joins the A811. Turn right and, after 9 miles (14 km), Stirling Castle looms in front *(see page 230)*. A left turn at the junction leads after 15 miles (24 km) to **Drymen**, from where it is a further 7 miles (11 km), still on the A8ll, to Balloch *(see page 229)*.

Few will wish to leave Glasgow without having visited the "Bonnie, bonnie banks" and visitors are fortunate in that **Balloch**, at the south end of **Loch Lomond**, is just 19 miles (30 km) from the city. An inviting haven is reached 6 miles (10 km) after leaving Glasgow and immediately before the Erskine Bridge exit. The **Auchentoshan Distillery** welcomes visitors and, after a tour of the plant, they can enjoy a nip of the whisky of that name. It is that *rara avis*, a lowland malt; furthermore – and most unusually – it is triple distilled.

Drive past the handsome **Erskine Bridge**, the last bridge on the River Clyde and the only toll bridge, and then **Bowling**, the starting point of the now defunct Forth and Clyde Canal which is readily recognised by its locks and the boats moored in the basin.

Soon, **Dumbarton** (14 miles/22 km from Glasgow) is reached and the road forks, with the A82 continuing directly to Balloch (for Loch Lomond) and the A814 proceeding to Dumbarton and Helensburgh from where Loch Lomond can be reached. Take the latter and soon, on the left, a short road leads to **Dumbarton Rock**, a massive 240-ft (75-metre) twin-peaked volcanic outcrop which rises sheer from the river.

It was from the castle that stood here that, in 1548, the five-year old Mary, already Queen of Scots, set sail for France, and it was this castle which she was attempting to reach when she was defeated in 1568 at the Battle of

Dumbarton Rock and Castle.

Langside. It is also believed that William Wallace, after being captured, was brought here before being sent to his execution in London.

The stiff climb to the summit of the Rock, past a sundial which was presented by Mary and then through a portcullis, is well worthwhile and is rewarded by superb views not only of the Clyde estuary but of the mountains to the north. Also worth visiting in Dumbarton is the **Denny Ship Model Experiment Tank**, which was the world's first ship model tank testing establishment and where such famous craft as the *Queen Mary* were tested.

From Dumbarton it is a further 8 miles (13 km) to Helensburgh. En route, **Cardross**, where Robert Bruce died, is passed. **Helensburgh**, immediately beyond which is **Rhu**, with the best marina on this shore of the Clyde, is the birthplace of John Logie Baird, the television pioneer, and of Henry Bell, who launched the *Comet*, Europe's first practical steamship to brave open waters. A

Below, Helensburgh. Right, Hill House.

right turn from the main road into steep **Colquhoun Street** leads, after a mile, to the **Hill House**, generally considered to be the best extant example of a Rennie Mackintosh domestic commission (open to the public). Worth remembering is that when the house was built in 1902 for Walter W. Blackie, the publisher, Helensburgh was not served by two electric trains an hour; today, these make the Glasgow-Helensburgh journey in 50 minutes.

Back on Colquhoun Street, continue eastwards from the main road on the B832 through **Glen Fruin** where an infamous bloody battle between the MacGregors and the Colquhouns was fought in 1603. A number of innocent onlookers were also killed.

After 5 miles (8 km) this road joins the A82. Turn left for 3 miles (5 km) to the picturebook village of **Luss** on the west shore of **Loch Lomond**. From here the visitor can proceed northwards along the loch or turn back to **Balloch** at the south of the loch (seven miles/11 km

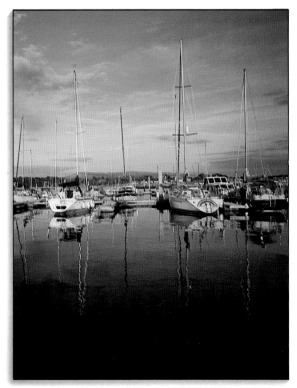

from Luss). In **Balloch Castle Country Park** the castle, built in 1808, serves as the Visitor Centre and sweeping picnic lawns offer lovely views of Loch Lomond and the mountains. A colourful walled garden is half-hidden in the grounds and unusual specimen trees flourish in the ornamental woodlands.

Probably the best way for the casual visitor to savour Loch Lomond is to board the stately *Countess Fiona* for a four-hour voyage on the waters. Stops are made at Luss, Rowardennan, Tarbet and Inversnaid, four of the loch's five principal villages (the fifth is **Balmaha**). The more energetic might wish to disembark at **Rowardennan** and then walk the 5 miles (8 kms) along the eastern shore of Loch Lomond to **Inversnaid**. This is part of the **Highland Way**, which runs from Glasgow to Fort William. Alternatively, the super-fit can disembark at Rowardennan and have time to make the ascent – and descent – of 3,192-ft (958-metre) **Ben Lomond** and catch the boat on its way back to Balloch.

To reach Stirling from Glasgow, take the ring road (M8), then the M73 followed by the A80 which becomes the M80, a total distance of 27 miles (43 km). The route is well marked. (Express trains depart from Queen Street station about every two hours and take 40 minutes.) The **Bannockburn Heritage Centre**, at the site of that one battle against the English which every schoolchild in Scotland knows, is 3 miles (5 km) south of Stirling.

At the Battle of Bannockburn, fought in 1314, Robert the Bruce defeated vastly superior English forces and won freedom for Scotland. All of this, and much more, can be seen in the Heritage Centre. Outside, a bronze equestrian statue of Bruce overlooks a rotunda which surrounds the Borestone in which the shaft of the hero's standard is said to have been set.

Strategic spot: The royal burgh of **Stirling**, standing on a bend of the River Forth was, for centuries, the most strategic spot in Scotland, controlling routes from the south to the north as well as from the east to the west and dominating much of Scotland's history. From the town, steep **Spittal Street** leads to the forecourt of **Stirling Castle**, which occupies a commanding position on top of a 250-ft (75-metre) rocky outcrop. Most of the castle, which is entered through an impressive gateway, is from the 14th to 16th centuries when it was a residence of the Stuart kings. This is where James II and V were born and both Mary, Queen of Scots and James VI spent several years here. Even before the Stuarts, a castle occupied this ground and frequently changed hands in the constant wars fought between the Scots and the English.

Admire the palace which James V had built around a central courtyard and which is one of Scotland's renaissance glories. Today, the most striking feature of this building, with ornate stonework largely cut by French, is the exterior facade. The castle's chapel was built on the instructions of James VI while the **Too neat to eat.**

125-ft (40-metre) Great Hall or Parliament House, with its exquisite carving and tracery, dates from James IV. It is being painstakingly reconstructed. The castle also contains the **Museum of the Argyll and Sutherland Highlanders Regiment**, with displays of regimental silver, uniforms and medals.

Superb views can be enjoyed from the spot where, at the northwest corner of the castle ramparts, Queen Victoria gazed across a balustrade which bears her initials. To the west, behind a broad lush plain, are the Campsie Fells and then, from west to north, Ben Lomond, Ben Venue, Ben Ledi and Ben Vorlich. To the northeast are the Ochils, and, much closer, the Wallace Monument and Cambuskenneth Abbey. A statue of Robert Bruce stands on the Esplanade and Queen Mary's lookout carries the inscription MR 1561.

Youth hostellers can expect a treat in Stirling. Their home is **Argyle's Lodging**, Scotland's choicest renaissance mansion which stands just before the castle esplanade. It dates from 1630 and was built by the Earl of Stirling, the founder of Nova Scotia. Further down the hill is **Mar's Wark**, an unfinished renaissance palace which was started about half a century before the Argyle Lodging. Some say that the Earl of Mar reduced nearby Cambuskenneth Abbey to ruins in order to obtain building stones for this palace which was to have been his town house.

Note the Royal Arms and several curious inscriptions above the entrance. Behind this is the 15th century **Church of the Holy Rude** where Mary Queen of Scots and James VI were crowned when babies. The oak roof over the nave is from the early 15th century and the 90-ft (27-metre) square battlement bears scars of a siege held in 1651. Observe, too, the five-sided apse from early in the 16th century.

Broad Street, known as the "Top of the Town", has many buildings of architectural and historic interest. These include the **Smith Institute** with its col-

Stirling Castle.

lection of Scottish folk material, mainly of Mary, and the handsome early 18th-century **Tolbooth** capped with a Dutch-like roof. A footbridge across the River Forth, about a mile due east from the town centre, immediately leads to the remains of **Cambuskenneth Abbey**, from where superb views across the Forth Valley can be enjoyed. (Alternatively, follow the A9 out of town to Causewayhead and then the signposts on the A91.)

This, one of Scotland's most important abbeys, was founded, probably by David I in 1147 and colonised by the Augustinians. Only the west doorway and the free-standing belfry survive. The latter, an extremely impressive three-storey structure, is one of Scotland's greatest Gothic campaniles. James III and his Queen were buried in front of the abbey's high altar. A monument to their memory was unveiled by Queen Victoria in 1864.

The route to Cambuskenneth Abbey also leads, after about 2 miles (3 km) to the beckoning Wallace Monument which commemorates the Battle of Stirling. En route, on the left, is the **Old Bridge** from about 1400 which was blown up in 1745 to prevent the Highlanders reaching the south. The **Wallace Monument** rises from a courtyard, in wooded country, on 362-ft (109-metre) Abbey Craig. A statue of Wallace surmounts the door and inside are marble busts of famous Scots, including Bruce, Burns, Adam Smith and Sir Walter Scott.

Also on view is Wallace's two-handed sword: the only snag is that experts claim that such swords were not used until the late 15th century. The vistas which reward those who climb the 246 steps of the square 220-ft (66-metre) tower are immense and include seven battlefields.

Below the monument, around Airthrey Loch, spreads the **University of Stirling**, the youngest of Scotland's six universities. Part of this beautiful campus, which occupies grounds landscaped by a pupil of Capability Brown, is **Airthrey Castle**, designed by Robert Adam. The University's **MacRobert Arts Centre** offers a variety of programmes ranging from opera to folk and jazz throughout the year and is also home of the Stirling Film Theatre.

The **Trossachs**, to the west of Stirling, is an area of remarkable Highland beauty which inspired such literary giants as William and Dorothy Wordsworth and Samuel Coleridge and, above all, Sir Walter Scott. It was Scott's colourful descriptions which attracted the very first tourists, including Queen Victoria, into Highland Scotland and those who are familiar with *The Lady of the Lake*, *Rob Roy* and *Waverley* will feel very much at home here. The glorious landscape is cut by deep glens filled either by foaming rivers or by sparkling clear lochs, each with its own distinctive characteristics.

Gothic masterpiece: For a half- or full-day of magic in the **Trossachs**, leave Stirling on the M9 and travel for 7 miles

Skiing on Loch Erinhead.

(11 km) to **Dunblane** with its small 13th century Gothic **Cathedral** whose west front, with central doorway and lancet windows, was considered by John Ruskin to be a masterpiece of Scottish church architecture. Leave Dunblane on the A820 and, after 5 miles (8 km), cross the bridge over the **River Teith** and enter **Doune**. The bridge was built in 1535 by the former tailor to James IV, reputedly to spite the local ferryman who had refused him passage.

Doune's **Castle**, which occupies a triangular site, protected on two sides by the rivers Teith and Ardoch and on the third by a deep moat, is one of Scotland's most magnificent examples of medieval architecture and was extensively restored in the 1880s. The massive keep gatehouse soars upwards for 95 ft (29 metres) and the main block rises four storeys high. Bonnie Prince Charlie imprisoned captives here and Mary Queen of Scots dined and slept here. Magnificent views can be enjoyed from the castle walls.

Killin, near Callander.

Visit also the **Doune Park Gardens** and the **Doune Motor Museum**, the latter housing an outstanding collection of vintage cars, including Hispano Suiza, Frazer Nash and the world's second oldest Rolls-Royce. Some are in running order and compete in the Doune Hill Climb (some weekends in April, June and September).

Continue due west from Doune on the A84 past **Drumvaich** to reach **Callander** where the rivers Teith and Leny meet in the lee of **Ben Ledi**. The streets of this prosperous Highland gateway, which as early as 1818 Keats found "vexatiously full of visitors", are lined by shops, hotels and bed-and-breakfast establishments.

It would be sinful, time permitting, not to make a short detour on the A84 which climbs northwards from Callander through the **Pass of Leny**, where falls tumble and salmon leap to the south end of **Loch Lubaig**. (The round trip is 12 miles/19 km.)

From Callander, the shapely peak of

Ben Venue acts as a beacon as the A84, which becomes the A821 winds and curves for 6 miles (10 km) along the north bank of **Loch Vennachar** to **Brig O' Turk**, a lovely village which has long attracted artists. Three miles (5 km) further on, turn right at the Y-junction, at the western end of Loch Achray. Drive between **Ben An**, to the north, and **Ben Venue**, to the south, through a short, narrow gorge of rocks and mounds covered with heather and deciduous trees, bog myrtle and fox-gloves to Loch Katrine. This mile-long stretch is the heart of the Trossachs which Scott described so evocatively.

Loch Katrine is 9 miles (14 km) long and 1 mile at its broadest and since 1859 has been one of the chief sources of the water supply of Glasgow. It is best enjoyed during the summer months by a cruise aboard the restored Victorian steamer *Sir Walter Scott,* although those with energy and/or those who are true *aficionados* of Scott will wish to stroll for a mile to the site of the Silver Strand whose view is described in *The Lady of the Lake*. Opposite this point is Ellen's Isle, named for Ellen Douglas, the heroine of the book.

Splendid views: Return to the Y-junction and take the **Duke's Road** (A821) south. This spectacular route climbs and twists through the **Achray Forest** for 6 miles (10 km) to Aberfoyle. Just before the summit, from where there are outstanding views, the **Achray Forest Drive**, 7 miles (11 km) of gravel road open from Easter to September, takes off to the left and touches on four lochans. Immediately before Aberfoyle, situated off to the left, is the **David Marshall Lodge**, another splendid viewpoint and the visitor centre of the **Queen Elizabeth Forest Park**.

Aberfoyle can justly claim to be a major gateway to the Highlands and it was the starting point for the first horse-drawn "coach tours" to the Trossachs which became fashionable after the publication of *The Lady of the Lake*. Here occurred the confrontation between **Loch Katrine.**

Bailie Nicol Jarvie and Rob Roy and here, at the end of the 17th century, the Reverend Kirk, an authority on the supernatural, was spirited away by the fairies.

Those with time will thoroughly enjoy the scenic side-trip to the immediate west on the B829 along the northern shore of **Loch Ard**, the eastern shore of **Loch Chon** and so to a T-junction, 10 miles (16 km) from Aberfoyle. Here, a drive of just a few hundred yards to the north leads to the south shore of **Loch Katrine** and one of the best viewpoints in the Trossachs, while a steep downhill drive of 4 miles (6 km) ends at **Inversnaid** on the eastern shore of Loch Lomond. From here it is but a short walk to **Rob Roy's Cave**. Those pushed for time can return from Aberfoyle to Glasgow on the A81.

A Burns Museum exhibit of Tam o' Shanter.

To proceed onwards with the Trossachs tour take the A81 for 5 miles (8 km) to **Port of Menteith** which stands on the northern shore of the lake of that name (note that this is not a loch but Scotland's only lake). The historically minded will wish to board the ferry for the short voyage to the island of **Inchmahome** and a visit to its priory. Here Robert the Bruce prayed before his epic victory at Bannockburn and here young Mary Queen of Scots played beneath the great walls of the priory.

Continue east on what is now the A873 through the hamlets of **Blairhoyle** and **Ruskie** and the pleasant village of **Thornhill** which lies just to the north of **Flanders Moss**, a National Nature Reserve and a remarkable remnant of the ancient raised peat bog which once covered much of the Forth Valley. Next, 8 miles/13 km from Port of Menteith, comes **Blair Drummond** which boasts Scotland's only safari park; here, lions and tigers roam, sea lions perform, monkeys amuse and a boat ride to Chimp Island excites. A safari bus is available for those without transport. Stirling is just 6 miles (9 km) away, but to visit Blair Drummond at the beginning rather than at the end of a Trossachs safari might prove fatal.

Best start an exploration of the **Burns Country** by visiting Ayr which is 36 miles (58 km) from Glasgow on the A77 or 50 minutes by train from Central Station (two trains an hour). There's quite a spectacular view from the road, a few miles before reaching Ayr, of the **Heads of Ayr** and the wide bay of which it forms the southern extremity.

Ayr, the largest of the Firth of Clyde resorts, has a long beach, many amenities and several places of interest to Burns devotees. The great man's statue stands outside the railway station and in nearby High Street is the **Tam o' Shanter Inn**, immortalised in the poem of the same name. Then there is the still functional **Auld Kirk** (1654–56) where Burns was baptised and the 13th-century **Auld Brig**, a *"poor narrow footpath of a street Where twa wheelbarrows tremble when they meet"*.

Two miles (3 km) beyond Ayr is Alloway with the **Land o' Burns Visitor Centre**. (To commence a Burns tour

here, do not enter Ayr at the roundabout immediately before the town but rather take the road marked **Alloway**.) Close by, the whitewashed, thatched cottage in which Burns was born, is immaculately maintained and furnished in the style of an 18th-century cottage. Adjacent to it is a museum of relics of the poet's life and works.

On the other side of the Visitor Centre is ruined **Alloway Kirk**, which was already a ruin in Burns' time and where his father is buried. This is where the warlocks and witches danced with "auld Nick" in *Tam o' Shanter*. The charming nearby **Auld Brig o' Doon**, which spans the river of that name, is where Tam made his escape from the witches. Looking down on the bridge is the Burns monument, designed as a Grecian temple, and housing a museum.

Kirkoswald, 13 miles (21 km) south of Ayr on the A77, is where Burns was sent to study when he was 16. Many years later he remembered some of the colourful characters he met and included them in *Tam o' Shanter*. The thatched cottage of Souter Johnnie, the village shoemaker and Tam's faithful drinking companion, is now a museum of Burnsiana and can be visited. In the garden at the rear the cobbler, Tam o' Shanter and the innkeeper and his wife are immortalised in stone.

Those who can tear themselves away from their pursuit of Burns will make for magnificent **Culzean Castle** and the country park of that name. The castle – whose Oval Staircase with its two-storeyed colonnaded gallery and the Round Drawing Room are breath-taking – is just a couple of miles north of Kirkoswald but can only be reached by a slightly circuitous route of about 10 miles (16 km) which involves travelling either to the northeast or to the southwest. There's no doubt which route enthusiast golfers will choose: that to the southwest goes through Turnberry.

Nature lovers: Culzean Castle, Robert Adam's masterpiece, is mainly 18th-century and occupies a commanding

Burns Cottage at Alloway.

position above the Firth of Clyde. Clearly visible is **Paddy's Milestone**, the tiny island of **Ailsa Craig**, which owes its sobriquet to the fact that it was the first sight of Scotland seen by Irish immigrants. The extensive grounds at Culzean became Scotland's first countryside park in 1970 and offer many attractions to nature lovers.

From Culzean, start the return trip to Glasgow on either the A7129 or the A77. Five miles (8 km) past Ayr branch right on the A719 and follow the signs to **Tarbolton** (3 miles/5 km) and the 17th-century **Bachelors' Club**, a building which was the home of a village debating society founded by Burns and some of his friends. It was also in Tarbolton in 1779 that Burns, "to give my manners a brush went to a country dancing school" against his father's wishes. Now make south for 1 mile on the B730 and turn left for 5 miles (8 km) on the B743 for Mauchline. En route, stop at the statue of "**Highland Mary**" which marks the spot where Mary Campbell of Auchnamore and Burns parted with an exchange of vows. (Highland Mary returned to Greenock where she died).

It was at **Mauchline** that Burns is said to have met and to have married Jean Armour after she bore him twins. They lived for a while in **Burns House**, now a museum. **Mauchline Churchyard** contains the graves of four of Burns' children and some of his friends. Opposite the Church is **Poosie Nansie's Tavern**, where Burns saw the revels which resulted in his cantata *The Jolly Beggars*. On the outskirts of the town, at the junction of A76 and B744, the **National Burns Tower** stands above Cottage Homes and houses a small museum.

Before turning north to Kilmarnock, some might wish to make a 6-mile (10-km) detour south on the A76 to **Auchinleck** where the diarist James Boswell was born and from where, in 1773, he and Dr Johnson set off on their tour of the Hebrides. Part of the local church is now a Boswell Museum, adjacent to which is the Boswell Mausoleum where

James is buried. The museum also commemorates another son of Auchinleck: William Murdoch, the 18th-century pioneer of gas lighting.

From here it is 13 miles (21 km) north on the A76 to **Kilmarnock** where the first edition (known as the Kilmarnock edition) of Burns' poems was published. The **Burns Monument** in **Kay Park** is a red-sandstone structure surmounted by a tower and contains a museum of Burnsiana. Also worth a visit is **Dean Castle**, which houses a collection of armour, musical instruments and tapestries. The surrounding **Country Park** has a riding centre.

From Kilmarnock, travel on the A71 for 8 miles (13 km) to **Irvine**, the last of Scotland's New Towns and a seaside resort. Here, Burns enthusiasts will make for the **Glasgow Vennel** where, in 1781, Burns lodged and learned the trade of dressing flax. The house is now a museum. The Irvine Burns Club, founded in 1826, claims to be the oldest Burns Club in the world.

Irvine is also the home of the inchoate **Scottish Maritime Museum** which, in addition to shore exhibits, has a number of craft moored alongside, including a Scottish puffer and a former Irvine Harbour tug, which may be visited. The **Magnum Centre**, claiming to be Scotland's largest leisure centre, offers opportunities for indoor curling and lawn bowls as well as more mundane ice-skating and swimming.

Immediately to the north of Irvine, just to the west of the A737, is **Eglinton Park** with its late 18th-century ruined castle. In 1839 an historic jousting tournament was held here in an attempt to revive the ceremony of ancient chivalry; since the late 1980s this has been revived and is now held annually.

Another unusual traditional competition is held on the first Saturday of July in **Kilwinning**, a mile to the north on the A737. Then, the Ancient Society of Archers holds a shoot re-enacting the ancient tradition of "shooting the papingo" which is set on top of the town steeple. Kilwinning claims to be the home of freemasonry in Scotland, the brotherhood having been introduced by European masons who built the 12th-century priory, the fairly extensive remains of which can be seen in the town centre.

Seaside resorts: From Irvine, one can drive south back to Ayr, a distance of 11 miles (18 km) on the A78 passing en route **Prestwick International Airport**. The land between the road and the sea is devoted to golf and is home to some of the finest links in the world. However, rather than taking this route, proceed northwards for 15 miles (24 km) on the A78 to Largs, passing the seaside resorts of **Ardrossan** (ferry for the island of **Arran**) and **Saltcoats**.

In **Largs**, visit the **Skelmorlie Aisle** and the **Pencil Monument**. The former, situated in the Old Burial Ground, is a magnificent renaissance jewel-box mausoleum with a ceiling painted with decorative local views and abstract scenes. The latter commemorates the Battle of

Eating out at Largs.

Largs (1263) at which King Haakon of Norway was defeated and subsequently had to secede to Scotland the Isle of Man and the Hebrides which the Norsemen had held for 400 years.

In the **Kelburn Country Centre**, about 3 miles (5 km) south of Largs, the oldest castle in Scotland to have remained in the hands of the same family stands among extensive wooded slopes. The castle, parts of which date from the 12th century, is the home of the Earl of Glasgow. The 18th century farm buildings form a village square and the grounds offer a wide variety of amusements, including pony trekking and a commando assault course. The glorious gardens have an extraordinary weeping larch, two yew trees more than 1,000 years old and Scotland's largest Monterey pine. (Those with a yen to stay in a baronial castle with a genuine Earl and Countess as hosts can have this wish fulfilled at Kelburne: note that the rates are steep and the hosts prefer parties of between 8 and 16 persons.)

Immediately facing Largs are the islands of **Great and Little Cumbrae**. On the former is the resort of **Millport**, whose cathedral claims to be Europe's smallest. The highest point on the island, at 417 ft (125 metres), is **Glaidstaine**, from where there are outstanding and exhaustive views. From Largs to Glasgow there is a choice between the A78, which hugs the coast until becoming the A8 at Greenock, or the inland A760, then the A737 to Paisley. The former route is 31 miles (50 km) while the latter is 41 miles (66 km).

For a trip to the fertile **Clyde Valley**, lined by garden centres, leave Glasgow by the M8 and at Junction 8 join the A73 which immediately becomes the M74. Leave this at Junction 5 for East Kilbride and drive to the handsome small town of **Bothwell** with its bridge dating to the 14th century. A monument here marks the **Battle of Bothwell Brig** which was fought in 1679 and resulted in the defeat of the Covenanters and five-month imprisonment for 1,200 of them.

Bothwell Castle.

Near the bridge the magnificent red sandstone ruins of **Bothwell Castle** loom beside the River Clyde. This, the best preserved 13th century castle in the land, was repeatedly fought over by the Scots and the English; after Robert Bruce's followers captured it, they knocked part of the impressive east tower into the River Clyde.

From Bothwell, travel to the home of the explorer and missionary David Livingstone in nearby **Blantyre**. He was born in 1813 in a one-room tenement in Shuttle Row, a block of flats built in 1780. The entire block has been beautifully restored and is now the **Livingstone National Memorial and Museum** which vividly traces the life of this remarkable man. An adjacent African Pavilion illustrates modern Africa and a social history museum houses agricultural, cotton spinning and mining exhibits from the district at the time of Livingstone. The great man's statue stands on the tower of the **Livingstone Memorial Church**.

From Blantyre, drive southeast on the A724 through industrial yet historically important **Hamilton**. Mary Queen of Scots rested here after escaping from Loch Leven Castle and in 1651 Cromwell made the town his headquarters. Visit the octagonal **Parish Church** designed by William Adam in front of which stands the pre-Norman **Netherton Cross**, an ancient Christian relic. On the east wall of the churchyard is the famous **Heads Memorial** commemorating four local Covenanters beheaded after a 1666 rising. Of interest are two **museums**, one military, the other local history, emphasising transport.

The **Hamilton Mausoleum** was built in the middle of the 18th century as a crypt for the 10th Duke of Hamilton but its echo, said to be the longest in the world, prevented it ever being used. The original bronze doors, removed and placed inside, have mouldings illustrating Bible stories and are facsimiles of the renowned panels on Ghiberti's doors at the Baptistry in Florence. The Mau-

Left, David Livingstone effigy at Blantyre. Below, Lammermuir Day parade at Lanark.

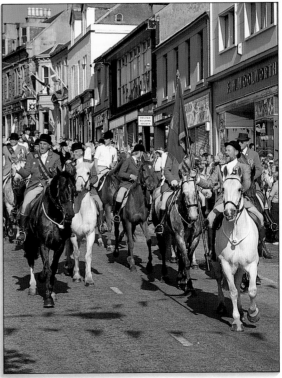

soleum now stands in the **Strathclyde Country Park** which has something for everyone and whose man-made lake is used for international rowing regattas.

Lovingly restored: Look south from the mausoleum to see, at the end of a tree-lined avenue, the **Chatelherault Hunting Lodge** erected in the 1730s at the command of the 5th Duke of Hamilton. Until the late 1980s this building was a ruin but was then lovingly restored. The lodge, which resembles a small French château, was designed by William Adam. The rooms are few but the decoration is quite superb.

The lodge is now the centre of a **Country Park** where one of the attractions is the Cadzow herd of white cattle, believed to be descended from animals introduced by the Romans. Only two herds of these animals exist: the other is in Northumberland. Another attraction is a stand of magnificent oak trees dating from about 1450. The grand avenue of trees which stretched southwards for 2 miles (3 km) to Hamilton Palace has

been replanted with yews and will soon grow again. Not the case, however, with grandiose Hamilton Palace which was destroyed in 1927.

Continue south on the A72 for 8 miles (13 km) to the village of Crossford. Turn right on a minor road which, after about 2 miles (3 km) comes to the tiny villge of **Tillietudlem**. A further 1,000 yards on, a negotiable track leads to 15th-century **Craignethan Castle**, a defensive gem from medieval times which is protected on three sides by cliffs and on the fourth by a moat. This is assumed to be the castle about which Scott wrote in *Old Mortality,* although he said: "I did not think on Craignethan in writing about Tillietudlem (Old Mortality), but there can be no objection in adopting it as that which public taste has adopted as coming nearest to the ideal of the place". Nowhere, in all her travels, did Mary Queen of Scots remain longer than at Craignethan which she visited after her escape from Loch and before her defeat at the Battle of

Grand designs at Chatelherault.

Langside; her ghost, it is said, puts in an occasional appearance.

Back on the A72 continue for 6 miles (10 km) on a delightful road which parallels the River Clyde, which has excellent fishing, to Lanark, 25 miles (40 kms) from Glasgow. Other than on its market day each Monday, **Lanark**, attractive as it is, has little to offer. However, travel from here for about a mile on a clearly signposted, twisting and steeply descending road and, at one's feet, in a wooded gorge through which flows the Clyde, is a handsome, virtually intact 18th-century village.

However, **New Lanark**, the cradle of Scotland's Industrial Revolution and now a World Heritage Centre, is no ordinary village. Once the largest cotton-spinning complex in Britain, it is urban rather than rural; the solid stone, Georgian-style buildings are three and four storeys high and stretch, in some instances, for hundreds of yards. The mills closed in 1968.

It all began in 1785 when David Dale,

utilising the power of the nearby falls of the River Clyde, built cotton spinning mills here. Robert Owen, his son-in-law, became the manager of the mills and village in 1800 and commenced what he asserted, with some justification, was "the most important experiment for the happiness of the human race that has yet been instituted at any time in any part of the world". Owen set up Britain's first infant school, dormitory accommodation for the apprentices, an adult education and social club with the high-falutin' title of "New Institution for the Formation of Character", and a workers' co-operative.

The mill closed in 1968 but strenuous and successful efforts to restore and revitalise it are being made by the New Lanark Association, one of whose founders was Kenneth Dale Owen, a great-great-grandson of Robert. Many of the old mill buildings have been restored as modern houses, shops and craft workshops. One is the **Visitor Centre**, where those interested can learn how Robert Owen's mills, in the days of satanic workshops, were able to marry better working conditions and improved output. To visit New Lanark is a heart-warming experience.

The village dyeworks is now home to a **Scottish Wildlife Centre** which tells the story of the Falls of Clyde and its natural heritage. From here, it is a delightful 30-minute walk along the Clyde to the **Cora Linn Falls** with their 90-ft (27-metre) fall and a viewing platform. A further 30 minutes lead to the **Bonnington Linn Falls**.

For an overview of the route travelled – and, on a clear day, for views as far north as Ben Lomond and the Island of Arran in the Firth of Clyde – drive west of Lanark on the A72 for 5 miles (8 km) and then turn left on the B7108 for about 2 miles (3 km). A secondary road to the left soon climbs to the viewpoint of **Blackhill** (951 ft/285 metres). Tired of the vistas? Then all around are the well-preserved remains of an Iron Age Fort and a Bronze Age Cairn.

New Lanark, cradle of Scotland's Industrial Revolution.

THE WORLD CAPITAL OF GOLF

Glasgow, displaying uncharacteristic modesty, does not style itself the "Golfing Capital of the World", yet it probably deserves the title. Fifty courses lie within the city limits and 90 are within 20 miles (32 km) of its centre. Spread the net wider and within 32 miles (48 km) there are about 150 courses. These range from pleasant, straightforward nine-hole affairs (about 30 courses, which will appeal to the perpetual hacker) to ferocious 18-hole tigers which will challenge the best.

It must be admitted, rather grudgingly, that golf was played in and around Edinburgh before the madness struck Glasgow. However, by 1589, there are reports of the Glasgow Kirk Session prohibiting the playing of the game in Blackfriars Yard. The first eye-witness account in the world of the game is a 1721 poem about golf on Glasgow Green by James Arbuckle, a Glasgow University student. Later, those Glasgow Green players founded the **Glasgow Golf Club** whose Tennant Cup, played for on their course at **Killermont**, 16 miles (24 km) north of the city, is the oldest open amateur tournament in the world.

The simplest way for the visitor to Glasgow to play golf is to make for one or other of the city's eight municipal courses, four of which are 9-hole. **Linn Park** and **Littlehill** get the nod as the best public courses. At the other end of the scale, but still easy to play – not in terms of skill but of logistics (simply pay the green fee) – is **Turnberry**, one of three locations within an hour's drive of Glasgow which has hosted the Open. Turnberry's two courses are quintessential links courses – and it is links courses which the avid golfer must experience on a visit to Glasgow.

(The word links refers to that stretch of land which connects a beach with more stable inshore land, and a links course is that sandy, undulating terrain which borders the shore. A feature of such courses is the ridges and furrows which result in the ball nestling in an infinite variety of lies. Another feature is that the wind which blows off the sea can suddenly whip up with enormous ferocity. A hole which, in the morning, was played with a driver and a 9-iron can, after lunch, demand a driver, long 3-wood and a 6-iron.)

Sixteen miles (25 km) north of Turnberry is **Ayr**, with three parkland courses open to the public. **Belleisle**, from the drawing board of the great James Baird, is considered by many to be the best parkland course in Scotland. Coalescing with Ayr, to the north, is **Prestwick** whose **Prestwick Club (Old Prestwick)** advertised in 1860 "A General Golf Tournament for Scotland". And so began The Open. (A stone cairn commemorates the first tee of the original Championship course.) **Prestwick's St Nicholas** is just as challenging while its flat **St Cuthbert**, a parkland rather than a links course, is that wee bit easier.

From Prestwick 13 miles (21 km) northwards to **Irvine**, there are a dozen superb links courses interrupted by only the occasional field or habitation. An attraction of these Ayrshire courses is that they usually remain playable throughout winter at times when the inland courses are closed because of frost or snow. **Troon**, a short drive (with a wood not in a car) from Prestwick is home of the Royal Troon Club Old course which possesses both the longest and shortest holes on any Open course. Its **Portland** course is somewhat easier. Troon also has three municipal courses of which **Lochgreen** is the most challenging.

Nearer Glasgow – only a couple of miles west of Glasgow Airport – is the **Langbank** public course, which offers magnificent views of the Vale of Leven and Ben Lomond. It is part of the **Gleddoch House Golf and Country Club**, which has an 20-room hotel with a first class restaurant, stables, squash courts and a small swimming pool.

Within, or on the fringe of Glasgow, are the excellent courses of **Haggs Castle**, **Pollok** and **Whitecraigs** to the south of the city, **Sandyhills** to the north and **Bridge of Weir** to the west. Twelve miles (19 km) south of the city is the challenging, windy, moorland **Bonnyton Moor** course, a **Glasgow Jewish Golf Club** which is open to those who are not of the faith. All these are private clubs whose greens are open to *bona fide* members of other clubs. ■

INSIGHT GUIDES
Travel Tips

FOR THOSE
WITH MORE THAN
A PASSING INTEREST
IN TIME...

Before you put your name down for a Patek Philippe watch *fig. 1*, there are a few basic things you might like to know, without knowing exactly whom to ask. In addressing such issues as accuracy, reliability and value for money, we would like to demonstrate why the watch we will make for you will be quite unlike any other watch currently produced.

"Punctuality", Louis XVIII was fond of saying, "is the politeness of kings."

We believe that in the matter of punctuality, we can rise to the occasion by making you a mechanical timepiece that will keep its rendezvous with the Gregorian calendar at the end of every century, omitting the leap-years in 2100, 2200 and 2300 and recording them in 2000 and 2400 *fig. 2*. Nevertheless, such a watch does need the occasional adjustment. Every 3333 years and 122 days you should remember to set it forward one day to the true time of the celestial clock. We suspect, however, that you are simply content to observe the politeness of kings. Be assured, therefore, that when you order your watch, we will be exploring for you the physical—if not the metaphysical—limits of precision.

Does everything have to depend on how much?

Consider, if you will, the motives of collectors who set record prices at auction to acquire a Patek Philippe. They may be paying for rarity, for looks or for micromechanical ingenuity. But we believe that behind each $500,000-plus

bid is the conviction that a Patek Philippe, even if 50 years old or older, can be expected to work perfectly for future generations.

In case your ambitions to own a Patek Philippe are somewhat discouraged by the scale of the sacrifice involved, may we hasten to point out that the watch we will make for you today will certainly be a technical improvement on the Pateks bought at auction? In keeping with our tradition of inventing new mechanical solutions for greater reliability and better time-keeping, we will bring to your watch innovations *fig. 3* inconceivable to our watchmakers who created the supreme wristwatches of 50 years ago *fig. 4*. At the same time, we will of course do our utmost to avoid placing undue strain on your financial resources.

Can it really be mine?

May we turn your thoughts to the day you take delivery of your watch? Sealed within its case is your watchmaker's tribute to the mysterious process of time. He has decorated each wheel with a chamfer carved into its hub and polished into a shining circle. Delicate ribbing flows over the plates and bridges of gold and rare alloys. Millimetric surfaces are bevelled and burnished to exactitudes measured in microns. Rubies are transformed into jewels that triumph over friction. And after many months—or even years—of work, your watchmaker stamps a small badge into the mainbridge of your watch. The Geneva Seal—the highest possible attestation of fine watchmaking *fig. 5*.

Looks that speak of inner grace *fig. 6*.

When you order your watch, you will no doubt like its outward appearance to reflect the harmony and elegance of the movement within. You may therefore find it helpful to know that we are uniquely able to cater for any special decorative needs you might like to express. For example, our engravers will delight in conjuring a subtle play of light and shadow on the gold case-back of one of our rare pocket-watches *fig. 7*. If you bring us your favourite picture, our enamellers will reproduce it in a brilliant miniature of hair-breadth detail *fig. 8*. The perfect execution of a double hobnail pattern on the bezel of a wristwatch is the pride of our casemakers and the satisfaction of our designers, while our chainsmiths will weave for you a rich brocade in gold *figs. 9 & 10*. May we also recommend the artistry of our goldsmiths and the experience of our lapidaries in the selection and setting of the finest gemstones? *figs. 11 & 12*.

How to enjoy your watch before you own it.

As you will appreciate, the very nature of our watches imposes a limit on the number we can make available. (The four Calibre 89 time-pieces we are now making will take up to nine years to complete). We cannot therefore promise instant gratification, but while you look forward to the day on which you take delivery of your Patek Philippe *fig. 13*, you will have the pleasure of reflecting that time is a universal and everlasting commodity, freely available to be enjoyed by all.

Should you require information on any particular Patek Philippe watch, or even on watchmaking in general, we would be delighted to reply to your letter of enquiry. And if you send us

fig. 1: The classic face of Patek Philippe.

fig. 4: Complicated wristwatches circa 1930 (left) and 1990. The golden age of watchmaking will always be with us.

fig. 6: Your pleasure in owning a Patek Philippe is the purpose of those who made it for you.

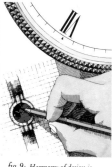

fig. 9: Harmony of design is executed in a work of simplicity and perfection in a lady's Calatrava wristwatch.

fig. 5: The Geneva Seal is awarded only to watches which achieve the standards of horological purity laid down in the laws of Geneva. These rules define the supreme quality of watchmaking.

fig. 7: Arabesques come to life on a gold case-back.

fig. 10: The chainsmith's hands impart strength and delicacy to a tracery of gold.

fig. 2: One of the 33 complications of the Calibre 89 astronomical clock-watch is a satellite wheel that completes one revolution every 400 years.

fig. 11: Circles in gold: symbols of perfection in the making.

fig. 8: An artist working six hours a day takes about four months to complete a miniature in enamel on the case of a pocket-watch.

fig. 12: The test of a master lapidary is his ability to express the splendour of precious gemstones.

fig. 3: Recognized as the most advanced mechanical regulating device to date, Patek Philippe's Gyromax balance wheel demonstrates the equivalence of simplicity and precision.

PATEK PHILIPPE
GENEVE
fig. 13: The discreet sign of those who value their time.

your card marked "book catalogue" we shall post you a catalogue of our publications. Patek Philippe, 41 rue du Rhône, 1204 Geneva, Switzerland, Tel. +41 22/310 03 66.

Reality check. Call home.

—— *AT&T USADirect® and World Connect®. The fast, easy way to call most anywhere.* ——

Take out AT&T Calling Card or your local calling card.** Lift phone. Dial AT&T Access Number for country you're calling from. Connect to English-speaking operator or voice prompt. Reach the States or over 200 countries. Talk. Say goodbye. Hang up. Resume vacation.

Austria*†††.....................022-903-011	Luxembourg..........................0-800-0111	Turkey*...........................00-800-12277
Belgium*.........................0-800-100-10	Netherlands*...................06-022-9111	United Kingdom..............0500-89-0011
Czech Republic*............00-420-00101	Norway..............................800-190-11	
Denmark.........................8001-0010	Poland†♦¹...........0◇010-480-0111	
Finland...........................9800-100-10	Portugal†.........................05017-1-288	
France...............................19-0011	Romania*.....................01-800-4288	
Germany...........................0130-0010	Russia*†(Moscow)................155-5042	
Greece*...........................00-800-1311	Slovak Rep.*...............00-420-00101	
Hungary*....................00◇-800-01111	Spain●...........................900-99-00-11	
Ireland..........................1-800-550-000	Sweden..........................020-795-611	
Italy*.................................172-1011	Switzerland*.....................155-00-11	

AT&T
Your True Choice

For a free wallet sized card of all AT&T Access Numbers, call: 1-800-241-5555.

Getting Acquainted

NOTE: Unless a separate exchange code is shown, all telephone numbers are for Glasgow (UK trunk dialling code 0141, international 44-141).

Geography & Population

Glasgow straddles the River Clyde, 14 miles (22 km) upstream from its estuary at Dumbarton (Strathclyde's ancient capital) and is at 55 degrees 51 minutes north, 4 degrees 17 minutes west. Glasgow proper covers an area of roughly 76 sq. miles (197 sq. km). Its population, like that of most UK cities, has been declining gradually since the 1930s; between 1978 and 1988 it plummeted from 815,000 to 703,000 as people moved out to surrounding areas. The decline has slowed to around 5,000 people a year and the current population is around 680,000.

It is generally believed that the siting of the city was due to the shallows of the Clyde creating a ford with good pastureland on both banks suitable for grazing animals. Walking along the Clyde today, one can see that south of the river it is very flat and that this flatness continues for a short distance onto the north bank. Looking further north and to the northwest, the horizon changes and is broken by a multitude of irregular oval-shaped hills known as drumlins. These small hills rise quite sharply to a height of 100 to 250 ft (30 to 75 metres). The Necropolis, at 225 ft (68 metres), is one of the highest.

The steeper slopes of these whalebacked hillocks face northwest and gentler banks point southeast, indicating the direction of the glacial advance through the valley. The Victorians tailored many of their handsome terraces around these slopes: an impressive example is the Park Conservation Area on Woodlands Hill.

By the late 19th century Glasgow had become the second city of the British Empire, with a population of over one million. This burgeoning population was in part the result of the Irish potato famines of the 1840s and the rapid depopulation of Scotland's highlands and islands. The city fathers fought hard to overcome the deprivations within the town but it is only within the past decade that inner city renewal has begun in earnest.

As recently as 1985, one-third of Glasgow's occupied housing stock was found to be unsatisfactory, many dwellings lacking baths or wash-hand basins, and there is still a shortage of good-quality council houses. Dampness is the most persistent problem. Around 52 percent of the city's dwellings are owned by the local authority and another 33 percent are owner-occupied; the remainder are rented privately or from housing associations.

As manufacturing has declined, service industries now form the core of the city's economy (74 percent of employment). However, there is still a lot of leeway to make up: in 1996, more than 50,000 residents were registered as unemployed (more than 15 percent of the total workforce).

Government & Economy

Scotland became part of the United Kingdom after the Act of Union with England in 1707. It retains its own legal system and national church, while the educational system, although different from the English, has been undergoing several reforms instigated by the central government in London. Since 1959, Scotland has returned a majority of Labour Party MPs to the Westminster parliament.

The Secretary of State for Scotland, a member of the Cabinet, is responsible to Parliament for the Departments of Home and Health, Education, Agriculture and Fisheries, plus Economic Planning and Development. The Scottish Office has its administrative headquarters in Edinburgh in New St Andrew's House.

Local government of Glasgow is by run by two elected councils: Glasgow District Council and Strathclyde Regional Council. The latter deals with education, planning, environment (including roads) and the police and fire services. The Region is very large, administering six sub-regions, stretching from Argyll to the Ayrshire coast and back into central Scotland. The District Council is responsible for housing, recreation and sanitation within the city; it has its headquarters at the City Chambers in the heart of Glasgow.

Throughout the centuries, Glasgow's economy has had a strong mercantile base. In the 18th century the city traded in tobacco, sugar and cotton and continued to do so into the 1800s. As the Clyde was widened and deepened, heavier industries such as shipbuilding became established. But they began to falter shortly before World War II and never really recovered. Light industry continues and the city is a burgeoning commercial centre. Tourism looks set to become a major growth area.

The resurgence of energy and wealth within the city is most visible in some of those areas which suffered from neglect and decay. Parts of the docks and the Merchant City are prime examples of this phenomenon and now provide scores of luxury dwellings for young urban professionals.

Time Zones

Scotland, like the rest of the UK, follows Greenwich Mean Time (GMT). In late March the clocks go forward one hour for British summer time and in late October are moved back to GMT.

Climate

George Square and the City Chambers lie closer to the Arctic Circle than Red Square and the Kremlin in Moscow. Fortunately, Glasgow has a milder climate than that experienced in Russia because of the city's proximity to the Atlantic with its warm currents.

There are no extreme temperature changes. Winters are generally mild (the mercury seldom falls much below zero) and summers cool with the mercury hovering in the mid-60s (F) or around 20°C. The city usually has less than 40 inches (100 cm) of rain a year. The most pleasant time to visit is May through September. In the summer the days are long with sunrise being as early as 5.30am and night not falling until after l0pm.

Culture & Customs

Glasgow has a history steeped in culture and learning and is the home of the second oldest university in Scotland. Even during its most impoverished times it continued to open magnificent galleries and concert halls, often finding funds from private individuals. There has always been a tremendous driving force behind theatre, music and art which has continued throughout this century.

Dr James Bridie, a man determined that Scottish writing and acting should have a venue of its own, created the Citizens' Theatre. Today, its directors and actors have established its international reputation on the basis of a wide selection of works ranging from Shakespeare to Pinter.

Music is well represented with two symphony orchestras, several chamber music groups and choirs and Scottish Opera. In addition, the city is the home of the Scottish Ballet. Contemporary visual arts are strengthening as the city continues to produce and to attract talented young people.

Language

A book could be written about the Glasgow vernacular – and indeed, an excellent one exists, written by Michael Munro (see *Further Reading*). Glaswegian is an infectious dialect which gives an excellent insight to the Glaswegian personality with its warmth tempered by aggression and black humour.

Planning The Trip

What To Wear

Unfortunately, not infrequent rain calls for raincoats and umbrellas. It is always a good idea to carry some warm clothing – just in case. Glaswegians appear to be impervious to the vagaries of the weather, preferring to look fashionable, come what may. Formal dress is a rarity, even in the smartest places.

Entry Regulations
Visas & Passports

An integral part of the UK, Scotland has the same passport and visa requirements as the rest of Britain. There is no border check of any kind for visitors travelling between England and Scotland. Enquiries should be made to the relevant embassy.

Customs

There are no restrictions on the amount of British or foreign currency you can bring into the country.

Following the introduction of the European Union's Single Market in 1993 there are no longer any official restrictions on the movement of goods within the community, provided those goods were purchased within the EU. However, British Customs have set the following "guide levels" on the following: cigarettes 800 pieces; cigarillos 400 pieces; cigars 200 pieces; tobacco 1kg; spirits 10 litres; fortified wines etc 20 litres; wine 90 litres and beer 110 litres. EU nationals no longer need to exit through a red or green channel.

Travellers from further afield are subject to the following allowances: 1 litre of spirits, or 2 litres of fortified or sparkling wine, or 2 litres of table wine (an additional 2 litres of still wine if no spirits are purchased); plus 200 cigarettes or 100 cigarillos, or 30 cigars, or 250g of tobacco; plus 60cc perfume, 250cc toilet water.

Any queries should be made to Customs and Excise at 21 India Street, Glasgow (tel: 221 3828).

Animal Quarantine

For full details of regulations and kennels in the UK, contact Animal Health Office, Crown Building, 1 Barrack Street, Hamilton, Scotland (tel: 01698-286666). Birds and mammals will normally be quarantined for six months, during which time regular visits to pets can be arranged.

Health

European Union nationals qualify for free medical care; for others, medical insurance is advisable. Everyone is entitled to free emergency treatment at a hospital casualty department.

Money

Scotland shares a common currency with the UK. Each Scottish bank issues its own notes, but English banknotes are perfectly acceptable. The £1 note has been retained in Scotland and is much more common here than the English £1 coin. City centre banks have bureaux de change, and all banks cash travellers cheques.

Banks are open Monday–Friday 9.30am–12.30pm and 1.30–4pm with city centre banks staying open at lunchtime. Thomas Cook at Glasgow Airport (tel: 887 7220) offers a limited banking service seven days a week 8am–8pm.

For those wishing to change money outside banking hours, the following are open on Saturday: Thomas Cook, 15 Gordon Street, G1, tel: 221 5522, 9am–4.30pm; American Express, 115 Hope Street, G2, tel: 226 3077, 9am–noon.; Greater Glasgow Tourist Board & Convention Bureau, 35 St. Vincent Place, G1, tel: 204 4400.

A number of foreign banks, other than English, have offices in Glasgow. These include:

Bank of China, 450 Sauchiehall Street, G2. tel: 332 3354.
Bank of India Ltd., 142a St. Vincent Street,G2. tel: 221 4153.
Bank of Ireland, 19 St. Vincent Street, G1. tel: 221 9353.
Habib Bank, A.G. Zurich, 52 Oswald Street, Gl. tel: 204 2197.
Habib Bank Ltd., 141 Norfolk Street, G15. tel: 420 1319.

Public Holidays

Local, public and bank holidays can be frustrating for visitors, but generally there will usually be a small shop open somewhere, during the major public holidays such as 25 and 26 December and 1 and 2 January. Glasgow's annual holiday, known as the Glasgow Fair, starts on the Saturday after the second Monday in July and lasts for two weeks. This is an excellent time to visit the city because it empties as quickly as an uncorked whisky bottle, making parking almost enjoyable.

By Air

Glasgow Airport is situated 8 miles (13 km) west of the city centre alongside the M8 motorway at Junction 28. It was designed in the early 1960s by Sir Basil Spence, who is perhaps better known for his less successful flats in the Gorbals. In 1989, the airport began expanding its facilities in anticipation of a big increase in air traffic in the 1990s.

British Airways runs an almost hourly "Shuttle" service between London (Heathrow) and Glasgow Monday–Friday with the first flight at 7.15am and the last at 8.15pm; you can buy tickets for a guaranteed seat up to 20 minutes before scheduled departure time. There is a slightly reduced service at the weekends. British Midland flies every two hours between London (Heathrow) and Glasgow Monday–Friday and Sunday, flights starting at 7.10am and ending at 9pm. Again, expect slightly fewer flights at weekends. Currently, there is little difference between the summer (March–October) and winter (October–March) schedules of either company, but this may change.

The one-way economy fare can be £67 or £87, depending on when you book. When traffic is light, it's worth buying a standby ticket, which can cost less than £50.

Air UK flies regularly between London (Gatwick) and Glasgow, and London (Stanstead) and Glasgow.

There are also flights between Glasgow and Birmingham (British Airways), Glasgow and Manchester (British Airways and Loganair), Glasgow and Leeds/Bradford (Capital Airlines), Glasgow and the East Midlands (British Midland). Loganair and British Airways serve the islands and highlands of Scotland while Air UK flies to the Channel Islands and Manx Airlines to the Isle of Man.

Although there are a fair number of direct flights from Glasgow to Europe, few are non-stop. Among the latter are BA and Air France to Paris: Lufthansa to Dusseldorf: SAS to Copenhagen and Stavanger; Air UK to Amsterdam; Scottish European Airways to Frankfurt; Aer Lingus, SAS and Air Ryan (summer service only) to Dublin and Iceland Air to Copenhagen, Iceland and the Faroe Islands. British Airways has direct flights (not non-stop) to Dusseldorf, Frankfurt, Munster, Hanover and Munich and both Scottish European Airways and Sabena have direct flights to Brussels.

A coach service runs between Glasgow Airport and Anderston and Buchanan Bus Stations. It departs every half hour during the day and takes about 25 minutes. For enquiries, telephone Citylink at 332 9191. Taxis are available outside the airport. The journey should take about 20 minutes and costs £10 plus tip.

Useful addresses and telephone numbers for reservations and enquiries are:

Aer Lingus, 19 Dixon Street, G1. tel: 248 4341.
British Airways, Atrium House, 50 Waterloo Street, G1, tel: 0345 222111.
British Midland, Merlin House, Mossland Road, Hillington, G52, tel: 0345 554554.
Loganair, Glasgow Airport. tel: 889 1311.
Lufthansa, 78 St. Vincent Street, Gl. tel: 0345 737747.
Manx Airlines, tel: 0345 256256.
Scandinavian Airlines, tel: 0345 090900.
Sabena World Airlines, Glasgow Airport. tel: 848 4766.

Also:
American Airlines, Glasgow Airport, tel: 848 7788.
Qantas Airways, 39 St. Vincent Place, G1. tel: 226 3955.
Singapore Airlines Ltd., 7 Nelson Mandela Place, G2. tel: 2040656.
South African Airways, tel: 221 0015.
Air UK, 177 West George Street, G2, tel: 248 8888.

Prestwick Airport is 40 minutes or so south of Glasgow. Northwest Airlines flies from here to New York and Boston and Air Canada flies from here to Toronto, Halifax, Vancouver and Calgary.

There are several reliable methods of transport between Glasgow and Prestwick. Buses are normally laid on to meet incoming flights, taking passengers to Glasgow's Buchanan Bus Street Station in just under one hour. In addition, Citylink, tel: 332 9191, runs an hourly service to Buchanan Street Bus Station. Alternatively, Prest-wick Railway Station is five minutes away and a free minibus service runs between the airport and the station. The train arrives at Glasgow's Central Station, taking 45 minutes. When travelling from Central Station to Prestwick Station, use the Freephone at Central to request the minibus facility on your arrival. Taxis are available outside the airport. The journey to Glasgow will take about one hour and costs around £30.

Useful addresses and telephone numbers for reservations and enquiries are:

General Enquiries: Prestwick Airport. tel: 01292 479822.
Air Canada, 45 West Nile Street. G1. tel: 226 5884.
Northwest Airlines, 38 Renfield Street, G2. tel: 226 4175.

By Rail

Glasgow, one of the main cities within British Rail's network, has two busy stations: Central, for trains heading for destinations to the south (including London) and Queen Street, for the northern towns, the Highlands and Edinburgh. (The West Highland Line is a route of renowned beauty, passing through some of the country's finest scenery.)

Trains from Glasgow Central (tel: 204 2844) arrive at London Euston (tel: 0171-387 7070) after 5½ hours. The first train for Euston leaves Glasgow Monday–Saturday 6.30am, the last at 11.50pm. Euston to Glasgow service: Monday–Friday starts at 7.20am, ending 11.50pm. This service is considerably reduced on Sundays, with the journey taking seven hours and even longer.

24-hour passenger enquiries, tel: 204 2844.
Sleeper Reservations (Monday–Saturday 7.00–22.00, Sunday 8.00–22.00), tel: 221 2305.
Motorail Reservations, tel: 204 2844.

By Road

During the early 1960s, as part of a fiercely criticised communications policy, Glasgow pushed an inner ring road through the heart of the city, destroying many splendid buildings. Charing Cross, once an imposing area of almost Continental elegance, now stands as a testament to 20th-century road engineering. This "channel of noise and smell", as the new road was described by many, must today be acknowledged as a excellent piece of planning and a necessary evil.

Glasgow would never claim that mistakes have not been made during its long and chequered history – it has frequently learned the hard way – but it is in part thanks to these past errors that its inner city renewal programme is the envy of many other cities. From the south, Glasgow is approached by the M74, which is the continuation of the M6. Edinburgh and Glasgow are linked by the M8, and the A82 carries traffic to and from the west coast.

By Bus

Scottish Citylink (tel: 332 9191) runs daily coaches between London's Victoria Coach Station and Glasgow's Buchanan Street Bus Station. Stagecoach (tel: 332 4100) and Red Knight (tel: 332 8100) also run frequent coaches between Buchanan Street and London's King's Cross. The journey takes between 7½ and 8½ hours depending on the number of stops made en route (check Express services at time of booking).

Porter Services

Porters are like gold dust at Central and Queen Street Railway Stations but they do exist. To be certain of help for disabled or infirm travellers, telephone the Station Assistant beforehand at Central (tel: 335 4352) or Queen Street (tel: 332 9811). At Glasgow Airport there are usually lots of grey-uniformed porters, but if you have any difficulty finding one, ask at the Information Desk on the first floor. Neither airport nor railway porters charge, but tipping, although not mandatory, is customary.

Disabled

For information on disabled facilities within the city, telephone **Forum on Disability**, 227 6125.

Gays

Lesbian and Gay switchboard 7pm–10pm tel: 221 8372.

Useful Addresses

Tourist Information

Greater Glasgow Tourist Board and Convention Bureau, 35 St Vincent Place, Glasgow G1 2ER, tel: 204 4400.

Strathclyde Transport Travel Centre, St Enoch Square, tel: 226 4826.

Tourist Information Desk, Glasgow Airport, tel: 848 4440.

Consulates

Brazilian Consulate, 25 Broomvale Drive, G77, tel: 616 0300.

Canadian Consul, 151 St Vincent Street G2. tel: 221 4415.

Costa Rican Consul, 18 Woodside Crescent G3. tel: 332 9755.

Cypriot Consul, 58 West Regent Street G2. tel: 332 7733.

Danish Consulate, 59 Waterloo Street G2, tel: 204 2209.

German Consulate, 158 West Regent Street, G2, tel: 221 0304.

Greek Consulate, 98 Bardonald Drive G12. tel: 334 0360.

Icelandic Consulate, 389 Argyle Street, G2. tel: 221 6943.

Italian Vice-Consulate, 170 Hope Street G2. tel: 332 4297.

Norwegian Consulate, 140 Hope Street G2. tel: 204 1353.

Pakistan Vice-Consulate, 137 Norfolk Street, G5, tel: 429 5335.

Peruvian Consulate, 211 Nithsdale Road G41. tel: 423 7214.

South African Consulate-General, 69 Nelson Mandela Place G2. tel: 221 3114.

Spanish Consulate, 389 Argyle Street. tel: 221 6943.

Swedish Vice-Consul, 36 Washington Street, G3, tel: 221 7845.

Swiss Consulate, 4 Victoria Crescent, Clarkston. tel: 644 1645.

Thai Consulate, 70 Wellington Street G2. tel: 248 6677.

Tunisian Consulate, 50 Peel Road, G74, tel: 644 3964.

The following countries have consulates in Edinburgh:

American Consulate General, 3 Regent Terrace, EH7. 0131-556 8315.

Australian Consulate, Hobart House, 80 Hanover Street, EH2. 0131-226 6271.

Austrian Consulate, 33–34 Charlotte Square, EH2. 0131-225 1516.

Practical Tips

Most offices are open Monday–Friday 9am–5 or 5.30pm and may be closed between 1 and 2pm.

The main Sunday church services are at 11am Many churches also hold a Sunday evening service.

Church of Scotland, St George's Tron Church, 165 Buchanan Street, G1, tel: 221 2141.

Episcopal Church of Scotland, Diocese of Glasgow, 5 St Vincent Place, G1, tel: 221 5720.

Catholic Church, Archdiocesian Office, 196 Clyde Street, G1, tel: 226 5898.

Church of Jesus Christ of Latter Day Saints, Julian Avenue, G12, tel: 357 1024.

Jewish Orthodox Synagogue, Garnethill, 29 Garnet Street, G3 tel: 332 4151.

The Central Mosque, Adelphi Street, G5 tel: 429 3132.

First Church of Christ Scientist, 87 Berkeley Street, G3, tel: 248 1698.

The *Herald*, published in Glasgow since 1783, provides sound coverage of national, international and financial news. Its east coast rival, *The Scotsman*, also a quality daily, has a slightly lower circulation. The *Evening Times*, the *Herald*'s sister paper, covers local news.

The *Daily Record*, part of the Mirror Group, is the most widely read Scottish tabloid, now finding itself in a circulation battle with the local edition of Rupert Murdoch's *Sun*, at the opposite end of the political spectrum. All the London-based national newspapers are readily available.

Scotland on Sunday is the country's only quality Sunday paper.

Scotland also produces a variety of business and literary magazines, along with a fair number of glossy freesheets which can be found in the smaller, upmarket shops throughout the city.

It remains a source of debate why Scotland, whose people are so politically aware, cannot sustain its own political weekly. However, the *Scottish Field* and the *Scots Magazine* are good-quality monthly magazines which deal with Scottish topics. *The List*, an Edinburgh-based listings magazine, provides comprehensive coverage of Glasgow events.

Radio & TV

BBC Radio Scotland (FM 92.5–94.6 MW 810kHz/370m) is a national network with news and talk programmes. Radio Clyde (FM 102.5 MW 1152kHz/261m) is the local commercial station. BBC Scotland and Scottish Television (STV) are the two television stations based in the city. Most of their output is a relay of the national BBC1 and ITV networks, but they substitute a few hours each day of Scottish news, features and drama.

Postal Services

The Head Post Office is in George Square, in the centre of town. It is open Monday–Friday 9am–5.30pm and Saturday 9am–12.30pm. Other city centre Post Offices are at 85–89 Bothwell Street G2, 216 Hope Street G2 and 533 Sauchiehall Street G3. Some Post Offices are housed within newsagents and open at slightly different times, with some closing for lunch and remaining closed on Wednesday afternoons. For information on services, tel: 0345 740740.

Telecoms

The traditional red telephone box has been almost replaced by modern glass booths. There are two types, one operated by coins (£1, 50p, 20p and 10p) the other by Phonecards which can be purchased from newsagents and Post Offices. Phone boxes are scattered throughout the city, and there are several inside the Post Office building at George Square. To enquire about BT services call 0800-289179. To call the operator, dial 100; Directory Enquiries,

192; Telephone Repair Service, 151; Talking Clock, 123.

Telex/Fax

Phone 0171-492 7111 to send a telex anywhere in the world. It is a 24-hour service and can be very busy during business hours.

George Square Post Office, tel: 242 4176, has a fax machine available for public use. Fax machines can often be found in city-centre photocopying shops.

Weights & Measures

Britain's shelves are filled with goods which state both imperial and metric weights, but the metric system is officially the correct one. Milk and beer come in pints and half-pints; fruit, vegetables, cheese etc. continue to be sold in pounds and ounces. Road signs give distances in miles.

Electricity

240 volts is standard. Hotels will usually have dual 110/240 volt sockets for razors.

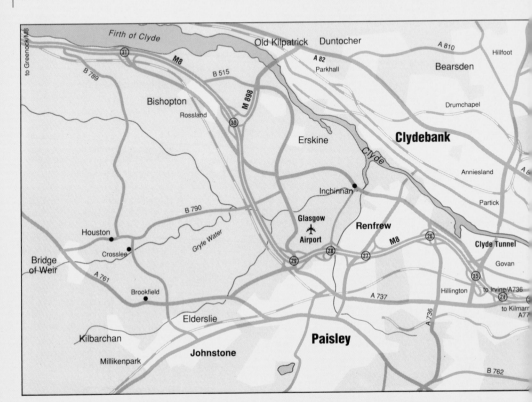

Security & Crime

In emergencies, dial 999. No money is required to make a 999 call from a phone box; dial, and ask for either the Fire, Police or Ambulance service. For non-urgent enquiries contact the nearest Police Station: City Centre, Cranstonhill Police Station, 945 Argyle Street, tel: 532 3200; West, Stewart Street, Cowcaddens, tel: 532 3000; North, Baird Street, tel: 532 4100; East, London Road, tel: 532 4600; South, Craigie Street, tel: 423 1113.

Medical Services

There are several 24-hour Accident and Emergency hospitals in the city: Glasgow Royal Infirmary, 82–84 Castle Street, tel: 211 4000; Royal Hospital for Sick Children, Yorkhill (close to the Kelvin Hall), tel: 201 0000; Western Infirmary, Dumbarton Road, tel: 211 2000. At the emergency clinic at the Dental Hospital, 378 Sauchiehall Street, tel: 211 9600, hours are Monday–Friday 9–10.30am and 2–3.30 pm, Sunday 10.30–noon; there is a charge for treatment on Sundays.

Getting Around

Orientation

Because Glasgow is built on so many hills, it is sometimes difficult to appreciate its area and wealth of architecture on foot. Yet walking is the best (if the most tiring) method of exploring. Do remember to lift your eyes occasionally from the hazards of the street to glance upwards at the wide range of Victorian building design and craftsmanship. Alternatively, for £1.60, unlimited travel for a day can be purchased on the city's underground railway, along with a small, informative booklet outlining 17 walks around the city tracing the history of the town through its buildings – ask for the Heritage Trail.

On a clear Friday afternoon, head for the University of Glasgow's Tower, which affords spectacular views of the city and surrounding areas. Telephone 339 8855 to confirm that the Tower is open; normally it opens on the first Friday in May and closes on the last Friday in September, with guided parties leaving at 2pm sharp.

Left Luggage

There are two Left Luggage offices in Glasgow. One is situated at Central Station, tel: 335 4362, open Monday–Friday 6.30am–11pm and 7.30am–11pm on Saturday and Sunday. The other is at Queen Street Station, tel: 335 3256, open Monday–Saturday 7am–10pm. Sunday 10am–6pm.

Public Transport

By Bus

Two main bus companies operate within the city centre: **Strathclyde Transport** (vivid orange), and **Kelvin Central** (blue-and-yellow). Kelvin Central has increased its fleet by introducing old London buses in order to oper-

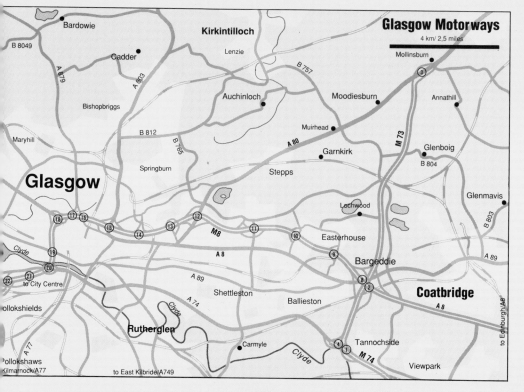

ate on as many routes as possible. Both companies tend to use the same bus-stops and cover most of the city with frequent services (running every 10–15 mins. until about 11pm when the much reduced Night Service operates). For information on these services, visit the **Travel Centre** at St Enoch Square, open Monday–Saturday 9.30am–7.30pm or telephone 226 4826 Monday–Saturday 7am–9pm; Sunday 9am.–7.30pm.

By Underground

Glasgow has a small, 15-stop underground, known locally as the Clockwork Orange (its coaches are the same lurid colour as the Strathclyde buses). It is an excellent way to get around the city on a wet day, costing 60p regardless of the number of stops. It operates Monday–Saturday from 6.30am–10 or 10.30pm and on Sunday between 11am and 6pm. Trains run every 4–6 minutes at busy times, with 8-minute intervals during evenings and on Sundays.

A Heritage Trail ticket (with accompanying leaflet), permits one day's unlimited travel on the system.

The original cable-operated Subway was first opened on 14 December 1896, though it closed again the same day after a collision under the River Clyde; it re-opened five weeks later. The loss-making company was bought by Glasgow Corporation in 1922. The last train was hauled by cable in 1935, when a full electric service began. In 1977 the dilapidated system was shut down for modernisation; the new Underground was inaugurated by the Queen on 1 November 1979.

The total length of the system is 6½ miles (10.4 km) and the track gauge is an exceptionally narrow 4 ft (1.22 metres). Around 14 million passenger journeys are made each year. The deepest station is Buchanan Street and the shallowest Cessnock. The maximum speed of the cars is 34 mph (54 kph).

By Taxi

Glasgow has 1,400 taxis. Unless it is pouring with rain, when demand exceeds supply, the black taxi cab is fairly easy to flag down. They run 24 hours a day and can be picked up from the taxi ranks outside Central Station, Queen Street Station and the two bus stations, at Anderston Cross and Buchanan Street. They may also be found on the following roads: Cambridge Street, Holland Street and Queen Margaret Drive (Great Western Road end).

The fare is displayed on the metre next to the driver. There is an extra late-night charge and normally a surcharge if the taxi is to travel to a destination beyond the city boundary. If travelling beyond the city limits it is prudent to obtain an estimate before setting off.

TOA Radio Taxis, tel: 332 7070; Glasgow Radio Taxis, tel: 332 6666; Glasgow Wide Taxis, tel: 429 2900.

Private Transport
By Car

CAR HIRE

There is a wide variety of self-drive van and car hire companies: Hertz, 106 Waterloo Street, tel: 248 7736; Mitchells Car Hire, Multi-Storey Car Park, Mitchell Street G1, tel: 221 8461; Mitchells Van Hire, 47 McAlpine Street (opposite Anderston Bus Station), G2, tel: 248 4981; Avis, 161 North Street G3, tel: 221 2827; Arnold Clark, 10 Vinicombe Street, G12, tel: 334 9501; Europcar, 556 Pollokshaws Road, G4l, tel: 423 5661; Eurodollar Rent-A-Car, Terminal Building, Glasgow Airport, tel: 887 7915; Budget, 101 Waterloo Street, G2, tel: 226 4141.

The following chauffeur-driven car hire companies also offer experienced guides: Kingston Chauffeur Drive, 197 Reid Street, G40. tel: 554 6066. Little's Chauffeur Drive, 1282 Paisley Road West, G52. tel: 883 2111.

PARKING

Parking meters are used extensively throughout the city centre and take 20p coins. There are 24-hour multi-storey car parks at Anderston Cross, Cambridge Street, George Street, Mitchell Street, Oswald Street and Waterloo Street.

Where to Stay

Hotels

Accommodation can be booked in advance by contacting individual hotels or the Accommodation Reservations Department, Greater Glasgow Tourist Board & Convention Centre, 35 St Vincent Place, Glasgow G1, tel: 204 4400. Rooms can be booked in person at the above address which is open May–September Monday–Saturday 9am–9pm, October–April Monday–Saturday 9am–6pm. There is also an accommodation booking service at Glasgow Airport which is open all year 9am–9pm. Or ask for a copy of the current edition of Greater Glasgow's *Where to Stay* which lists hotels, guest houses, self-catering accommodation and camp sites in and around the city; obtainable from Tourist Offices.

Those who are intending to stay in the city for any length of time should book before arriving as Glasgow lacks reasonably priced accommodation within the city centre, a fact which first became apparent during the 1988 Garden Festival.

Scottish Tourist Board (STB) approved accommodation displays a sign bearing the word "listed" or one to five crowns to denote the facilities such as en suite bathrooms, television and central heating. In addition the STB grades accommodation into three categories: Approved, Commended or Highly Commended. This grading gives an idea of the quality of service and comfort. Approximate guide to prices per person per night in a double room: $ = below £40; $$ = £40–£65; $$$ = £65+.

Babbity Bowster, 16–18 Blackfriars Street, tel: 552 5055. Six rooms. This small hotel, more renowned for its food than its accommodation and very popular with the media, occupies a listed building in the Merchant City. $.

Central, Gordon Street, tel: 221 9680. 168 rooms. This, part of Central Station, is Glasgow's oldest hotel. During the 1980s it enjoyed a face-lift in an attempt to return it to former glories. Rooms vary in size and facilities; you might wish to view room before unpacking. $$.

Copthorne, George Square, tel: 332 6711. 138 rooms. Situated in the heart of George Square next door to Queen Street station. $$$.

Dalmeny, 62 St Andrews Drive, tel: 427 1106/6288. 10 rooms (not all with private facilities). More of a guest house than a hotel, situated in its own large garden in the south-side of the city, about 3 miles (5 km) from town. $.

Ewington, 132 Queens Drive, tel: 423 1152. 42 rooms. A well-appointed terrace hotel in a leafy street beside Queen's Park and about 2 miles (3 km) from the city centre. $$.

Excelsior, Glasgow Airport, tel: 887 1212. 290 rooms. This Trust House Forte hotel has an unusually large number of single rooms. A courtesy bus runs between hotel and city centre. $$.

Forte Crest, Bothwell Street, tel: 248 2656. 251 rooms. Luxury hotel close to the motorway and the Anderston Bus Station. $$.

Glasgow Moat House, Congress Road, tel: 306 9988. 285 rooms. Glasgow's newest hotel; a skyscraper of reflective glass beside the Clyde and the Scottish Exhibition and Conference Centre. $$$.

Gleddoch House, Langbank, Renfrewshire, tel: 01475 540711. 30 rooms. On leaving the airport turn right rather than left on the motorway and after a couple of miles arrive at this delightful hotel which is part of a country club whose facilities – first-class 18-hole golf course, stables, squash courts and small swimming pool – are available to guests. $$$.

Hospitality Inn, 36 Cambridge Street, tel: 332 3311. 306 rooms. First-class hotel in the heart of the city. $$.

Kelvin Park Lorne, 923 Sauchiehall Street, tel: 334 4891. 98 rooms. Very handy for Kelvingrove Art Gallery, Transport Museum and University of Glasgow. $$.

Kirklee Hotel, 11 Kensington Gate, tel: 334 5555. 9 rooms. Old red sandstone hotel situated in attractive West End residential crescent about a mile from the city centre. $.

MacDonald Thistle, Eastwood Toll, Giffnock, tel: 638 2225. 56 rooms.

Strategically placed hotel on the south-side about 5 miles (8 km) from city centre. $$.

One Devonshire Gardens, 1 Devonshire Gardens, Gt. Western Road, tel: 339 2001. (27 rooms). An exquisite West End hotel in a residential district. Each room is different and the service deluxe old-fashioned. $$$.

Sherbrooke Castle, 11 Sherbrooke Avenue, tel: 427 4227. 25 rooms. A Scottish baronial castle situated in its own grounds in the southside about 3 miles (5 km) from the city centre. Handy for the Burrell and Pollok Country Park. $.

Stakis Grosvenor, Grosvenor Terrace, Gt. Western Road, tel: 339 8811. 93 rooms. Large hotel with striking facade close to the Botanic Gardens, University of Glasgow and trendy Byres Road and to the Hillhead underground. $$$.

Stakis Ingram, Ingram Street, tel: 248 440l. 90 rooms. A stone's throw from George Square. $$.

Swallow, 5l7 Paisley Road West, tel: 427 3146. 119 rooms. Slightly to the southwest of the city and close to the Cessnock underground. $$.

Tinto Firs, 470 Kilmarnock Road, tel: 637 2353. 27 rooms. A *hotel propre* rather than a *hotel meuble* in a quiet, residential district on the southside of the city. Handy for the Burrell and Pollok Country Park. $$.

Wickets, 52 Fortrose Street, tel: 334 9334. 10 rooms. Comfortable and well appointed hotel in the West End. Pleasant situation beside cricket ground. Close to Kelvingrove Art Gallery and Museum and Transport Museum and Kelvin Hall underground. $.

Guest Houses

Most guest houses are in residential areas in the south-side and the West End, about one to 2 miles from the city centre. Those in the city are few and far between and can scarcely be described as quiet. Parking too, can present a problem except for enthusiastic early morning meter feeders. Bed and breakfast per person per night: $ = less than £20; $$ = £20–£30.

Alamo Guest House, 46 Gray Street, tel: 339 2395. Pleasant, quiet road alongside Kelvingrove Park. $.

Chez Nous, 33 Hillhead Street, tel: 334 2977. Close to Glasgow University and Hillhead underground. $.

Iona Guest House, 39 Hillhead Street, tel: 334 2346. Well-established and comfortable: close to the Botanic Gardens. $.

McLays Guest House, 268 Renfrew Street, tel: 332 4796. Well-appointed, comfortable guest house only a few minutes from the city centre. $.

Mrs C. Divers, Kirkland House, 42 St Vincent Crescent, tel: 248 3458. Open all year. In the quieter part of this beautiful crescent. $$.

Mrs R. Easton, 148 Queen's Drive, tel: 423 3143. Open all year. Pleasant situation by Queen's Park. $.

The Town House, 4 Hughenden Terrace, tel: 357 0862. Situated to the west of the city. Well-established and comfortable guest house in a rather handsome listed building. $$.

Self-Catering

Cairncross House, Kelvinhaugh Place, tel: 330 5385. Self-catering in West End halls belonging to Glasgow University. Open summer holidays. From £70 a week for a room sleeping one or two persons.

Forbes Hall, Rottenrow East, tel: 553 4148. Fairly central flats within the University of Strathclyde sleeping four to six: from £220 a week. Open June until September.

Campgrounds

There is a lack of large campsites in and around Glasgow; many are mainly residential with only a few plots to rent, so telephone in advance to check.

Craigendmuir Caravan Park, Campsie View, Stepps, tel: 779 2973. Accommodates caravans, touring caravans and tents. From £5.50 per night. Take the M80 out of town and follow the signs for Stepps.

Tullichewan Caravan Park, Old Luss Road, Balloch, tel: 01389 759475. This is one of the largest sites close to Glasgow; take the turning for Balloch off the A82. From £3.75 for tents and from £5.75 for caravans.

Youth Hostels

The Scottish Youth Hostel Association (12 Renfield Street, tel: 226 3976, information only) runs a Grade 1 hostel at 7 Park Terrace (tel: 332

3004) in the West End. Accommodation in comfortable dormitories, costs £5 a night for an adult. Cooking facilities and a shop are available. You must be a member of the SYHA: a year's membership, purchased at the hostel, costs from £1.40 for five to 15-year-olds, up to £5.15 for an adult. Advance booking is recommended from March until September. The hostel is open all year.

YMCA Hostel, 33 Petershill Drive, tel: 558 6166. This is a mixed hostel. Weekly rates from £235.

Eating Out

Where To Eat

A wide selection of good restaurants, some excellent, can be found in Glasgow and it is possible to eat well, without wine, for under £10. Rough guide to prices for a three-course evening meal excluding wine: $ = under £10; $$ = £10–£20; $$$ = over £20.

Scottish

(These restaurants do not serve only Scottish food.)

Babbity Bowster, 16 Blackfriars Street, tel: 552 5055. Friendly upstairs restaurant serving Scottish food. Renowned for its Burns Night supper. $$.

Rab Ha's, 83 Hutcheson Street, tel: 553 1545. Interesting dishes with fresh fish and game. $$.

International

City Merchant, 97 Candleriggs, tel: 553 1577. Excellent value pre-theatre menu. $. At all times good à la carte. $$. Snacks in downstairs bar for $.

Two Fat Ladies, 88 Dumbarton Road, tel: 339 1944. Bingo addicts will know how this restaurant got its name. Simple new restaurant with excellent food and ambience opened by New Zealand restaurateur. $$.

The Buttery, 652 Argyle Street, tel: 221 8188. Victorian dining room where the staff, fortunately, are not over-attentive. Delicious food but quite expensive. $$$.

The Belfry, 652 Argyle Street, tel: 221 0630. Very comfortable and restful restaurant below The Buttery offering a reasonably priced menu. $$.

One Devonshire Gardens, 1 Devonshire Gardens, Gt. Western Road, tel: 339 2001. Set-price menus in Edwardian style hotel/restaurant. $$$.

The Ubiquitous Chip, 12 Ashton Lane, tel: 334 5007. Attractive covered garden courtyard is part of this restaurant which has an outstanding, competitively priced wine list. $$$.

Fish

The Rogano, 11 Exchange Place, tel: 248 4055. One of the city's oldest restaurants decorated in 1930s Art Deco, giving a slightly austere feel. When the fish is good (other food also served) it is excellent. $$$.

Il Pescatore, 148 Woodlands Road, tel: 333 9239. Small restaurant serving Italian fish dishes. $$.

Jimmy's, 264 Gorbals Street, tel: 420 3652. Major section of a large, well-established pleasant pub converted to fish and chip restaurant (the only food served). $.

Italian

L'Arena Di Verona, 311–313 Hope Street, tel: 332 7728/7203. Excellent, uncomplicated meals in delightful, relaxing atmosphere. Pre-theatre menu, $. A la carte. $$.

La Parmigiana, 447 Great Western Road, tel: 339 8293. Small restaurant with excellent lunch menu. $$.

La Taverna, 7a Lansdowne Crescent, tel: 339 7128. Tasty Italian fare at realistic prices. Lunch a snip at half-price. Dinner $$.

Ristorante la Fiorentina, 2–20 Paisley Road West, Paisley Road Toll, tel: 420 1585. Up-market Italian restaurant south of the river but near the city. $$$.

La Lanterna, 35 Hope Street, tel: 221 9160. Unpretentious Italian restaurant with good food. $$.

Rotunda Pizzeria, 28 Tunnel Street, tel: 204 1238. Slightly expensive pizzeria with an interesting outlook for those who manage to book a window table. $.

The Fire Station, 33 Ingram Street, tel: 552 2929. Friendly staff in large old fire station – pasta a speciality. $. Monday–Friday, 5–7pm pasta dishes at half-price.

Di Maggio's Pizzeria, 61 Ruthven Lane (off Byres Road), tel: 334 6000. One of the better pasta restaurants in town and much favoured by students. $.

Sannino, 61 Bath Street, tel: 332 8025 and 61 Elmbank Street, tel: 332 3565. The largest pizzas in town in a friendly atmosphere. $.

Indian

Café India, 171 North Street, tel: 248 4075. Large restaurant with a pleasant ambience. Extensive wine list. $$.

Koh-i-Noor, 236 North Street, tel: 221 1555. Decor leaves a bit to be desired but staff are pleasant and helpful. $$.

Ashoka Tandoori, 108 Elderslie Street, tel: 221 1761/4763. Excellent sister restaurant of Balbir's Brasserie. Try to sit upstairs, which is not so dark and gloomy as the large room below. $$.

Chinese

Loon Fung, 417 Sauchiehall Street, tel: 332 1240. Cavernous room with pleasant staff and good menu. $$.

Peking Inn, 191 Hope Street, tel: 332 7120. Delightful Cantonese/Pekinese restaurant serving tasty seafood. $$.

Ho Wong, 82 York Street, tel: 221 3550. Slightly more up-market, serving Cantonese dishes. $$.

The Americas

Back Alley, 8 Ruthven Lane (off Byers Road), tel: 334 7165. Enjoy the Alley's classic steaks and burgers in a relaxing environment.

Chimmy Chungas, 499 Great Western Road, tel: 334 0884. Lively Mexican restaurant serving filling dishes. $$.

Metro, Unit 7, Merkland Court, tel: 334 1142. Good value cajun and European fare in basement restaurant. $.

Other Nationalities

Greek Golden Kebab, 34 Sinclair Drive, tel: 649 7581. Eccentric and variable. $.

Kosher Restaurant, 49 Copelaw Street, tel: 423 27ll. Inexpensive, large portions in plain surroundings on the southside of the city. $

Whistler's Mother, 116 Byres Road, tel: 334 2666. Dutch bistro with cosmopolitan foods including tasty, tangy salads. $.

Maxaluna, 410 Sauchiehall Street, tel: 332 1003. *The* eating place for the young and beautiful. Enjoy their Chino-Latino-Americano dishes whilst relishing the bar's wonderful decor. $$

Vegetarian

Many of the bistros/brasseries offer at least one vegetarian dish. Most of the larger restaurants will cater for vegetarians but it is wise to phone beforehand to forewarn them. The following are strictly vegetarian.

Balbir's Vegetarian Ashoka, 141 Elderslie Street, tel: 221 4763. Delicious meals in pleasant, modern atmosphere. $.

The Granary, 82 Howard Street, tel: 226 3770. Comfortable and friendly atmosphere in city centre. Excellent baking. $.

Others

Sloans, Argyll Arcade, tel: 221 8917. An old, pleasant, traditional pub-restaurant serving steak pies, mince, chips and custard. $.

The Chapter House at Pickering & Inglis, 26 Bothwell Street, tel: 221 8913. A bright coffee shop in the rear of a bookshop specialising in religious books. Serves light meals, salads and superb baking. $.

Willow Tearoom, 217 Sauchiehall Street, tel: 332 0521. The only Mackintosh tearoom still functioning. A feast for the eyes and the stomach. Invariably extremely busy at lunch. $.

Bistros/Brasseries

Glasgow has become more continental in its eating habits during the past five years, with numerous places doubling as café/bars during the day and restaurants at night.

Baby Grand, Elmbank Gardens, tel: 248 4942. Crowded café-bar with continental atmosphere and grand piano. $$.

Café Gandolfi, 64 Albion Street, tel: 552 6813. The grandfather of modern Glasgow café life. Tasty dishes but very busy at lunch time. $.

Café Noir and Metro, 151 Queen Street, tel: 248 3525. The Noir is a pleasant café while the Metro serves an international cuisine including cajun and Mexican. $$.

D'Arcy's, Princes Square, Buchanan Street, tel: 226 4039. See and be seen by everyone in this shopping mall. Excellent wine list. $$.

De Quinceys, 71 Renfield Street, Tel: 333 9725. The decor of this former bank with coloured tiles on the walls and ceiling is most attractive. Reasonable meals at reasonable prices. $.

Janssens, 1355 Argyle Street, tel: 334 9682. Well placed for Kelvingrove Art Gallery and offering a more interesting menu than most.

Nico's, 379 Sauchiehall Street, tel: 332 5736. Good for breakfast when large coffees and hot chocolate are served to accompaniment of classical music. In evening music and atmosphere is upbeat. $.

O'Henry's Café Bar, 14 Drury Street, tel: 248 3751. Atmospheric bars on several levels with good food. $.

Papingo, 104 Bath Street, tel: 332 6678. Pleasant brasserie with Scandinavian-style decor. $$.

October Café, Princes Square, Buchanan Street, tel: 221 0303. Yuppie glamour in up-market shopping mall. Good wine list. $$.

Qui, The Italian Centre, John Street, tel: 552 6099. Attractive coffee shop on ground floor; Italian restaurant with excellent ambience in basement. $$.

The Brasserie, 176 West Regent Street, tel: 248 3801. Excellent for food with slightly *nouvelle* presentation. $$.

The Granary, 10 Kilmarnock Road, tel: 632 8487. Cheerful place with consistently high standards on the southside of the city.

Drinking Notes

Pubs

The Glasgow pub still exists, even though the visitor or the returning Glaswegian is much more likely to notice the slick new brasseries with their highly polished facades and gleaming tables.

Most pubs sell a selection of "real ale" of varying strengths known as 60 shilling, 70 shilling and 80 shilling. Imported bottled beers are *de rigueur* in brasseries, with "real ale" putting in a rare appearance. Most city pubs now also serve basic food.

The majority of city pubs are open from 11am until 11pm on Sunday through Thursday and from 11am until midnight on Friday and Saturday. During festivals some pubs remain open until 2am A few traditional favourites where entertainment is often provided

unconsciously by Glaswegians are:
Bon Accord, 151 North Street.
Corn Exchange, 88 Gordon Street.
Exchequer Bar, 59 Dumbarton Road; also has a beer garden.
Fixx II, 86 Miller Street.
Griffin, 226 Bath Street. This watering hole has three bars: serious drinkers make for the Griffin; the Griffiny has a lounge; and the Griffinette is just that wee bit more classy.
Halt Bar, 160 Woodlands Road: popular with artists and film makers; regular live music.
Horseshoe Bar, 17/21 Drury Street: the longest continuous bar in Europe.
Ingram, 138 Queen Street.
Scotch Corner Bar, 221 Buchanan Street: stocks more than 150 different whiskies.

Wine Bars

Bull and Bear, 158 Buchanan Street. More a wine bar than a pub: in the Stock Exchange building.
Smiths, 47 West Nile Street.

Attractions

Places of Interest

Historic Buildings

City Chambers. George Square, tel: 221 9600. Tours Monday–Friday at 10.30am and 2.30pm. Lavishly decorated inside with marble pillars, delicate plasterwork and mosaic floors. An excellent example of the wealth in the city in the late 1800s.

Glasgow Cathedral, Castle Street, tel: 552 3205. April–September Monday–Saturday 9.30am–7pm; Sunday 2–5pm. October–March Monday–Saturday 9.30am–4pm; Sunday 2–4pm. Outstanding example of pre-reformation Gothic architecture from the 12th century.

Glasgow School of Art, 167 Renfrew Street, tel: 353 4500. Monday–Friday 10am–noon and 2–4pm. (Fee for tour). One of the best examples of Charles Rennie Mackintosh's work to be found in the city. Started in 1896, it is built on the steep incline of a drumlin. Look out for the fabulous oriels on the western section (built 1907) rising to a height of 65 ft (21 metres).

Headquarters of Charles Rennie Mackintosh Society, 780 Garscube Road, tel: 946 6600. Tuesday, Thursday, Friday noon–5.30pm; Saturday 10.30–1pm; at other times by arrangement. These are in the former and recently renovated Queen's Cross church which is from the Mackintosh drawing board. Library, small Mackintosh exhibition and refreshments.

Hutchesons' Hall, 158 Ingram Street, tel: 552 8391. Monday–Friday 9am–5pm. This 1802 building has an impressive hall.

Merchants' House, 7 West George Street, 22l 8272. May–September: Monday–Friday 10am–4pm. Home of the Glasgow Chamber of Commerce with two superb halls.

Mitchell Library, North Street, tel: 305 2999. Monday–Friday 9.30am–9pm; Saturday 9.30am–5pm. The largest public reference library in Europe is housed in an impressive building. The west section contains theatre, café and conference rooms which may be entered via Granville Street. For those interested in learning more about Glasgow, a visit to the Glasgow Room on the third floor is obligatory.

Stock Exchange, Nelson Mandela Place, tel: 221 7060. Monday–Friday 10am–4.30pm. Modern interior within exceptional example of Venetian Gothic architecture.

Trades House, 85 Glassford Street, tel: 552 2418. Monday–Friday 10am–5pm. Designed by Robert Adam with magnificent interior.

Templeton Carpet Factory. On the northern edge of Glasgow Green. An extraordinary building, based on the Doge's Palace in Venice, with a brightly coloured facade belonging to a warmer climate. Now a business centre.

Churches & Graveyards

Glasgow Cathedral as it stands today was begun in the middle of the 12th century by Bishop William de Bondington. St Mungo, Glasgow's patron saint, was buried here in AD 603. Observe the excellent collection of post-war stained-glass windows.

Several old churches of note are scattered throughout the city. One of the more central is St George's Tron in Buchanan Street. Modern churches of note are rare within the city, but St Charles Roman Catholic Church in Kelvinside Gardens has a wonderful, calming atmosphere, with Benno Schotz's "Stations of the Cross" as an added bonus.

The Necropolis by Glasgow Cathedral was modelled on the Père Lachaise Cemetery in Paris and is filled with temples, pillars and obelisks erected by the then wealthy of the city. More than 250,000 graves lie in the South Necropolis, off Caledonia Road. Both paupers and millionaires were buried here.

Public Galleries & Museums

(Admission, unless stated to the contrary, is free.)

Burrell Collection, Pollok Country Park, tel: 649 7151. Monday–Saturday 10am–5pm; Sunday 2–5pm. Enormous, catholic collection including Daumier cartoons, ivories, glass and tapestries. Several rooms of William Burrell's home, Hutton Castle, have been recreated as requested by Burrell when donating the collection to Glasgow.

Collins Gallery, University of Strathclyde, Richmond Street, tel: 552 4400 ext 2558. Monday–Friday l0am–5pm; Saturday noon–4pm. Contemporary exhibitions of photography, sculpture and paintings.

Dome of Discovery, South Rotunda, Govan Road. A fun science museum with lots of opportunity to touch.

Haggs Castle, 100 St Andrews Drive, tel: 427 2725. Monday–Saturday l0am–5pm; Sunday 2–5pm. Small 16th-century castle turned into a museum for children.

Hunterian Art Gallery, University of Glasgow, tel: 330 5431. Monday–Friday 9.30am–5pm; Saturday 9.30am–1pm. Excellent collection of 19th and 20th-century French and Scottish works plus substantial print collection including many Whistlers. Superb recreation of the house once occupied by Mackintosh situated in the gallery's tower. Open Monday–Friday 9.30–12.30 and 1.30–5; Saturday 9.30–1. (Admission charge to Mackintosh house.)

Hunterian Museum, University of Glasgow, tel: 330 4221. Monday–Friday 9.30am–5pm; Saturday 9.30am–1pm. Includes extensive coin and medal collection dating back to ancient Greece.

Kelvingrove Art Gallery and Museum, Kelvingrove Park, tel: 221 9600. Monday–Saturday 10am–5pm; Sunday 2–5pm. Britain's best civic collection of British and European paintings. Also displays of arms and armour, the Glasgow style, porcelain, silver, pottery and natural history, archaeology, history and ethnography.

McLellan Galleries, 270 Sauchiehall Street, tel: 331 1854. Hours vary. Major venue for temporary local and touring exhibitions of paintings and sculpture.

Museum of Transport, Kelvin Hall, tel: 221 9600. Monday–Saturday 10am–5pm; Sunday 2–5pm. Fascinating exhibits with a fine collection of tramcars and railway locomotives. The Clyde Room has an outstanding collection of model ships.

People's Palace, Glasgow Green, tel: 554 0223. Monday–Saturday 10am–5pm; Sunday 2–5pm. The social history of Glasgow is explained through its exhibits.

Pollok House, Pollok Country Park, tel: 632 0274. Monday–Saturday 10am–5pm; Sunday 2–5pm. A beautiful 18th-century Robert Adam house with superb collection of Spanish paintings and works of others, including William Blake.

Provand's Lordship, 3 Castle Street, tel: 552 8819. Monday–Saturday 10am–5pm; Sunday 2–5pm. Only surviving medieval house in the city. One room has been left as it would have been when the hospital chaplain was resident.

Regimental Museum of the Royal Highland Fusiliers, 518 Sauchiehall Street, tel: 332 0961. Monday–Thursday 9am–4.30pm; Friday 9am–4pm. Uniforms and other militaria relating to the regiment's fascinating 300-year history.

The Tenement House, 145 Buccleuch Street, tel: 333 0183. Saturday & Sunday 2–4pm (November–March); Daily 2–4pm (April–October). Between 1911 and 1965 one lady lived in this house, changing none of its features. Today it remains as it was, with gas lighting, lace curtains and old newspaper cuttings. (Admission charge.)

Private Galleries

Glasgow has a host of small privately-run galleries which supplement the large civic collections with frequently changing exhibitions. Entry is normally free.

T & R Annan, 164 Woodlands Road, tel: 332 0028. Monday–Friday 10am–5pm; Saturday 10am–12.30pm. "A family firm established in 1855," selling original paintings and prints mainly in traditional style. Also home of Annan collection of old photographs.

Barclay Lennie, 203 Bath Street, tel: 226-5413. Monday–Friday 10am–5pm; Saturday 10am–1pm. Specialises in 19th and 20th-century paintings and sculpture.

Compass Gallery, 178 West Regent Street, tel: 221 6370. Monday–Saturday 10am–5.30pm. A gallery renowned for helping young artists launch their work.

Cyril Gerber Fine Art, 148 West Regent Street, tel: 204 0276/221 3095. Regularly changing exhibitions concentrating on Scottish artists. Monday–Friday 9.30am–5.30pm; Saturday 9.30am–12.30pm.

Gallery of Modern Art, Queen Street, tel: 331 1854. Glasgow's newest art gallery, featuring the work of local artists on four floors. Monday–Saturday 10am–5pm; Sunday 11am–5pm.

Glasgow Print Studio, 22 King Street, tel: 552 0704/552 6838. Monday–Saturday 10am–5.30pm. Offers print making facilities to artists.

Mackintosh & Company, situated in the Glasgow Style Gallery, 1 Bothwell Lane, tel: 357 3601. Monday–Friday 9.30am–5.30pm; Saturday 10am–5.30pm. Art nouveau glass, metalwork, furniture in the Glasgow Style and quality copies of Rennie Mackintosh furniture, mirrors and fabrics.

The Original Print Shop, 25 King Street, tel: 552 6838. Monday–Saturday 10am–5.30pm. The best selection of contemporary, limited edition, original prints in Scotland. Also regular changing displays mostly by Scottish artists.

Glasgow Centre for Contemporary Arts (CCA), 350 Sauchiehall Street, tel: 332 7521. Tuesday–Saturday 10am–9pm; Sunday 2pm–5.30pm. Frequently changing contemporary exhibitions in spacious rooms. Also recherché bookshop and café.

Washington Gallery, 44 Washington Street, tel: 221 6780. Monday–Friday 10am–11pm; Saturday 2–5pm. In a street of ageing warehouses, this smart first-floor gallery exhibits con-temporary artists and frequently has some of the older names on its walls.

City Parks

Several of Glasgow's more than 70 public parks have interesting features.

Victoria Park lies to the west of the city and has a remarkable covered Fossil Grove (330 million-year-old tree stumps) which was discovered accidently in 1880 when a new path was under construction.

Rouken Glen Park is a magnificent country estate with waterfall. Walk through the tropical **Butterfly Kingdom** and be surrounded by exotic butterflies and moths. Open daily at 10am from the end of March until the beginning of November (tel: 620 2084).

Botanic Gardens on Great Western Road opposite the Grosvenor Hotel. Open daily from 7am–dusk, tel: 334 2422. The glasshouses open around lunchtime and close 4.15 in winter and 4.45 in summer. The large glasshouse known as the Kibble Palace is the gardens' main attraction. It is well over 100 years old and contains a fine display of plants from temperate regions, interspersed with sculptures.

Country Parks

Glasgow is fortunate in that not only is there a Country Park within the city boundaries but it is surrounded by a further 16 such parks. Some of these are:

Pollok Country Park (2060 Pollokshaws Road, Glasgow G43 1AT, tel: 632 9299) is home to the Burrell Collection, Pollok House with its art collection, a herd of Highland cattle and a police-dog training school. It has many attractive woodland and parkland walks, picnic areas and a "Walk about a bit" trail.

Balloch Castle Country Park (leave the B854 in Balloch at the southern tip of Loch Lomond, tel: 01389 58216) has beautifully landscaped grounds which offer excellent views of Loch Lomond. A history trail and a tree trail will appeal to those who require further stimulation.

Castle Semple Country Park (10 miles/16 km southwest of Paisley with access from the A760, tel: 01505 842882) has, as its main feature, a large shallow loch which is open throughout the whole year for sailing, windsurfing, rowing and canoeing.

There is a bird observation centre and woodlands walks. Fishing permits are available.

Chatelherault Country Park (1 mile southeast of Hamilton on the A72, tel: 01698 426213) surrounds a William Adam lodge and includes the wooded gorge of the River Avon, a site of Special Scientific Interest. The ancient Cadzow oak trees and the Cadzow herd of white cattle are both intriguing.

Culzean Country Park (12 miles/20 km southwest of Ayr) has as its main feature a magnificent Adam's Castle. In the grounds are a treetop walkway, an adventure playground, swan ponds, a deer park and formal gardens and woodlands. Superb views. Caravan/camping park available.

Eglinton Country Park (southeast of Kilwinning off the A78 and A737, tel: 01294 51776) has the ruined Eglinton Castle as its hub and offers formal gardens, woodland, river and loch walks.

Kelburn Country Centre, on A78 between Largs and Fairlie, tel: 01475 568685. mid-March to mid-October daily 10am–6pm; remainder of year only the Grounds are open from 11am–5pm. The Castle is open only in May: tours commence at noon, with last tour at 4pm.

Muirshield Country Park (3 miles/5 km northwest of Lochwinnoch and reached from the B786, tel: 01505 842803) is a high valley with woodlands, rhododendrons and rough moorland. Features are a nature trail and scenic walks.

Strathclyde Country Park (between Hamilton and Motherwell with access from either the A725/M74 or the A723/M74 intersection: tel: 01698 266155) has a nature reserve. It is also a great place for sports enthusiasts, having an international rowing course, water sports centre, golf course, pitch and putt and a jogging trail. In addition, there is Strathclyde loch, woodlands and a nature trail and the Hamilton Mausoleum. Caravan/camping park available.

Greater Glasgow & Beyond

Auchentoshan Distillery, Dalmuir, before Erskin Bridge, tel: 01389 79476. Monday–Friday 9am–4.30pm (last tour 3.35pm.) A most unusual triple distilled lowland malt is produced here.

Bachelors' Club, Sandgate, Tarbolton, tel: 01292 541424. Easter–October daily 10am–6pm. Other times by appointment. Robert Burns helped found this club which is now filled with Burns memorabilia while the lower rooms are set up as a typical cottage interior of his time.

Bannockburn Heritage Centre, off M80, 2 miles (3 km) south of Stirling, tel: 01786 812664. March–October 10am–6pm. Audio-visual presentation of events leading up to Battle of Bannockburn.

Bothwell Castle, situated near Uddingston Cross, tel: 01698 816894. April–September weekdays 9.30am–7pm; Sunday 2–4pm. October–March weekdays 9.30am–4pm; Sunday 2–4pm. (Closed Thursday afternoon & Friday in winter). Imposing red sandstone castle on bank of Clyde, considered to be the best surviving 13th-century castle in Scotland.

Burns Cottage and Museum, Alloway, Ayr, tel: 01292 41215. June–August 9am–7pm; April, May, September, October 10am–5pm (Sunday 2–5pm); November–March 10am–4pm (not Sunday). Birthplace of Robert Burns and leading museum of Burnsiana. Start of the Burns Heritage Trail.

Burns House Museum, Castle Street, Mauchline, tel: 01290 50045. Easter–October Monday–Saturday 11am–12.30pm and 2–5.30pm; Sunday l.30–5.30. At other times enquire next door. Burns and family lived here. Also fascinating collection of Mauchline ware, for which town was famous in 19th century and display of curling memorabilia.

Burns Monument, Alloway, Ayr, tel: 01292 41321. April–mid-October daily 9am–7pm, November–March 10am–5pm. Grecian alongside the lovely River Doon.

Burns Monument and Museum, Kay Park, Kilmarnock, tel: 01563 26401. Admission by arrangement. Lovely views from museum which houses displays on life and works of Burns and has extensive Burns library.

Cambuskenneth Abbey, Stirling. April–September Monday–Saturday 9.30am–7pm. Sunday 2–7pm. This abbey was founded in the 12th century and used on occasions for the meeting of the Scottish Parliament.

Cameronians Regimental Museum, Mote Hill, of Muir Street, Hamilton, tel:

01698 428688. Daily 10am–noon and 1–5pm except Wednesday when closed in afternoon. Memorabilia relating to history of regiment from 1689 to the present.

Coats Observatory, 49 Oakshaw Street, Paisley, tel: 889 3151. Monday–Friday 2–5pm; Saturday 10am–1pm and 2–5pm. Public viewing, October–March on Thursday 7–9.30pm. Two large working astronomical telescopes along with seismic and meteorological equipment. Access suitable for disabled.

Colzium Museum, Colzium House, Lennox Estate, Kilsyth, tel: 01236 735077. Wednesday 2–5pm; April–October 5.30–8pm. Local history displayed in beautiful Victorian mansion.

Countess Fiona, Maid of the Loch Ltd., Balloch Pier, Balloch, tel: 01389 52044. Cruises on Loch Lomond from Balloch Pier during May–September.

Craignethan Castle, 5 miles (8 km) northwest of Lanark, tel: 0131 226 2570. April–September Monday–Saturday 9.30am–7pm; Sunday 2–4pm; October–March Monday–Saturday 9.30am–4pm; Sunday 2–4pm. 15th-century castle with later additions illustrating outstanding examples of military fortification.

David Livingstone Centre, Blantyre, tel: 01698 823140. Approached by M74 or A724 and about 8 miles (13 km) south of Glasgow. The home of Scotland's most celebrated explorer and missionary. Museum and visitor centre open all year seven days a week from 10am–6pm.

David Marshall Lodge, off A81, one mile north of Aberfoyle. Mid-March–mid-October daily 10am–6pm. Visitor centre with magnificent views.

Denny's Ship Model Experimental Tank, Castle Street, Dumbarton, tel: 01389 63444. Monday–Friday 10am–4pm. The world's first commercial experimental tank.

Doune Castle, Doune, tel: 0131 226 2570. April–September Monday–Saturday 9.30am–7pm; Sunday 2–7pm. October–March Monday–Saturday 9.30am–4pm; Sunday 2–4pm. Splendid ruins of one of the best preserved medieval castles in Scotland.

Doune Motor Museum, Doune, tel: 01786 841203. April–October daily 10am–5pm. Superb collection of vintage and post-vintage cars.

Dumbarton Castle, Dumbarton, tel: 0131 226 2570. April–September Monday–Saturday 9.30am–7pm; Sunday 2–7pm. October–March Monday–Saturday 9.30am–4pm; Sunday 2–4pm. It was from here that Queen Mary left for France in 1548, at the age of five.

Dunblane Cathedral, Dunblane, tel: 0131 226 2570. April–September, Monday–Saturday 9.30am–7pm; Sunday 2–5pm; October–March, Monday–Saturday 9.30am–4pm; Sunday 2–4pm. 13th-century masterpieces of Scottish architecture.

Finlaystone Estate and Country Park, Langbank, tel: 01475 54285. Monday–Sunday 9am–5pm. Country park with woodland walks and views of the River Clyde. House has doll collection.

Glasgow Zoo Park, Calderpark, Uddingston, tel: 771 1185. Open all year 10am–5pm winter, 10am–6pm summer. Wide range of animals and reptiles; paths suitable for wheelchairs.

Glengoyne Distillery, on the A81, beyond Strathblane, tel: 332 6361. Open April–November 10.30am–3.15pm. Guided tours about every 30 minutes and the opportunity to sample a Highland malt.

Greenbank Gardens, south of city off the B767, tel: 639 3281. Attractive gardens open all year 9.30am–sunset.

Hamilton District Museum, l19 Muir Street, Hamilton, tel: 01698 283981. Monday–Saturday 10am–5pm. This museum in a 17th-century coaching inn is rich in local material.

Hamilton Mausoleum, 18th-century chapel renowned for its echo.

Hill House, Upper Colquhoun Street, Helensburgh. Originally a private house designed by Charles Rennie Mackintosh for the publisher Walter Blackie. Open all year, daily 1–5pm (last tour 4.30).

Inchmahome Priory, situated on the island in Lake of Menteith, 4 miles (6 km) east of Aberfoyle. Access from Port of Menteith. tel: 01786 62421. April–September Monday–Saturday 9.30am–7pm; Sunday 2–7pm. Ruined priory where infant Mary Queen of Scots sent for refuge in 1547.

Irvine Burns Club Museum, Wellwood Eglinton Street, Irvine, tel: 01294 74511. 2.30–5pm. Burnsiana, including letters from Tennyson, Dickens and Garibaldi.

Land O'Burns Centre, Murdoch's Lane, Alloway, Ayr, tel: 01292 43700. October–May daily l0am–5pm; June, September, 1–6pm; July and August 10am–9pm. An interpretation centre at start of Burns Heritage Trail with exhibits and audio-visual programme.

McLean Museum & Art Gallery, 9 Union Street, Greenock, tel: 01457 23741. Monday–Saturday 10am–noon and l–5pm. Material relating to social industrial and maritime history of Inverclyde District. Important collection of Scottish paintings.

New Lanark (tel; 0555 61345) and the **Falls of Clyde** (tel: 01555 65262). Well signposted off the A74. Nature Reserve is open all year. Village is open seven days a week 11am–5pm.

Newark Castle, Port Glasgow, tel: 01475 41858. April–September: Monday–Saturday 9.30am–7pm; Sunday 2–7pm. October–March Monday–Saturday 9.30–4pm; Sunday 2–4pm. Standing on the River Clyde, the oldest part of this castle dates to the 15th century. The castle contains small collections of historical prints of Port Glasgow.

Paisley Abbey and Place of Paisley, tel: 889 7654. Monday–Friday 10am–12.30pm and 1.30–3pm, Saturday 10am–noon and 1.30–3pm. Birthplace of the Stewart dynasty.

Paisley Museum & Art Galleries, High Street, tel: 889 3151. Monday–Saturday 10am–5pm. Superb collection of Paisley shawls.

Scottish Maritime Museum, Laird Forge, Gottries Road, Irvine, tel: 01294 7828. March–mid-October 10am–4pm. Several local craft moored at pontoon may be visited

Skelmorlie Aisle, Largs. April–September Monday–Saturday 9.30am–7pm; Sunday 2–7pm. Magnificent renaissance mausoleum.

Sma' Shot Cottages, 11/17 George Place, Paisley. tel: 889 0530. May–September Wednesday & Saturday 1–5pm. Restored and furnished artisan's house of the Victorian era.

Smith Art Gallery and Museum, 40 Albert Place, Dumbarton Road, Stirling, tel: 01786 71917. Wednesday, Thursday, Friday & Sunday 2–5pm; Saturday 10.30am–5pm. The story of Stirling from William Wallace to the present.

Souter Johnnie's Cottage, Main Street, Kirkoswald, tel: 01655 6603. Easter–September noon–5pm; other times by appointment. This thatched cottage displays Burns relics and life-size figures of Burns characters.

Stirling Castle, Visitor Centre, tel: 01786-62517. Open April-September Monday-Saturday 9.30am–5.15pm. Sunday 10.30am–4.45pm. Castle and palace built on volcanic rock. The public can visit most of the buildings, lawns and gardens; the views are spectacular. The visitor centre is situated in the esplanade.

Summerlee Heritage Trust, West Canal Street, Coatbridge, tel: 01236 431261. Open daily 10am–5pm. Possibly the world's noisiest museum, with working steam cranes and locomotives and an operational tramway.

Thomas Coats Memorial Church, High Street, Paisley, tel: 889 9980. May–September Monday, Wednesday, Friday 2–4pm. Other times by arrangement. One of Europe's most magnificent Baptist churches.

Wallace Monument, Causewayhead, nr. Stirling, tel: 01786 72140. February, March & October 10am–5pm; April & September 10am–6pm; May through August 10am–7pm. A monument to one of Scotland's national heroes; superb views.

Weaver's Cottage, Shuttle Street, Kilbarchan, tel: 01505 5588. April, May, September and October Tuesday, Thursday, Saturday, Sunday 2–5pm. June–August daily 2–5pm. A typical 18th-century weaver's home with working looms. Attractive garden.

Glasgow City Walks, tel: 942 7929. Guided walks in Glasgow's city centre including such features as the Cathedral and Merchant City.

Discovering Scotland Tours, 153 Queen Street, tel: 204 0444. Tours of surrounding areas including Loch Lomond, Stirling, Ayr, etc.

Clyde Marine Motoring Company Ltd, Princes Pier, Greenock, tel: 01475 721281. Pleasant cruises to various Clyde Coast resorts and islands during the summer season.

Waverley Excursions, Anderston Quay, tel: 221 8152. Cruises down the river and around the islands of the Firth of Clyde on "the last sea-going paddle steamer in the world".

Clyde Helicopters, City Heliport, SECC, tel: 226 426l. Scenic 15 and 30-minute trips or longer excursions. Private charter and trips to top country restaurants.

Culture

Concerts

During the winter the Royal Scottish National Orchestra (RSNO) presents regular Saturday evening concerts and the BBC Scottish Symphony Orchestra presents Friday evening concerts. In the summer month the RSNO has a short Promenade season. For other concerts by numerous chamber music and choral groups see the daily press.

May is the month for Mayfest, an international festival which is now rated as the second largest in Britain. Jazz musicians flock to Glasgow in June for the annual Jazz Festival and in July there is a Folk Festival. August is the big blow when Glasgow hosts the World Pipe Band championships.

City Hall, Candleriggs, tel: 227 5024. A wide variety of entertainment is presented in this hall which has excellent acoustics.

Glasgow International Concert Hall, Corner Killermont and Buchanan Streets. The city's premier concert venue with seats for 2,500 people.

Henry Wood Hall, Claremont Street, tel: 204 4540. Home of the RSNO.

Scottish Exhibition and Conference Centre, Finnieston Street, tel: 248 3000 (Information). The rather soulless SECC is injected with life when it hosts concerts by visiting rock bands.

Stevenson Hall, Royal Scottish Academy of Music and Drama, 100 Renfrew Street, tel: 332 5057. Venue for Friday night concerts by the BBC Scottish Symphony Orchestra and for many other delightful classical offerings.

Dance

Scottish Ballet, 261 West Princes Street, tel: 331 2931. A Glasgow-based touring company which performs regularly at the Theatre Royal and at their Robin Anderson auditorium in West Princes Street.

Opera

Scottish Opera, 39 Elmbank Crescent. For performance information, contact the Theatre Royal, tel: 332 9000. Scottish Opera is in residence at the

Theatre Royal from September to June. Strong company with magnificent stage sets and a large and varied repertoire.

Theatres

Atheneum Theatre, 100 Renfrew Street, (tel: 332 5057). Beautiful theatre in the Royal Scottish Academy of Music and Drama.

Citizens' Theatre, 119 Gorbals Street, tel: 429 0022 (box office). Repertory company internationally renowned for its adventurous productions.

King's Theatre, Bath Street, tel: 227 5511 (box office). Light drama, music events and amateur shows are shown in this comfortable old theatre.

Mitchell Theatre, Granville Street, tel: 227 5511. This well-designed theatre, a part of the Mitchell Library, mounts concerts and amateur shows.

Pavilion Theatre, Renfield Street, tel: 332 1846 (box office). Somewhat old-fashioned commercial theatre favoured by comedians. Variety shows and the occasional concert.

Theatre Royal, Hope Street, tel: 332 9000 (box office). This beautifully furbished theatre is the home of Scottish Opera and is used by major visiting theatre and ballet companies.

Glasgow Centre for Contemporary Arts (CCA), 350 Sauchiehall Street, tel: 332 7521. Small studio theatre which can be slightly claustrophobic. Enjoyable productions by touring companies.

Tramway Theatre, Albert Drive, tel: 227 5511 (box office). A cavernous theatre suitable for epic productions.

Tron Theatre, 63 Trongate, tel: 552 4267 (box office). The place to see new Scottish works; very lively atmosphere and popular bar.

Cinemas

MGM Filmcentre, Sauchiehall Street, tel: 332 1592. Five screens showing the latest commercial releases.

Glasgow Film Theatre, 12 Rose Street, tel: 332 8128. Two screens. This specialises in foreign language and minority films but does not turn up its nose at quality new releases.

Grosvenor, Ashton Lane, tel: 339 4298. Two screens in West End. Late-night screenings.

Odeon, Renfield Street, tel: 332 8701. Recent popular releases on six screens.

Musical Venues

PUBS & BARS

Certain pubs have a tradition of live music, often at the weekends. The following is a short selection.

Blackfriars, 36 Bell Street, tel: 552 5924. Regular venue for jazz, blues and folk.

Bonhams, 192 Byres Road, tel: 357 3424. Busy, colourful bar with jazz sessions Sunday lunchtime.

Fixx II, 86 Miller Street, tel: 221 1568. The place to find up-and-coming bands. In the past Deacon Blue, Hue and Cry and Wet Wet Wet have played here.

Grand Ole Opry, 2 Govan Road, nr. Paisley Road Toll, tel: 429 5396. Glasgow cowboys enjoy the Hoots Mon Corral where there is live country music nightly and where the drinks are cheap. Suitable for the whole family but to get a table be there by 7.30pm.

Halt Bar, 160 Woodlands Road, tel: 332 1210. Horseshoe-shaped bar with traditional pub feel. Rock, folk or jazz with music most nights.

Saints & Sinners, 272 St Vincent Street, tel: 221 5279. Rock music in hot and crowded room.

Nice 'N' Sleazy, 421 Sauchiehall Street, tel: 333 9637. A popular night spot, regularly playing host to many bands which cater to those with an "alternative" taste in music.

King Tuts Wah Wah Hut, 272 St Vincent Street, tel: 221 5279. All serious Glaswegian gig goers have heard of this renowned establishment, which puts on performances most nights of the week.

Nightclubs

Glasgow has always enjoyed a thriving club scene. Over the years there have been many hotspots, some of which have achieved truly legendary status amongst a ceaseless throng of club enthusiasts who have many a night danced away their cares in a crowded, sweaty environment.

The scene in Glasgow caters for almost every taste from dance music to "indie". To make sure of up-to-date information, check the local media such as The List, which has a thorough and comprehensive guide to club life in both Glasgow and Edinburgh.

Cotton Club, 5 Scott Street, tel: 332 0712. Wednesday–Sunday. Hot and lively atmosphere with the occasional band playing, otherwise chart sounds. Over-21s.

Follies, 193 Pitt Street, tel: 332 1111. Thursday–Sunday. Upmarket venue in large converted church. Over-21s. No denim.

Bennets, 90 Glassford Street, tel: 552 5761. Mainly gay. The Shimmy Club on Tuesdays, is its straight night which has an enthusiastic following.

Fury Murrys, 96 Maxwell Street, tel: 221 6511. Wide range of music but favours Rock.

Sub Club, 22 Jamaica Street, tel: 248 4600. Dark, sweaty and very popular; finding room on the dance floor is the only problem.

The Tunnel, 84 Mitchell Street, tel: 204 1000. Considered to be one of the top ten clubs in the country, this stylish spot caters for the young, trendy and energetic. Favours dance music.

The Arches, Midland Street (off Jamaica Street), tel: 221 9736. A serious nightspot for the committed club goer, this huge converted warehouse provides hypnotic dance beats till the early hours of the morning.

Cabaret

There is no regular cabaret venue in the city, but the **King's Theatre** (Bath Street, tel: 227 5511) and the **Pavilion** (Renfield Street, tel: 332 1846) have occasional comedy and variety acts.

Gambling

The law requires that you become a member of a casino about 48 hours before you play. Membership is free. Men are expected to wear a jacket and tie.

Berkeley Casino Club, 508 Sauchiehall Street, tel: 332 0992.

Chevalier Casino, 95 Hope Street, tel: 226 3856.

Princes Casino, 528 Sauchiehall Street, tel: 332 8171.

Regency Casino, 15 Waterloo Street, tel: 221 4141.

Shopping

Glasgow Style

Spendthrift by nature, Glasgow has bred some curious shopping attributes, *writes Anne Simpson*. **Argyle Arcade** can boast the largest number of jewellery shops per square footage, under one roof, in the world. Not even Geneva or Rio de Janiero can match it for concentrated volume. As for London's Burlington Arcade, its hallmarked atmosphere comes nowhere near this one's mesmeric gleam. And can anywhere in the Marks & Spencer empire compete with Glasgow's manic descent on the crispy prawn wontons and choux pastries on a Friday afternoon? It is as if the empty plate of Armageddon haunts the Glasgow psyche at weekends.

But it is **Princes Square** that exists as the true temple for the shopper of extravagant passion and taste. Gracefully glassed in around the honeyed warmth of an old sandstone courtyard, the square has an almost *fin de siècle* ornateness which has captured royal attention: the Prince of Wales, who opened it officially, wrote glowingly of its aesthetic charms in his book *A Vision of Britain*.

Too-overdressed for some architectural tastes, the centre nevertheless draws style pundits from all over Britain and abroad, seeking anything from the French and Italian fashion labels of Comme de Garçons (at the Whistles shop) and Byblos and Giglo (at Sax) to the voluptuous shapes and rich textures of Nancy Smillie's distinctive Scottish pottery. Here, too, at One, you will find modern bric-a-brac, fine and spare in line, or decorative, eclectic furnishings at Illuminati, while Ted

Baker, Hunter's and Rells beckon the dudes with figurative ties and folklorico shorts and braces.

Beyond the square, on the opposite side of **Buchanan Street**, there is Frasers, one of the most highly regarded department stores in Scotland. But no-one should travel to Glasgow without also stopping into the gentrified Merchant quarter of the city where Ichi Ni San is worth visiting for upmarket ready-to-wear. Nearby in-House offers some of the most memorable modern European furniture and accessories in Britain.

And you don't need to be going anywhere these days to feel drawn to Glasgow's **Central Station**. The concourse, with its reworked Victoriana, has become the emporium of spontaneous indispensables; the emergency bow tie; addictive fruit gums in the shape of cola bottles; the stuff of a venison pâté sandwich from a delicatessen open until midnight, and the briefest of underclothes teased into discreet, little packages. But obviously this being a terminus for countless lives, a lot of people are in transit to somewhere and, given that, it is nothing short of amazing how many people seem to embark on journeys without thinking to pack their smalls.

This is perhaps the only firm conclusion to be drawn from an afternoon spent observing the brisk business at Knickerbox and Sock Shop, now housed in the great mahogany bow where once crowds would stare hypnotised by the decrepit flip-and-flap of a British Rail timetable and its bulletin of regrets for delayed arrivals, late departures and almost whimsical cancellations. The following day – when strike action had driven trains into silence – those very same clothes shops were closed. Only the cobbler, situated close by, was busy then, a small signal, this, that in Glasgow pedestrians remain as resolute as stones.

A group of fashion and graphic designers – including Lex McFadyen at Cook Street Studios, Claire Heminsley of lucahoots at the same address, Spencer Railton in the basement of his home, and Jane Harris at Pollokshields – spunkily work against the mainstream to prove that there is a demand for clothes which go beyond the safe commercialism of Next, and a demand, too, for "art fashion" where a

genuine nihilism affects the garb. McFadyen's boldest commissions, for instance, evoke something of Jean-Paul Gaultier's audacity, and Railton is the man who showers his evening gowns with satirical sequins to achieve a look that unequivocally proclaims Dame Edna Everage rather than Ines de la Fressange.

Jane Harris, on the other hand, almost sculpts and colours her silks – by way of Fortuny-style pleating and shimmeringly contrasting dyes – into exquisite shell-like garments; rippling chrysalis jackets and fluted waistcoats which, because of their work intensity, can only be made to order and are reminiscent of Issey Miyake's mysterious and wondrously constructed clothes, the origami of fashion. On interiors, Ronnie Bridges' strength as a designer can be seen in the sophisticated, steely ambience of the fashion shop Ichi Ni San, at Candleriggs.

Shopping Hours

High street shops are open 9am–5.30pm Monday to Saturday, and until 7 or 8pm on a Thursday. Smaller shops may not open until 10am, closing at 6pm or later. Most of the city centre bookshops stay open until 10pm during the week, and are open on Sunday afternoons. Several shops in and around Argyle Street are open on Sundays from l0am until 5pm. Many local grocers and the large out-of-town shopping centres are open on Sundays. The majority of off-licences in the city are open and will sell alcohol on Sundays.

Scottish Specialities

In order to look like a true Scot, pay a wee visit to **Geoffrey Highland Crafts**, 309 Sauchiehall Street (tel: 331 2388), a major kilt maker and seller of all things tartan. **Macgregor and Macduff**, 41 Bath Street (tel: 332 0299), and **Mackay and Stewart**, 8–10 Orchard Street, Paisley (tel: 885 2367) sell similiar Scottish attire. **R.G. Lawrie**,110 Buchanan Street (tel: 221 0217) has a wide range of Scottish items including kilts, tartans and Scottish glass and silver.

Those wishing to blow about their new garb will find makers of bagpipes at **James Begg**, 85 Renfield Street (tel: 333 0639). To play the pipes in tune contact **Fiona McKenzie** (6c Castle Way, Kildrum, Cumbernauld, tel: 01236 7730937).

Wonderful Scottish woollies – and you may need them in Glasgow – are found in abundance at **Edinburgh Woollen Mill**, 75 St Georges Place (tel: 221 2252) and **Pitlochry Knitwear**, 130 Buchanan Street (tel: 221 1044). To round off a Scottish buying spree visit the shop of the **National Trust for Scotland** at 158 Ingram Street (tel: 552 8391).

Shopping Areas

As in all large UK cities, the chain stores dominate the high street. In the city centre there are three main shopping areas, Sauchiehall Street, Buchanan Street and Argyle Street. Parts of all three are pedestrianised although, at times, one wonders about Buchanan Street which is by far the smartest of the three and which still has a couple of old-style shops breaking the vast areas of glass frontage.

Sauchiehall Street stretches all the way from the top of Buchanan Street to the east end of Kelvingrove Park, with the main shopping area situated between Charing Cross and Buchanan Street. **Marks and Spencer** (tel: 332 6097), **C & A** (tel: 333 9441), **BHS** (tel: 332 0401) and **Littlewoods** (tel: 332 0997) have large stores here, alongside other well-known names such as **The Body Shop** and **Laura Ashley**.

Nevisport (261 Sauchiehall Street, tel: 332 4814) sells a large range of mountaineering and skiing equipment. Those wishing to ward off the winter chills without looking sporty will make for the small fur shops closer to Charing Cross.

For those searching for a wide selection of records, cassettes or CDs, head for **Casa Cassettes** (325 Sauchiehall Street, tel: 332 1127); they also stock numerous recordings of Scottish music. **Henderson the Jeweller** (217 Sauchiehall Street, tel: 331 2569) is housed in a refurbished Mackintosh building with the famous **Willow Tearoom** (332 0521) on the first floor. Across the road at 350 (tel: 332 7521) the **Glasgow Centre for Contemporary Arts (CCA)** stocks a recherché selection of books and

mounts exhibitions (with items for sale) of contemporary art.

Bath Street is the home of two auction houses; **Christie's** (164 Bath Street, tel: 332 8134) and **Phillips** (207 Bath Street, tel: 221 8377). Both Christie's and Phillips hold sales of furniture, paintings, silver and jewellery on various mornings throughout the week. For people without the time or the patience for viewing and bidding, try **Tim Wright Antiques** (147 Bath Street, tel: 221 0364). **Cooper Hay Rare Books**, one of the best antiquarian book dealers in Glasgow, is at 203 Bath Street (tel: 226 3074).

West Regent Street has several good quality shops dotted along its length, with most situated at basement level. **Muirhead Moffat**, which deals in fine antiques, is at 182 (tel: 226 4683). **Compass Gallery** (178 West Regent Street, tel: 221 6370) is filled with work by up-and-coming Scottish artists at reasonable prices. Further down at number 148 is **Cyril Gerber Fine Art** (tel: 221 3095), the sister gallery of the Compass, exhibiting 19th and 20th-century artists which naturally, are more expensive. **Victorian Village** (57 West Regent Street, tel: 332 0808) is a warren of small antique shops offering old fragile clothing, silver, glass, medals etc.

Thomsons (79 Renfield Street, tel: 332 6380) is one of the few shops specialising in coffee and tea within the city. An excellent place for all things photographic is **Tom Dickson's** (87 Renfield Street, tel: 332 0556). Better still is **Jessop Photo Centre** at 254 Sauchiehall Street (tel: 331 2201). Wanting to smell some country fragrances? Check out **Blooms** (80 West Nile Street, tel: 332 8366), which supply a wide choice of fresh flowers – don't let its window display put you off.

The oldest bookshop in Scotland is **John Smith's** (57 St Vincent Street, tel: 221 7472). Sadly, its shelves and island displays leave too little room for the customer, especially on a Saturday – which may contribute to the staff having rather less time for the customer than one would wish. The shop has a very good antiquarian section. Delicious smells waft out from **Health Foods** (73 St Vincent Street), which sells fresh bread and healthy yoghurts. **Graham Robert & Co** (71 St

Vincent Street, tel: 221 6588) stocks a fine selection of tobacco, cigars etc.

Austin Reed, the menswear shop, is at 35 Gordon Street (tel: 248 3811) while at 23 is **Greaves** (tel: 221 3322) which offers all sorts of sporting equipment from golf clubs to waterskis. Further along the road is **Waterstones** (tel: 221 0890), a delightful and large bookstore with knowledgeable staff.

At the corner of Gordon and Buchanan streets is **Henry Burton** (tel: 221 7380), a small, independent gentlemen's and ladies' outfitters established in 1847. The atmosphere is very civilised and the staff are patient and helpful. **Frasers** (21 Buchanan Street, tel: 221 3880) is the smartest department store in town, with large floor areas devoted to men's and women's clothing. Across the road at 64 is **Burberry** (tel: 221 6222) which is next door to **Jaeger** (tel: 221 7957).

Princes Square (Buchanan Street) is the ultimate in easy and expensive shopping. Built within a listed building, this glass-domed centre offers a food court with shops offering the latest fashions and luxury produce. There are plenty of pit stops for the "shop till you drop" set, with a wine bar, brasserie and coffee shop plus a self-service restaurant on the second floor. The Square opens at 9.30am but most of the shops don't open until 10am, closing at 7pm.

More than 20 jewellers are found under the glass-roofed **Argyle Arcade** which was built in 1827 and which is approached from either Buchanan Street or Argyle Street.

Argyle Street is where you will find more of the large retailers such as **Next** (tel: 221 6142), **The Gap** (tel: 248 9110), Littlewoods (tel: 248 3713) and **Marks & Spencer** (tel: 552 4546). The new **St Enoch Centre** is the largest glass-roofed construction in Europe, with most of the well-known high street stores represented. Before shopping, park the car in the seven-level car park and the kids in the centre's ice-rink.

The fashion-conscious do not have far to venture to find the latest names. **The Warehouse** (92–94 Argyle Street, tel: 221 9382) stocks both men's and women's clothing. **Ichi-Ni-San** (26 Bell Street, tel: 552 2545) sells a range of the more expensive labels, including

Giuliano Fujiwara and Moschino. Also in this neck of the woods is **Slater Menswear** (165 Howard Street, tel: 552 7171) which has made the *Guinness Book of Records* as the "world's largest store selling only men's suits and accessories". The firm carries 17,000 suits and sells 2,000 a week. All top makes are on sale at cut-rate prices.

Stockwell China Bazaar (67/77 Glassford Street, tel: 552 5781) has three floors of china, crystal and earthenware. Gift hunters searching for the more unusual might try **Iona Records** (155 Stockwell Street, tel: 552 0969) which holds a large and interesting stock of Jazz and Folk.

The West End has a multitude of small, absorbing shops interlaced with good food shops. **Roots and Fruits** (451 Great Western Road, tel: 339 5817) sells a wide selection of fruit and vegetables; organic produce at the rear of the shop. Two doors down, Roots and Fruits has opened an excellent flower shop. **Peckhams** (100 Byres Road, tel: 357 1454) is an extremely useful delicatessen staying open until midnight.

The Barras (244 Gallowgate, tel: 552 7258) is a large covered and open market with more than 1,000 traders. Everything is sold here, from the kitchen sink to clothing. Open Saturday and Sunday 9am–5pm. Less exciting is the **Candleriggs Market** on Albion Street (tel: 552 5908) which is open only on Fridays, Saturdays and Sundays.

Practical Points

Exports

Some shops operate a VAT refund scheme for visitors, which allows visitors to claim back the 15 percent value-added tax on goods which they intend to take out of the country. Ask the shopkeeper for details.

Complaints

Contact **Consumer Advice** at 9 Queen Street, tel: 204 0262, or the **Citizens' Advice Bureau** at 87 Bath Street, tel: 331 2345.

Sport & Leisure

Participant Sports

Facilities

Glasgow and its surrounding towns have many council-run sports facilities. These include swimming pools, tennis courts, lawn bowl greens, croquet courts, boating ponds, putting greens, pitch and putt courses and golf courses all of which are open to the public at very reasonable rates. These, apart from swimming pools, are found in public parks which are open from 8am–dusk. Best of these parks, in terms of facilities, are:

Alexandra, Sannox Gardens, G3l, tel: 554 4887.

Bellahouston, Dumbreck Road, G51, tel: 427 0558.

Kelvingrove, Dumbarton Road, G11, tel: 334 6363.

Linn, Clarkston Road, G44, tel: 637 3096.

Maxwell, Glencairn Drive, G4l, tel: 423 8693.

Queen's, Langside Road, G42, tel: 632 0772.

Ruchill, Bilsland Drive, G20, tel: 946 3269.

Springburn, Broomfield Road, G21, tel: 557 5780.

Tollcross, Tollcross Road, G32, tel: 778 1046.

Sports Centres & Complexes

Bellahouston Sports Centre, Bellahouston Road G52, tel: 427 5454. Squash, gymnasium, indoor tennis and badminton. Non-members cannot book in advance.

Bishopbriggs Sports Centre, 147 Balmuildy Road, Bishopbriggs, tel: 772 6391. Swimming pool, indoor bowls and facilities for the disabled.

Pollokshaws Sports Centre, Ashtree Road, Pollokshaws, tel: 632 2200. Badminton, swimming pool, indoor bowls and Turkish baths.

Golf Courses

Best of the eight municipal courses are:

Littlehill, Auchinairn Road, Bishopbriggs, (tel: 772 1916).

Linn Park, Simshill Road, (tel: 637 5871 or 424 4451).

Other courses, which are open to the public, although best telephone first to make sure of availability, are:

Bonnyton Golf Club, Eaglesham (tel: 01355 2781).

Bridge of Weir, Golf Road, Bridge of Weir (tel: 01505 612609).

Haggs Castle, Dumbreck Road (tel: 427 3535). (This course is near the Burrell Collection and the Haggs Castle Children's Museum.)

Langbank (Gleddoch House Golf & Country Club), Langbank (tel: 01475 54304).

Pollok Golf Club, 90 Barrhead Road, G43, (tel: 632 4351). (This course is near the Burrell Collection).

Sandyhills Golf Club, 223 Sandyhills Road (tel: 778 1179).

Whitecraigs Golf Club, 72 Ayr Road, Whitecraigs (tel: 639 1681).

The top out-of-town courses are:

Prestwick Golf Club, 2 Links Road, Prestwick (tel: 01292 77404).

Royal Troon Golf Club, Old Course, Craigend Road, Troon, (tel: 01292 311555).

Turnberry Golf Club, Turnberry Hotel, Ayrshire, (tel: 01655 202).

Other Sports

Kilmardinny Riding Centre, Milngavie Road, Bearsden, tel: 942 4404.

St Enoch Centre Ice Rink, St Enoch Square, tel: 221 5835.

The Summit Centre, Minerva Way, G3, tel: 204 2215. Ice rink open to the public for skating, Saturday 9.30am–12am and 2pm–4.30pm and 7pm–10pm; Sunday 1.30pm–4pm and 7pm–10pm.

Spectator Sports

Football

Glasgow is the Brazil of the north, being absolutely "fitba' mad". Celtic and Rangers are undoubtedly Scotland's most famous teams and both have their grounds within Glasgow. Celtic FC, Celtic Park, 95 Kerrydale Street (tel: 556 2611). Rangers FC, Ibrox Stadium, Edmiston Drive (tel: 427 8500).

National and international matches are played at Hampden Park, Somerville Drive, G42.

Athletics
Kelvin Hall International Sports Arena, Argyle Street, tel: 357 2525. Occasional track meets.

Greyhound racing
Shawfield Stadium, Rutherglen Road, tel: 647 4121. Racing every Monday, Tuesday, Thursday, Friday and Saturday at 7.45pm.

Rugby
Several local teams have grounds around the city: Balgray (Kelvinside Academicals), Great Western Road G12; Old Anniesland (Glasgow High School), Crow Road G11; and Garscadden (Glasgow University), Garscadden Road South G15.

Further Reading

Non-Fiction
Berry & White *Glasgow Observed* (John Donald 1981).
Blair, Anna *Tea at Miss Cranston's: A Century of Glasgow memories*.
Burrow *A Shipbuilding History 1750–1932* (Alexander Stephen 1932).
Corrance & Boyd *Glasgow* (Collins 1981).
Cunnison, J & Gilfillan, J.B.S. (eds.) *The Third Statistical Account of Scotland: Glasgow* (Collins 1958).
Daiches, David *Glasgow* (Granada 1982).
Gallaghar, Tom *Glasgow, The Uneasy Peace* (Manchester University Press 1987).
Gibb, Andrew *The Making of a City* (Croom Helm 1983).
Glasgow Herald Book of Glasgow (Mainstream Publishing, 1990).
Gomme, Andor & Walker, David *Architecture of Glasgow* (Lund Humphries 1987).
House, Jack *Heart of Glasgow* (Richard Drew 1987).
Lindsay, Maurice *Portrait of Glasgow* (Robert Hale 1972).
McDowall, John T*he People's History of Glasgow* (S.R.Publishers 1970).
McLellan, Duncan *Glasgow Public Parks* (John Smith 1894).
Muir, Edwin *Scottish Journey* (Mainstream 1975).
Munro, Michael *The Patter* (Glasgow District Libraries 1985).
Worsdall, Frank *The City that Disappeared: Glasgow's Demolished Architecture* (Richard Drew 1981).
Worsdall, Frank *The Tenement: A Way of Life* (Chambers 1979).
Worsdall, Frank *Victorian City* (Richard Drew 1982).

Fiction
Banks, Ian *Espedair Street* (Fortuna 1988).
Berman, Chaim Ickyk *The Second Mrs Whitberg* (Allen and Unwin 1976).
Davis, Margaret Thomson *The Breadmakers* Trilogy (Allison and Busby 1972)
Gray, Alasdair *Lanark* (Edinburgh: Canongate 1981).
Hanley, Clifford *Dancing in the Streets* (Mainstream 1983).
Hanley, Clifford *Glasgow: A Celebration* (Mainstream 1984).
Kelman, James *A Disaffection* (Secker and Warburg 1989).
McCrone, Guy Fulton *Wax Fruit Trilogy* (Constable 1947).
McIlvanney, William *Lanark* (Hodder and Stoughton, 1977).
Munro, Neil *Para Handy and other Tales* (Wm. Blackwood, 1980).

Other Insight Guides
Among the 190 **Insight Guides**, the following cover the British Isles: *Scotland, Edinburgh, Wales, London, Oxford, Ireland* and *Dublin*.

Compact Guides
A companion series of **Insight Compact Guides** provides encyclopaedic information in a highly portable form, with text, pictures and maps all carefully cross-referenced for easy on-the-spot use. Titles include: *Scotland, London, Cornwall, Devon & Exmoor, New Forest, South Downs* and *Ireland*.

Pocket Guides
Insight Pocket Guides provide carefully timed itineraries and personal recommendations from a local host to help you make the best use of limited time in a destination. Each contains a full-size, fold-out map. Destinations include S*cotland, London, Southeast England* and *Ireland*.

Art/Photo Credits

All photography by DOUGLAS CORRANCE except for:

Annan Collection 49, 55
British Museum 30
Currie, Ken/Raab Galleries 83
Edinburgh University Library 27
Glasgow Libraries 22/23, 46, 47
Glasgow Museums & Art Galleries 26, 40, 45, 54L
Guildhall Art Gallery, London 34
Her Majesty the Queen 38/39
Hunterian Art Gallery 53
Imperial War Museum 50/51
People's Palace Museum 42, 43, 54R
Scottish Opera 77
Towneley Hall Art Gallery, Burnley 33
Bill Wassman 2

Maps Berndtson & Berndtson

Visual Consultant V. Barl

Index

A
B
C
D
E
F

H
I
J
a
b
c
d

f
g
h
i
j
k
l